Praise for
THE COMPATRIOTS

T0031641

"Soldatov and Borogan are two of the most revered experts on the subject of Russian secret services.... [*The Compatriots*] reads like a bunch of Hollywood plots bundled together into one mind-bending narrative.... A great read that now forms a perfect trilogy with two previous books—*The New Nobility*, which describes how secret services captured the Russian state under Putin, and *The Red Web*, which looks into the Kremlin's attempts to control the Internet."
—NPR.org

"A fine and timely new book.... In *The Compatriots*, authors Andrei Soldatov and Irina Borogan show that what has become the institutional practice of Moscow's security organs was honed in the early decades of Soviet government, when it perfected its methods against members of the Russian diaspora."   —*New York Review of Books*

"[An] engaging history.... *The Compatriots* offers a Russian perspective on fears, usually heard in the West, about the 'active measures' of propaganda and disinformation, as well as the arts of infiltration and assassination."   —*Financial Times*

"Veteran Russian journalists Andrei Soldatov and Irina Borogan have tried to make sense of one strand in their country's complex history, the role of Russians who were either sensible or cunning enough to leave at crucial moments, mainly for a West from which Russian mentalities have often been estranged."   —*Washington Times*

"These brave and intrepid journalists have produced a convincing argument."   —*Russian Review*

"Borogan and Soldatov have uncovered a series of thrilling narratives about the strange, desperate, and passionate world of Russians abroad. Each one is worth a film in itself but when combined with the insights into the intelligence operative who monitored, wooed, duped, bribed, or killed them, the authors have come up with a novel, refreshing, and illuminating look into the enigma of the Russian soul."

—Misha Glenny, author of *McMafia: A Journey Through the Global Criminal Underworld*

"Through a series of endlessly compelling stories, Soldatov and Borogan make the case that Putin is carefully grooming and manipulating the vast Russian émigré community to serve the interests of their mother country. You can't follow Russian politics without Soldatov and Borogan's reporting. In *The Compatriots*, they once again deliver the fascinating inside story that's absent from the American press."

—Joseph Weisberg, creator and executive producer of *The Americans*

"Talk about courageous journalism! Here's an inside exposé of Russian poisonings, assassinations, and political meddling written by two Russian investigative journalists, Andrei Soldatov and Irina Borogan. They narrate a century of the Kremlin's dirty tricks through manipulation of Russians living abroad—making them serve the dark purposes of the state. Reading this book, you understand that there are still many brave, patriotic Russians who want what's best for their country, not just Vladimir Putin. If you liked watching *The Americans* on TV, then *The Compatriots* is a must-read. This isn't spy fiction, but spy fact."

—David Ignatius, columnist for the *Washington Post* and author of *The Quantum Spy*

THE
COMPATRIOTS

ALSO BY ANDREI SOLDATOV AND IRINA BOROGAN

*The New Nobility: The Restoration of
Russia's Security State and the Enduring Legacy of the KGB*

The Red Web: The Kremlin's Wars on the Internet

THE ——
COMPATRIOTS

THE RUSSIAN EXILES WHO FOUGHT
AGAINST THE KREMLIN

ANDREI SOLDATOV AND
IRINA BOROGAN

PUBLICAFFAIRS

NEW YORK

PublicAffairs
Hachette Book Group
1290 Avenue of the Americas, New York, NY 10104
www.publicaffairsbooks.com
@Public_Affairs

Printed in the United States of America

Originally published in hardcover and ebook by PublicAffairs in 2019
First trade paperback edition November 2022

Published by PublicAffairs, an imprint of Perseus Books, LLC, a subsidiary of Hachette Book
Group, Inc. The PublicAffairs name and logo is a trademark of the Hachette Book Group.

The Hachette Speakers Bureau provides a wide range of authors for speaking events. To find out
more, go to www.hachettespeakersbureau.com or call (866) 376-6591.

The publisher is not responsible for websites (or their content)
that are not owned by the publisher.

Print book interior design by Amnet Systems.

The Library of Congress has cataloged the hardcover as follows:
Names: Soldatov, Andreï, author. | Borogan, I. (Irina), author.
Title: The compatriots : the brutal and chaotic history of Russia's exiles,
emigrés, and agents abroad / Andrei Soldatov and Irina Borogan.
Other titles: Brutal and chaotic history of Russia's exiles, emigrés, and
agents abroad
Description: First edition. | New York : PublicAffairs, 2019. | Includes
bibliographical references and index.
Identifiers: LCCN 2019021344 (print) | LCCN 2019980308 (ebook) | ISBN
9781541730168 (hardcover) | ISBN 9781541730182 (ebook)
Subjects: LCSH: Russians—Foreign countries—History. | Refugees—Soviet
Union. | Political refugees—Foreign countries. | Secret
service—Soviet Union. | Soviet Union—Politics and government.
Classification: LCC DK35.5 .S65 2019 (print) | LCC DK35.5 (ebook) | DDC
305.8917/1—dc23
LC record available at https://lccn.loc.gov/2019021344
LC ebook record available at https://lccn.loc.gov/2019980308

ISBNs: 9781541730168 (hardcover), 9781541730182 (ebook), 9781541730175 (paperback)

LSC-H

Printing 1, 2022

CONTENTS

PART II: MARKET FORCES

PART III: PUTIN'S PROJECT

PART IV: MEANS OF OUTREACH

SOVIET/RUSSIAN FOREIGN INTELLIGENCE ORGANIZATIONS AND DEPARTMENTS IN CHARGE OF KEEPING TABS ON RUSSIAN ÉMIGRÉS

- 1920—INO (*Inostranny Otdel*; Foreign Department) at Cheka (the All Russian Extraordinary Commission, known as the Soviet secret police, established in 1917)
- 1922—INO at GPU (*Glavnoye Politicheskoye Upravlenie*; Chief Political Department) and then at OGPU (*Obyedinyonnoye Gosudarstvennoye Politicheskoye Upravleniye*; Joint State Political Department)
- 1929—Administration for Special Tasks at INO of OGPU and the Fifth Section at INO (emigration)
- 1934—INO, renamed in 1939 into the Fifth Department at NKVD (*Narodny Kommisariat Vnutrennikh Del*; People's Commissariat of Internal Affairs)
- 1936—Seventh section at GUBG NKVD
- 1938—Fifth section at GUGB NKVD
- 1941—First Directorate at NKGB (*Narodny Kommisariat Gosudarstvennoy Bezopasnosti*; People's Commissariat of State Security)
- 1945—Ninth Section (Emigration) at First Directorate at NKGB
- 1946—Section 10-A (Emigration) at the First Directorate of the MGB (*Ministerstvo Gosudarstvennoy Bezopasnosti*; Ministry of State Security)

- 1947—Section EM at KI (*Komitet Informatsii*; Information Committee)
- 1949—Third Section at First Directorate (External Counterintelligence) of the MGB
- 1951—Third Section at First Chief Directorate (Foreign Intelligence) of the MGB
- 1953—Ninth and then Fifth Section (External Counterintelligence) at the Second Chief Directorate of the MVD (*Ministerstvo Vnutrennikh Del*; Interior Ministry)
- 1954—Ninth Section within the First Chief Directorate (Foreign Intelligence) of the KGB
- 1963—Second Service (External Counterintelligence) of the First Chief Directorate of the KGB
- 1974—Department K (External Counterintelligence) of the First Chief Directorate of the KGB. The Fourth Section of Department K was specifically tasked to deal with the émigré organizations.
- 1975—Nineteenth Section within the First Chief Directorate of the KGB
- 1991—SVR (*Sluzhba Vneshney Razvedki*; Foreign Intelligence Service or External Intelligence)
- 1991—GRU (*Glavnoye Razvedivatelnoe Upravlenie–GRU VS Rossii*; military intelligence agency known as the Main Intelligence Directorate of the General Staff of the Armed Forces of Russia)
- 1995—FSB (*Federalnaya Sluzhba Bezopasnosti*; Federal Security Service)

CAST OF CHARACTERS

LEADERS OF NATIONS
Joseph Stalin
Leonid Brezhnev
Richard Nixon
Mikhail Gorbachev
Boris Yeltsin
Vladimir Putin

STALIN'S SECRET SERVICES
Vasily Zarubin, chief of station in the United States
Mikhail Trilisser, head of the Foreign Intelligence Department (INO)
Nahum Eitingon, chief operative in charge of high-profile assassinations
Liza Gorskaya, operative; Zarubin's third wife
Yakov Blyumkin, operative, head of illegal station in Istanbul
Jacob Golos, head of Soviet spy ring in New York
Earl Browder, chairman of Communist Party in the United States
George Koval, "illegal" in New York
Caridad Mercader and **Ramon Mercader**, Eitingon's assets

COMMITTEE OF STATE SECURITY (KGB)
Yuri Andropov, chairman

Vladimir Kryuchkov, head of the foreign intelligence branch—the First Chief Directorate—and later chairman

Leonid Shebarshin, head of the First Chief Directorate

Alexander Vassiliev, KGB operative, journalist, and later historian

Yuri Sagaidak, KGB operative, journalist, and later financier

YELTSIN'S SECRET SERVICES

Evgeny Primakov, head of SVR Foreign Intelligence agency

Yuri Kobaladze, SVR's head of public relations

Alexander Litvinenko, FSB officer, refugee in London, and author

PUTIN'S SECRET SERVICES

Sergei Naryshkin, head of SVR Foreign Intelligence agency

Sergei Tretyakov, SVR deputy head of station in New York

Anna Chapman, SVR agent in the United States (New York)

Mikhail Semenko, SVR agent in the United States (Washington, DC)

Evgeny Buryakov, SVR operative, New York station

EITINGON/ZARUBIN FAMILY

Zoya Zarubina, spy and translator; daughter of Vasily Zarubin and stepdaughter of Nahum Eitingon

Alexei Kozlov, financier, inmate, activist, and Russian-German businessman; grandson of Zoya Zarubina

Olga Romanova, journalist and head of Russia Behind Bars; wife of Alexei Kozlov

KARA-MURZA FAMILY

Vladimir Kara-Murza (senior), journalist and NTV news anchor

Vladimir Kara-Murza Jr., journalist and politician; son of Vladimir Kara-Murza

Zhenya Kara-Murza, wife of Vladimir Kara-Murza Jr.

AMERICANS

George Kennan, diplomat, historian, and author of the "containment" policy

Henry Kissinger, secretary of state

Louis Fischer, journalist

George Fischer, author and researcher; son of Louis Fischer

Bert Jolis, Office of Strategic Service veteran, diamond trader, and fund-raiser for Resistance International

Bill Browder, investor, anti-Kremlin campaigner; grandson of Earl Browder

RUSSIAN OPPOSITION

Boris Nemtsov, Yeltsin's vice prime minister and politician

Vadim Prokhorov, lawyer to Boris Nemtsov and Vladimir Kara-Murza Jr.; no relation to Mikhail Prokhorov

COMPATRIOTS

Leon Trotsky, founder of the Red army and Stalin's archenemy in exile

Svetlana Alliluyeva, Stalin's daughter and writer

Mikhail Baryshnikov, dancer

Alexander Solzhenitsyn, soldier, prisoner, and writer

Natasha Gurfinkel, senior vice president of Bank of New York

Vladimir Galitzine, aristocrat and vice president of Bank of New York

Lucy Edwards, vice president of Bank of New York

Vladimir Bukovsky, dissident and founder of Resistance International

Mikhail Tolstoy, member of parliament and organizer of the First Congress of Compatriots

Alexei Jordan, aristocrat, financier, and leader of the United Russian Cadet Corps in the United States

Boris Jordan, financier and media manager; son of Alexei Jordan

Peter Holodny, priest, financier, and treasurer of the White Church

Masha Gessen, journalist, author, and LGBTQ activist

Masha Slonim, journalist and granddaughter of Stalin's foreign minister

Ilya Zaslavskiy, oil company manager and activist at Free Russia Foundation

Garry Kasparov, chess champion and opposition activist

OLIGARCHS

Boris Berezovsky, go-between and go-getter, and former ally of Putin exiled to London

Vladimir Gusinsky, media magnate and founder of NTV and Russian Television International; in exile

Mikhail Khodorkovsky, oil tycoon, prisoner, and leader of Open Russia movement; in exile

Alexander Lebedev, KGB officer in London, banker, and media magnate in Russia and the United Kingdom

Mikhail Prokhorov, nickel tycoon, owner of the Brooklyn Nets, media magnate, and owner of *Snob* (Global Russians club)

*"There is no business like it. We are politicians. We are soldiers.
And, above all, we are actors on a wonderful stage."*
LEONID NIKITENKO,
a chief of the Nineteenth Section of the KGB,
in charge of recruiting agents in the Russian émigré communities in the West

"A strong diaspora can only exist if there is a strong state."
VLADIMIR PUTIN,
president of Russia, former colonel of the KGB

FOREWORD TO THE
PAPERBACK EDITION

It is the middle of June 2022 and the fourth month of the war in Ukraine. We are writing this at a café in what used to be the BBC headquarters, now part of King's College.

Four years ago, when we began working on a book about Russian political emigration, we lived in Russia. Back then we felt a little bit uneasy about the theme of the book because nobody from our families had emigrated. Although some of our relatives were victims of Stalin's oppressive measures—some lost all their property, others were killed—our families never considered leaving Russia for good.

In the introduction to the first edition of this book we wrote: "We are Russian investigative journalists based in Moscow. (Full disclosure: Although we have traveled extensively, including while researching this book, we have never lived abroad for more than a few months.)"

That has now changed. For many months we were wary of the word "emigrant" when describing ourselves. But that is what we are. We emigrated from Russia, and there are few options to return.

We've been writing about Russia's security services for more than twenty years, but two years ago the Kremlin effectively banned any writing on the subject. When the war started, our website Agentura.ru was blocked by the Russian authorities—not once, but twice. And in June, we learned that Andrei had been added to both Russia's domestic and international wanted lists—on criminal charges of "spreading false news about the Russian troops in Ukraine"—the charges the Kremlin has been using extensively against those who spoke against the Russian invasion of Ukraine.

We left Russia in September 2020, and the next year many Russian investigative journalists followed and moved to Europe. They did so because they couldn't keep working in the country anymore: many of them were put under criminal investigation or placed on the list of "foreign agents"—a special derogatory term the Kremlin has used against its critics, stopping short of an outright accusation of treason (that would come later).

When the war started, the Kremlin made it a crime to call the war a war. The government attacked social media in an attempt to have a full monopoly on information in the country. Almost all liberal media, or what was left of it, either closed or stopped their operations as they faced the very real threat of their journalists ending up in jail for reporting on the war.

Hundreds of reporters fled Russia. They moved to Georgia, Armenia, Lithuania, Latvia, Poland, and the Czech Republic. Some ended up in Turkey and Israel or elsewhere. They were just a tiny part of a much bigger wave of Russians leaving the country in droves. The ghost of general mobilization forced more than one hundred thousand IT specialists out of the country. Long known for its engineers and computer scientists, Russia is one of very few countries in which local internet platforms can compete successfully with global platforms, such as Google and Facebook. Before the war, many of these professionals were employees of US and other Western companies; others ran their own companies and did work for foreign clients. After February 24, 2022, however, it became clear that this kind of international work would no longer be possible. The sweeping Western sanctions hampered access to Western technologies, and many tech workers were unable to be paid by their Western clients or even connect to the servers of their companies. Moreover, many were young people in their mid-twenties to forties who feared being drafted into the army if they stayed.

They were joined by the liberal intelligentsia of big cities like Moscow and St. Petersburg—professors, researchers, and historians. Until then, they had been employed by universities, museums, or other research organizations. Many worked on projects supported by Western foundations and had previously pursued their work mostly free from the Kremlin's shadow. Many also had ties to Western universities. But in today's Russia, this kind of independent work is seen as unpatriotic. The fleeing intellectuals did not think that their lives were in danger, but their careers were, and many of them lost their jobs because of their liberal views.

Finally, there were businesspeople and managers of big corporations, including state-owned companies, as well as the Russian banks. These Russians no longer felt comfortable in a country that was closing its borders and isolating itself from the outside world, and many of them had been working for companies that were subject to Western sanctions or might become subject to them in the future. When the war started, many of these people abruptly left their jobs and fled to Europe and the United Arab Emirates.

Nearly all of the new émigrés had three things in common: a high level of education, a metropolitan background, and a liberal outlook. The war also forced most to develop an interest in politics. They understood that their hope to return was only possible with a regime change.

These émigrés didn't want to sit and wait for that change to happen. At the time of this writing, the journalists and intellectuals in exile have already achieved dramatic success—they have kept their connection with the Russian audience alive, thanks to globalization and the internet. Since the start of the war, the intellectual and liberal part of Russian society has been relying on them in their daily consumption of uncensored news.

In a nutshell, the new exiles are the brain of the nation, eager to have a say in the fate of the country. And that makes, we believe, the new emigration essential to Russia's future—the promise the previous waves of Russian exiles have failed to fulfill.

THE
COMPATRIOTS

INTRODUCTION

Toward the end of December 2017, a skinny, young Russian with expressive eyes, a stubbly beard, and a slight limp walked into a coffee shop in downtown Washington, DC. His name was Vladimir Kara-Murza (junior), and he was a Russian political émigré and anti-Kremlin lobbyist. He had lived in DC for years but often traveled back and forth to Moscow, irritating the Kremlin. On a trip to Moscow in spring 2015, he had been poisoned and nearly died. During his treatment in a Washington hospital, he received a visit from an FBI agent who said he had been assigned to Kara-Murza's case. When Kara-Murza recovered, he flew back to Moscow, and in February 2017 he was poisoned a second time, experiencing identical symptoms. That was why, ten months later, he was still limping.

The young Russian took a seat next to the window and a minute later was joined by a tall man in his midforties: the FBI agent. The agent had called for a meeting, promising to bring Kara-Murza some information about his poisoning. At this point, they had known each other for two years.

"We think we found the active substance you were poisoned with," the FBI agent said.

He told Kara-Murza that the agency was preparing a detailed report and explained that the heads of the Russian secret services would be soon visiting Washington: "We are going to hand the report over to them—that there was an attempted murder of a Russian citizen on Russian territory for political reasons."

The FBI's intent, the agent implied, was to send a message that they were not very happy about politically motivated poisonings in Moscow. But some in the agency were more troubled by the strange events happening on their own turf—in Washington.

A year and a half earlier, a Russian former press minister and presidential aide had been brutally beaten near his Dupont Circle hotel. He managed to make it to his room and then died there, not far from the coffee shop where Kara-Murza and the FBI agent were sitting. Those who had beaten the ex-minister to death were never found, and the rumor in Moscow was that he had fallen out of line with the Kremlin just before the incident.

The FBI wanted to make its concerns clear to the Russian intelligence community, and the upcoming visit provided a unique opportunity. The heads of all three major Russian spy agencies—SVR, the foreign intelligence agency; FSB, the domestic security service; and the GRU, military intelligence—had never before traveled together to a Western capital, but they planned to do exactly that at the end of January 2018.

Three weeks after their coffee shop meeting, the FBI agent called Kara-Murza again. He didn't offer to meet this time. He just told Kara-Murza that laboratory results on the poison were inconclusive and that the plan to deliver a report had been called off. Then he hung up.

The heads of the three Russian intelligence agencies flew to Washington, as planned, at the end of January. It was very unlikely, given the circumstances, that the report on Kara-Murza was mentioned at the highly secret meeting.[1] The following month, another Russian, former spy Sergei Skripal, would be poisoned in Britain by two agents of Russian military intelligence.

Almost thirty years after the collapse of the Soviet Union and twenty since Vladimir Putin came to power in the Kremlin, Russians abroad were suddenly in the crosshairs.

In January 2018, as the heads of all three Russian spy agencies went to Washington, we went to Paris.

In the heavy rain, across the enormous Champ de Mars, the Eiffel Tower seemed unreachable. We were standing at the epicenter of France's military glory: behind us stood the stately classic complex of the École-Militaire—the famous center for French military education—and all around us the avenues were named after French marshals.

We decided to keep walking. It was a nice walk, even in the rain; after the winter in Moscow, it felt good to see something other than snow. From the Champ de Mars we headed down the Avenue Rapp—named after a Napoleonic general who led an attack at Austerlitz that completely decimated the Russian emperor's elite Chevalier Guard. Our destination was the Pont de l'Alma, a bridge named after a Crimean War battle in which an expeditionary French and British force defeated the Russian army.

But our intentions for sightseeing were not historical in nature. Right at that junction stands a brand-new complex: four buildings with facades covered in beige limestone. The building in the middle, topped by five onion-shaped domes, is the Holy Trinity Cathedral—part of the Russian Orthodox Spiritual and Cultural Center.

We wanted to see it because although the center had been in operation for only two years, it had already sparked large-scale "spy mania." Among the rumors circulating was that the French counterintelligence services had surrounded the complex with jamming devices to prevent the Russians from using the center's facilities for electronic eavesdropping. And we knew that the officials at the French Foreign Ministry, located on the nearby Quai d'Orsay, were pissed off by the Russian government's request that the center's employees be granted diplomatic immunity.

We entered through the main doors. Two bulky security guards told us—very politely and in Russian—to open our bags. They checked the insides thoroughly.

We crossed the main hall and entered an internal courtyard, where the rain was still coming down. But when we tried to sneak into the next building, we were stopped; a man appeared from nowhere and gestured at us to stop and go back. It was clear that we had entered an area that was under careful watch. In an instant, we were struck by that familiar feeling of being on Russian territory—specifically, the territory of a Russian government institution abroad.

Indeed we were. The center is the property of the administration of the Russian president, and it is run by people experienced in promoting Russia's foreign policy. The head of the center was a career Russian diplomat. And Bishop Nestor, the prior of Holy Trinity Cathedral, was no stranger to Russian diplomacy himself; he had spent four years serving in the Ministry of Foreign Economic Relations, an alliance the Moscow Patriarchate called "a symphony between the state department and the church."[2]

We walked back to the main hall, where a handful of French visitors were wandering around, looking at photographs on the walls. Announcements were posted everywhere about an upcoming concert featuring a male choir and an exhibition marking the centenary of the Bolshevik persecution of the Orthodox Church. Indeed, the center was getting ready to embark on an entire year of events commemorating the suffering of the church under the Communists.

The message was clear: Orthodox believers in France, mostly Russian emigrants and their descendants, were invited to come to a church that was clearly under Moscow's control. There, they would be embraced by the new Russia, one no longer divided into two groups—the Russian diaspora and Russians still living in Russia—but constituting a single *Russky Mir* (Russian world), whose members were all "compatriots."

Putin latched on to the concept of *Russky Mir*—the worldwide community of Russian-speaking people whose identity is firmly connected to Russia's history, culture, and language—in the early 2000s.[3] It is a community whose members are, by definition, closely tied to Russia. No wonder Putin liked the idea; it could serve as a good political instrument for promoting Russia's influence abroad. According to Putin, this "Russian world" now consists of more than thirty million people, with ten million living in Europe.[4] And, he decided, the church would provide them all with spiritual guidance.

To make this work for the Russian émigrés, two things were needed. First, prominent emigrant families would need to cooperate with Moscow. Second, the Russian Orthodox Church had to be united and the abyss bridged between the priests inside and outside the country.

Putin achieved both sets of conditions. He was not the first to take steps in this direction; his predecessor Boris Yeltsin had started a conversation with the émigrés in the final year of the Soviet Union. But Putin's goals were completely different.

Russia's diaspora is the third largest in the world, exceeded only by those from India and Mexico (China is fourth), according to UN statistics.[5] That didn't start recently. Russians began leaving the country in large numbers in the late nineteenth century, fleeing pogroms, tsarist secret police persecution, the Russian Revolution, then Stalin and the KGB. This exodus created a rare opportunity for the Kremlin. Moscow's masters and spymasters scored their biggest successes—recruiting among the Western establishment, stealing the secrets of the American atomic bomb—through networks of spies, many of whom were emigrants driven from Russia. During the 1930s and 1940s, dozens of spies were in New York City gathering information for Moscow.

The history of Russian espionage is soaked in blood, as Russian agents proved themselves ruthless and efficient at killing their fellow emigrants abroad. The Kremlin had learned well that to ensure political stability, it was not enough to have people inside the country under control; the émigré communities had to be brutally policed too. After all, the mighty Russian empire had been taken down by a bunch of emigrant revolutionaries who, at the end of World War I, had seized the opportunity to return to the country. Their descendants in the Kremlin had good memories, which they put to good use.

Did that story end with the collapse of the Soviet Union? No.

Mikhail Gorbachev opened the borders, and in the 1990s, Russians started to leave the country in much bigger numbers. Emigration remained a golden opportunity for the Russian spymasters but also a challenge. Post-Soviet Russia lived without politically motivated emigrations for only ten years. When Putin came to power, he immediately returned to the practice of forcing his enemies out of the country.

We are Russian investigative journalists now in exile in London. For more than twenty years we have been focused on researching the ways in which the Kremlin controls the Russian people. Our first book, *The New Nobility*, was about the secret services—Moscow's traditional means of "running a tight ship." In our second book, *The Red Web*, we described the Kremlin's desperate attempts to bring the internet to heel. So it seemed like the next natural step was to look at another serious challenge to the Russian authorities—the people who have moved outside Russia's borders—and to explore the ways in which the Kremlin is dealing with them.

In this book, we tell the story of how, throughout the twentieth century and into the twenty-first, the Kremlin has considered the presence of Russians in Western countries—particularly the United

States—both its biggest threat and its biggest opportunity. Successive regimes in Moscow sought for years to use the Russian émigré community to achieve their goals. But they also sought to neutralize any potential dangers posed by Russians abroad, experimenting with tricks and methods that would also come in handy closer to home.

Part I covers the Soviet period from the time of Lenin's death, when Soviet intelligence first began to develop ways to deal with the threat of emigration and ways of exploiting it, through the end of the Soviet Union. Much of that initial tool kit has been in use ever since. We also describe how the Americans struggled to make use of Russian émigré groups in the Cold War landscape.

Part II looks into the 1990s and how the opportunities created by Russia's opening borders were exploited—by Russian American financiers, by Russian spies, and by different waves of Russian émigrés.

Part III shows how Putin changed the game, announcing and promulgating his own view of emigration, namely, that it was high time for Russian "compatriots" to advance Russia's positions beyond its borders.

Finally, we describe in Part IV how Putin reintroduced political emigration—forcing Russians into exile and finding ways to signal to those who had left that Moscow's hand could reach them anywhere and everywhere.

Russia's borders remain porous, for the first time in its history, and that gives us hope. We tell the stories of some people who have found ways to fight the tactics of the current regime, both in Russia and from abroad. Their efforts, unsurprisingly, have raised the stakes and prompted the Kremlin to employ more desperate methods. That makes the world more dangerous, and more unpredictable, both for Russians abroad and for the countries that have welcomed them.

PART I

SPIES AND DISSIDENTS

CHAPTER 1

TALENT SPOTTING

L enin, "The Vozhd,"* was dead. Endless queues of silent mourners snaked through the snow as far as the eye could see, from Red Square all the way down to the Moskvoretsky Bridge. Some held large portraits: Lenin's bold, distinctive head; face framed by a goatee and a moustache; the famous squint. The mourners moved slowly forward in the freezing January air, toward the hastily built wooden cube at the foot of the Kremlin's wall. They wanted to see his body: the short man with small hands who was now lying there in an open coffin. LENIN read the sign over the entryway of the wooden cube. Long lines of servicemen in swishing greatcoats, large red stars on their helmets, formed a second line as they protected the wooden cube. Closer to the cube stood yet another line of guards—the chekists, the operatives of the Soviet secret police. One of them, a young man with fair hair and a flaccid chin, was in particular danger of freezing: Vasily Zarubin had already spent hours on Red Square and had not been able to leave to put on warmer clothes.[1]

Finally, Zarubin's shift ended. He crossed the square hastily and turned right, onto Nikolskaya Street. From there, he walked briskly

---

* Leader or guide in Russian.

to the imposing, five-story building on Lubyanka Square that had been occupied by the Soviet secret police since 1918. Stamping his feet against the cold, Zarubin cursed himself; he had responded to the urgent summons from Moscow so quickly that he had forgotten to dress for the frigid weather. Now he was paying for his oversight.

The guards at Lubyanka admitted the young chekist into the secret service headquarters, which, in addition to offices, housed a deadly prison. As Zarubin felt the prickly sensation of warmth returning to his frozen extremities, he received his instructions for his next assignment: he was being sent to China to spy on a community of Russian exiles who had fled the revolution.

Within the halls of Lubyanka, Zarubin was considered an experienced operative. He was thirty years old and had spent ten of them at war—first in the World War, then in the civil war, and, finally, suppressing peasant revolts in central Russia. But for all his experience, he had deficits: Zarubin had never been abroad, and, as the son of a railroad worker, his formal education extended only to primary school. His real and only education was in the trenches. With his fair hair, pale skin, and Slavic features, Zarubin looked very Russian—something that would help him in his next assignment. After all, Harbin, China, was home to a large community of Russian exiles, and Zarubin's looks would help him infiltrate this group.

Felix Dzerzhinsky, head of the Soviet secret police, was sure that anti-Bolshevik groups like the one in Harbin were just waiting for the right moment to reclaim Russia. Lenin's death would provide just such an opportunity: the departure of a charismatic leader rendered the new regime vulnerable. Dzerzhinsky responded to this threat by dispatching dozens of his operatives to countries in which Russian émigrés had found refuge. In the case of Harbin, this was relatively easy to accomplish. China and Russia had recently established diplomatic relations, and the Soviet authorities had already set up a consulate in the city.

Zarubin traveled to Harbin with his beautiful and intelligent wife, Olga, and their young daughter, Zoya. On arrival, he reported to the Soviet consulate where, as its newest officer, he officially served as deputy head of the economics division.

Zarubin was to have a long and productive career in Soviet intelligence. The émigré "problem," his first assignment, would become his lifelong occupation.

In agreeing to take this assignment, Zarubin was following an already long-standing tradition. As the famous Soviet dissident and political émigré Vladimir Bukovsky once said to us, "This was the way the Russian empire was built: the expansion of Russia was the result of a long process, in which the Russian people fled Russian power, and the power chased the people."[2]

Indeed, in the years and decades to come, Soviet secret police chiefs—Dzerzhinsky and his successors—would continue sending operatives abroad to deal with the threat, real or imagined, posed by Russian political emigration.

The year 1924 found Zarubin stuck in Harbin. Summer came and went, and by the time September rolled around, he thought he was beginning to get used to the place. He walked to work from the suburbs every morning, and to him, the city felt like Moscow, where his family had lived before World War I. The architecture was in the same messy, provincial style—mostly two- and three-story houses with first floors made of brick and upper floors of wood, sloppily scoured. Now he headed to the more fashionable part of town, up on the hill, known as *Novy Gorod* (New City). Here, fancy apartment buildings in the modern style added to the mix; they had huge windows, decorated with exquisite trellis work, and Art Nouveau front doors. Overweight, suspicious policemen in black uniforms patrolled streets bearing Russian names and guarded storefronts featuring pre-reform Cyrillic signage. It was a bit like time travel: seven years had passed since the Bolshevik revolution and four years since the end of bloody and brutal civil war, but in Harbin, at first glance, it looked like none of it had ever happened.

With his modest suit, Russian looks, and Russian language, Zarubin seemed to belong in this provincial city. But the Soviet spy was a hostile agent in a foreign country. Not only was Russia 320 long miles to the north—below the Russian signage on the shop windows, he could see the city's standard Chinese characters—but the city had an unusual history. Twenty years earlier, the tsar had rented a ten-mile chunk of Chinese territory for the construction of a railroad intended to connect the Trans-Siberian Railroad with Vladivostok. A fishing village—Harbin—was chosen as the location for the railroad's administrative center on China's soil. Russian engineers arrived and quickly built a Russian-style city, complete with Orthodox churches, schools, and typical street plan. With the permission of the Chinese authorities, the tsar placed Harbin under Russian administration. By the start of World War I, Harbin had grown to a midsized, essentially Russian city.

Then, on a dark October night in 1917, the Bolsheviks seized power in Russia in a military revolt. Many Russians chose to flee from the new masters. Those who found themselves in Russia's center fled west, taking either the sea road—through Crimea and then to Constantinople—or north, to Finland, with the hope of ultimately reaching Berlin and Paris, but also Prague and Belgrade. Those who happened to be in the east of the country headed farther east, often toward Harbin. Thus, by 1924 there were more than one hundred thousand Russians in the city. The Chinese happily agreed to keep things the way they had been before the revolution, which meant letting tsarist bureaucrats continue to run the town. Indeed, when Zarubin arrived, prerevolutionary Russian rules still governed daily life in Harbin.

Another consequence of the Chinese approach was that numerous White Guard organizations—remnants of the army that had fought against the "Red," or Bolshevik, guard—felt safe in the town. They didn't believe that the power struggle back in Russia was truly over and were biding their time in Harbin, waiting for the moment when they could return to their native land and seize power.

Dzerzhinsky, the chief of the Soviet secret police and a founder of the Cheka, was well aware of this. He was convinced that the White Guard would never give up. As a result, he put immense pressure on his operatives to do everything in their power to undermine the exiled White Guard organizations and their allies. In March 1924, he sent his deputy a note regarding "the fight against émigré terrorist organizations."[3] In it, Dzerzhinsky asked if the secret service was keeping comprehensive blacklists of members of these White Guard organizations. What about their relatives, in Russia and abroad? Dzerzhinsky wanted them all watched.

In early September, the Russian general Pyotr Wrangel founded the Russian All-Military Union, or ROVS, the military wing of the world Russian émigré community. Four years earlier, Wrangel had fought the Bolsheviks in Crimea, lost, and led the defeated White army into exile. By late 1924, in Harbin and elsewhere, Wrangel's ROVS was actively training its members, preparing them for their return to Russia.[4]

Zarubin hastened to a two-story mansion guarded by a fence. The monumental gate defiantly displayed the hammer and sickle on a globe, under the yellow-painted rays of a metal sun, framed by ears of wheat. The Soviet Union's emblem had been adopted as the proletarian state's coat of arms only the year before, and the colors on this rendering were still bright. Behind the gate, the mansion housed the Soviet consulate. Zarubin had been coming here every day, month after month, for almost half a year. But he was deeply frustrated: six months into his tenure as a Soviet secret police operative in Harbin, Zarubin had yet to accomplish anything at all.

As Zarubin passed beneath the Soviet coat of arms and into the consulate, he reflected on his situation. He had, he thought, very little chance of success. For starters, he was a known employee of the Soviet Consulate, so he couldn't pretend to be an émigré. There were other problems too: Zarubin's lack of education and social polish made it hard for him to mix with the local émigrés. The qualities he had developed in his brutal decade in the army were not those that could help him in a town full of tsarist administration officials, army officers, bohemians, and members of the intelligentsia. Besides, although the secret service had trained him to be a ruthless secret police operative, they hadn't taught him any spy tradecraft. In short, he couldn't knock on the door of a respectable house in town. Or could he?

The thing that distinguished Harbin from all other cities populated by Russian exiles was that it was still largely run by Russians. Simultaneously, the city's Soviet consulate was officially recognized by China. Thus, Zarubin's place of employment conducted official business with the White Russian–run city administration. It would be perfectly normal for a Soviet official (like Zarubin) to pay a visit to Harbin's city council. This, he thought, could be a way in.

Most of the city council's officials—exiles who had decided to take responsibility for the town they found themselves in—hailed from the Russian intelligentsia. One member of the city council, the official in charge of hospitals and public gardens, had once been a highly respected explorer of the remote and wild Kamchatka Peninsula. The former explorer had a daughter named Anna. She was a pretty but deeply lonely girl with fragile features.[5]

True, Zarubin had brought his wife, Olga, to Harbin with him. Olga was a smart and educated young woman who had married him in 1918—just a year after the revolution, it was a time in which a girl's marriage to a chekist could well save her entire family's life. And they had their daughter Zoya, only four years old, with them. But, reasoned Zarubin, Anna didn't need to know these details. As the daughter of a city official, Anna could be his in—an entry point to access the city elite. Zarubin arranged a meeting.

He started an affair, as planned. He got his agent. But then, something unexpected happened. He fell in love with her.

Consequences quickly followed. Olga received an anonymous letter from Zarubin's colleague, a fellow secret police officer, exposing the affair. She was deeply offended. Next, the information was passed to the head of the Soviet intelligence station in Harbin. The commander sensed danger: his officer was no longer reliable. Normally, in the bloodthirsty Soviet secret police, Zarubin's career would have ended here, but his chief liked him.

The only way to help Zarubin was to transfer him to another department, so his chief sent a telegram to Moscow. It was addressed to Mikhail Trilisser, head of the Soviet secret police's foreign department (intelligence operations abroad). The son of a shoemaker from Astrakhan, Trilisser had been a Bolshevik since 1901, and during the civil war, he had served on the Russia-China border as an undercover Bolshevik operative, spying against the White Guard, the Chinese, and the Japanese. He had a soft spot for the operatives from the Far East.

Trilisser agreed to give Zarubin a second chance.[6] Zarubin was called back to Moscow for training. Anna, Zarubin's lover, went with him. Zarubin's wife, Olga—now also employed by the secret police—stayed in Harbin, along with their daughter.

In Moscow, Trilisser decided Zarubin was worth keeping around. Even if his time in Harbin had been a disaster, he was stubborn, conventionally brave, and moderately ambitious. He was also Russian, and in the Soviet intelligence service, formed by and filled with Latvians, Jews, and Georgians, ethnic Russians were rare.

At just that moment, Russians were in huge demand. Stalin, Lenin's successor, had just officially proclaimed that "the building up of socialism in one country"[7] was possible—thus signifying the abandonment of any immediate plans to start a worldwide revolution. Among other things, this proclamation was a message to the secret police: a directive to become more Russia-oriented, more "national."

So Zarubin was saved. He was soon assigned to the Soviet embassy in Finland, another place where the Russian émigré community had nested.

In the end, he traveled to Finland alone. Anna was trapped in Moscow. She had made a mistake, falling for Zarubin, and for years to come, she desperately tried to find her way back to Harbin. There was no space for people like her in Russia—the Soviet authorities never trusted returned emigrants—and they didn't make it easy for her to leave. She was caught trying to cross the border and spent five years in Stalin's gulag.

Without Zarubin, there was no one to deal with the Russian émigré organization in Harbin. That was unacceptable to the Soviet secret police, who saw Harbin's émigré community as a crucial threat. Moscow urgently needed to send in another agent.

Trilisser, the chief of the Soviet foreign intelligence, picked Nahum Eitingon. A tall, handsome operative with black hair and black eyes, Eitingon was strikingly different from Zarubin.

Eitingon was young, just twenty-five years old, but already very sure of himself. A Jew born in a small town near Mogilev in the Pale of Settlement, he had witnessed the brutality of the tsarist regime firsthand: his native town fell victim to a pogrom when Eitingon was just six years old. This was followed by World War I and German occupation. He survived, becoming one of many Jews who developed their survival instincts at an extremely high, deeply personal price. People like him made for a generation of highly committed and professional Soviet operatives.

In 1917, when Eitingon was eighteen years old, he joined the Socialist Revolutionaries. Essentially a party of terrorists, they were masters of *konspiratsiya*, a set of strict security procedures taken to ensure the integrity of a clandestine operation. They had killed a long list of tsarist officials. Soon, however, Eitingon switched sides. He joined the Bolsheviks and then the Cheka, the Bolshevik secret police. He was given an order to persecute Socialist Revolutionaries, his old comrades. They were now branded "counterrevolutionaries" because they dared to question Bolshevik policies. Eitingon didn't hesitate: he immediately carried out his new orders. Where Zarubin was prone to emotionality, Eitingon was ice cold and sharp as a knife.

His commanders in the Cheka praised Eitingon for his effectiveness and "productiveness."[8] By early 1920, he was attached to the "Eastern" department of the secret police. There, his job was to supervise the fight against counterrevolutionaries across a very large region, stretching from the Caucasus to Siberia and to the Far East on the border with China. Next, he studied with the military academy's Eastern faculty in Moscow.

By 1925 Eitingon was better trained, better educated, and far more experienced than Zarubin, whose place he was about to take in Harbin.

Before Eitingon left for China, Trilisser called him into Dzerzhinsky's office. The founder of the Cheka was laconic. His only parting words were, "Do everything you can that is useful for the revolution."[9]

When he arrived in Harbin, Eitingon almost immediately started an affair with Zarubin's abandoned wife. The two promptly began living together. As with his decision to persecute his former comrades, here again, in love, Eitingon never hesitated—it was in his nature to take action.

Meanwhile, in a cheap hotel in Bucharest, a pretty, twenty-four-year-old, university-educated woman with black hair and piercing brown eyes committed murder. A fierce supporter of Romania's Communist Party, she had spent the evening in her room awaiting a Communist courier. When she heard a knock at the door, she opened it. It was a fellow comrade, someone she knew. But the man aimed a pistol at her. Then he demanded she hand over a packet from Moscow containing instructions from the Comintern, the Moscow-based international organization whose proclaimed goal was to instigate a worldwide Communist revolution.

She said she didn't have the papers, and the man with the pistol told her to put on her coat. She knew what was coming—her brother, a leader of the militant wing of the Romanian Communist Party, had just been killed by Siguranza, the brutal Romanian secret police. While dressing, she found her pistol. She took one shot and didn't miss.[10] Like Eitingon, she never hesitated. She didn't make mistakes either.

Trilisser spotted her talent and called her to Moscow. During her long career in Soviet intelligence, she would have many names, but the one she would finally be known by was Liza Gorskaya.

In the years to come, Zarubin, Eitingon, and Gorskaya—a disciplined Russian, a resourceful and ruthless Jew, and a well-educated, fierce, cosmopolitan woman—would all become successful Soviet operatives. All three would be instrumental in defining and executing the Kremlin's strategy for dealing with the threat posed by Russians abroad.

CHAPTER 2

IDENTIFYING TARGETS

The year 1929 began well for Eitingon, who was now heading the Soviet foreign intelligence's *rezidentura* (station) in Harbin. He had attracted the notice of his superiors in Moscow during his four years in China, and his most recent operation was his most spectacular yet. Soviet intelligence had long suspected that the local Chinese warlord, an uncrowned king of northern China known as the Old Marshal, had close ties to the Japanese. Moscow didn't like that. Japan had plans to turn this region of China into its military base, which threatened Russia.

While the Old Marshal was traveling by train from Beijing to Harbin, a bomb went off just as his personal car passed the bridge. The Old Marshal was mortally wounded and died the same day. The Chinese blamed the Japanese military, but the operation had in fact been Eitingon's. It propelled him into the elite of the Soviet foreign intelligence; afterward, the Soviet secret police awarded him the Red Banner Order, the greatest of the Soviet honors. Eitingon was not yet thirty years old.[1]

Trilisser trusted him completely. For more than a year, Eitingon enjoyed a free hand in carrying out operations all over China. He ran several important agents in the Russian émigré community, and his spies gave him access to top-secret correspondence between Japan's General Staff and its military missions in northern China. Here again, Eitingon proved himself brutally effective when dealing with his White Russian compatriots—the enemies of the revolution. He had one of his agents pass a tip to Japanese intelligence saying that twenty of their Russian émigré assets had switched sides and asked secretly for Soviet passports. The Japanese believed Eitingon's disinformation and promptly killed all of them. In the foreign branch of the Soviet secret police, Eitingon was a rising star.

On May 27, 1929, all this abruptly ended. At 2:00 p.m., dozens of Chinese policemen—some of them former White Guard servicemen now working for the Chinese—rushed the gate beneath the hammer and sickle on a globe, gained entry to the Harbin consulate's mansion, and arrested thirty-nine people on the spot.

Earlier that morning, the Chinese police had been warned by a Russian émigré that an important meeting was to take place around 2:00 p.m. in the mansion's basement—probably a Comintern conference plotting to instigate Communist rebellion. Indeed, Harbin's police were already on the alert—they had seen dozens of suspicious people entering the consulate all day. So the police commissar ordered a raid.[2]

Eitingon was armed and did not want to be caught by the police with a pistol on his body. Once again, he didn't hesitate. There was a good chance that the police would not search a little girl, so he quickly called for his now nine-year-old stepdaughter, Zoya Zarubina. He gave her his gun, and the child smuggled it out of the consulate. Eitingon then made sure that most of the rezidentura's secret documents were burned before the Chinese got them.

Still, the raid caused a scandal in Moscow. The rezidentura was compromised—there was no denying that.

Trilisser summoned Eitingon back to Moscow. More than three thousand miles lie between Moscow and Harbin, and it took Eitingon more than a week by train to arrive in the capital.

* * *

The June sun melted Moscow's asphalt, and Muscovites were choked by heat and dust; the authorities had begun blowing up churches all over the city under the pretext of making way for new streets. The attack on the consulate in Harbin was in the news, but the newspapers were more focused on providing colorful descriptions of counterrevolutionary conspiracies and requests by workers to put an end to them. Tension filled the air, and the pace of the city changed. Passersby overtook Eitingon, and he saw the strain in their faces. But he also saw excitement: a carnival had just arrived in Moscow. It was a massive show that was overtaking the streets. No fewer than fifty-four trucks carrying gigantic papier-mâché figures—dwarfs in cylinders labeled "Capitalist France and countries of Small Entente," a group of ugly puppets called "A wedding of the Pope and Mussolini," a truck with an elephant's trunk to symbolize colonial India—drove through the city, glorifying Soviet achievements and denouncing Western capitalists, before enthusiastically setting up camp on Red Square.[3] At the same time, some of Moscow's businesses had gone on strike because of low salaries, and long queues formed in front of shops. There were shortages of white bread.[4]

Eitingon didn't care much about the mood of Muscovites. Unlike Zarubin, Eitingon had little personal history there, and he was generally not a sentimental man: when he left his native town behind, he cut his ties to his past. For him, Moscow had always been Russia's powerhouse—nothing more and nothing less. Now he walked briskly to the large, looming building on Lubyanka Square and prepared himself to meet the Old Man, as Trilisser—a bespectacled, forty-year-old man with the type of brush mustache that Hitler later made famous—was called by his subordinates. As he made his way up to the third floor, to Trilisser's office, Eitingon ran into several colleagues he hadn't seen for years. Their confused and frightened faces stunned him.

For the past six months, the Soviet foreign intelligence department had been trembling with uncertainty as the chekists found themselves at the heart of Kremlin political intrigue. Ever since

Lenin died, the two archrivals—Joseph Stalin and Leon Trotsky—had kept their factions in the party at each other's throats, fighting for power. Trotsky's supporters held mass demonstrations in Moscow, but Stalin, cunning and calculating, was gaining ground and tightening his grip on the flamboyant Trotsky. Stalin delivered the final blow in January 1929. Trotsky, already in exile in Soviet Central Asia, thousands of miles from Moscow, learned that the decision had been made to throw him out of the country permanently.

Trotsky struck back at once. His supporters printed thousands of copies of a proclamation that included a transcript of a conversation between two high-ranking party officials, Bukharin and Kamenev. In the conversation, the officials weighed the opposition's odds against Stalin. According to the transcript, Kamenev wanted to know who the anti-Stalin opposition could rely on within the Soviet secret police. "Yagoda and Trilisser are with us," was Bukharin's answer.[5] The two were deputy heads of the Soviet secret police.[6]

Within the week, the head of the service, along with Genrikh Yagoda and Trilisser, wrote to Stalin. They claimed, rather desperately, that Bukharin's words had no grounds.[7] Stalin appeared to believe them, but it didn't calm the waters. Felix Dzerzhinsky had died two years earlier, and his successor was constantly ill and often absent from the office. Few believed he could protect his people, including his two most trusted deputies—Yagoda and Trilisser. Of the two, Yagoda was relatively safe—he had proven himself loyal to Stalin two years earlier when he crushed a pro-Trotsky manifestation in Moscow—but Trilisser was vulnerable.

Months passed and nothing happened. Nervousness was palpable at the foreign intelligence offices on the third and fourth floors of Lubyanka. People there knew how patiently Stalin could wait to exact his revenge for someone's mistake (indeed, both Yagoda and Trilisser would eventually be "purged" by Stalin, and Yagoda would fall and be executed first). Besides, foreign intelligence was a relatively small organization, with just over one hundred people, so there was no place to hide. If Trilisser were to fall, lots of people would fall along with him. The best way to avoid trouble was to go on assignment abroad as soon as possible—an idea that quickly became a truism among Soviet spies.

Zarubin was already safely out. After Finland, he had been sent to Denmark, an assignment that put his life on a completely new track. He went to Copenhagen as an "illegal": an agent with no diplomatic cover, who pretended he was not Russian. The illegals were the crème de la crème of the Soviet espionage world. Zarubin still had trouble mastering a foreign language, and he still lacked proper training in spy tradecraft, but he was considered a hardened Communist. Better yet, he was disciplined and understood the need for rules—a rare thing among the first generation of Soviet operatives. With his fair hair and blue eyes, he looked Northern European—at least in the eyes of his superiors. Thus, with Trilisser's approval, Zarubin went to Copenhagen using the passport of a naturalized American of Finnish extraction. (The passport was bona fide—it belonged to a man who didn't need it while he worked on a contract in the Soviet Union.) This infiltration strategy would be used more than once. Soviet intelligence loved to have its illegals in Europe pose as Americans. They believed that the bearer of an American passport was treated with more respect by the European police than people with European passports. It was also more difficult for European authorities to reach out to the US authorities for a background check. To bureaucrats in the "Old World," the United States was still a remote land. Zarubin's instructions were to sit tight in Copenhagen in the guise of a businessman. He was to keep a low profile.

In Moscow, Eitingon continued waiting for an assignment. Finally, Trilisser made a decision: Eitingon would go to Turkey to run a legal rezidentura in the Soviet consulate in Constantinople (the city was renamed Istanbul the following year). One of his tasks was to keep an eye on local émigré communities—Ukrainian,

Azerbaijani, and North Caucasian, in particular. He was also expected to spy on the White Guard organizations, just as he had in Harbin.

Eitingon considered himself lucky. In August 1929, when the Central Committee of the Communist Party finally started the purge of Moscow's Soviet foreign intelligence service, he was already in Constantinople.

What he didn't understand, though, was that of all the cities in the world, Constantinople had just become the most dangerous for Soviet operatives.

CHAPTER 3

THE COST OF LOVE

The Bolshevik political regime in Moscow started off by killing its enemies. But when it came to fellow revolutionaries who had fallen out of step with the party, the Bolsheviks were more forgiving. These former comrades in arms were not murdered; rather, they were expelled from the ruling elite or forced from the country.

This changed when Stalin took power. Always paranoid, Stalin did not like the idea of his former comrades potentially competing for influence from abroad. So the new Soviet leader instructed his spies to hunt them down, wherever they were. Soviet spies abroad targeted the party leaders who had just yesterday been part of the political regime, many of whom were still held in high regard by the country's elite—including the secret police. Stalin's vindictive approach would change the nature of Soviet intelligence forever.

A few months before Eitingon arrived in Constantinople, in February 1929, Leon Trotsky had been shipped by Soviet operatives to the Turkish capital from Odessa aboard the Soviet cruise liner

Ilyich. This time, *Ilyich* had no other passengers apart from Trotsky, his family, and two of Stalin's agents, so the secret police could keep Trotsky completely under control all the way from Central Asia to Turkey. They wanted to continue this around-the-clock monitoring in Constantinople.

But the task was not simple. Only yesterday, Trotsky had been a powerful, high-ranking party official. A legend of the revolutionary days, he was still popular within the party, including within the very secret service now charged with spying on him.

There were two foreign intelligence stations in Constantinople in 1929. The legal rezidentura existed within the consulate, and its agents were diplomats. That rezidentura was run by Eitingon. The illegal rezidentura had no diplomatic cover, and its chief was Yakov Blyumkin, a brisk thirty-one-year-old operative with five-o'clock shadow who always kept his hair trimmed short. Blyumkin ran the illegal rezidentura from a bookstore that specialized in the trade of antiquarian Jewish books.

The parallel existence of legal and illegal Soviet stations was a legacy of the harsh conditions the Bolshevik party had faced under the tsar. In tsarist Russia, the Bolshevik party's status fluctuated between legal and illegal, so the party set up a parallel system of underground cells to take over in case tsarist police shut down the legal party cells. During World War I, this system was expanded abroad as the Bolsheviks created a parallel underground network in many European countries and in the United States.

After the revolution, Lenin decided that the Bolshevik approach had been a success story and should be replicated. Moscow forced a two-tiered system on friendly Communist parties in Europe, which were obliged to create illegal, underground party cells in addition to their existing legal cells. According to the thinking in Moscow, this second, parallel system would serve as insurance in case the local authorities decided to ban the Communist Party. The Soviet secret police, as the party organization tasked with the most sensitive tasks, quite naturally followed suit: before long, the Soviet secret police had opened parallel illegal stations anywhere Soviet Russia had an embassy.

In Constantinople, the illegal rezidentura was in good hands. The "bookseller" Blyumkin was a resourceful operative, famous for his survival instincts. He had first made his mark in July 1918 when, as a young chekist and a member of the Social-Revolutionary party (in the first years after the revolution, Lenin allowed some fellow revolutionaries from other parties to be part of his repressive machine), he walked into the German embassy in Moscow and shot the German ambassador dead in cold blood.[1] Blyumkin, who had hoped the assassination would prevent the signing of a separate peace with Germany, pursued by Bolsheviks but opposed by his party, survived the ensuing mess and managed to flee his unhappy superiors in Moscow. Next he showed up in Ukraine, where he also survived the chekist investigation into the assassination. He won back his former bosses' trust and went on to forge a remarkable career in the foreign branch of the Soviet secret service. Throughout the 1920s, he popped up in various locales from Iran to Mongolia and continued plotting and conspiring. In Constantinople, Blyumkin was largely on his own, running his operations at the illegal rezidentura independently, but he needed to maintain contact with the legal rezidentura. For that, he had an agent: the young Romanian operative Liza Gorskaya.

Gorskaya had come a long way since Trilisser first spotted her in 1924. From Bucharest, she moved to Vienna, where, undercover as a translator, her career in Soviet intelligence began. She soon obtained Soviet citizenship. Her membership in the Romanian Communist Party was transferred to the Bolshevik party. Along the way, she got rid of her given name (Ester) and became Liza, and she adopted the Russian-looking surname Gorskaya. She also left behind her marriage to a Romanian Communist. Then she was sent to Moscow to receive intensive training in spy tradecraft.

She was a promising operative, fluent in French, German, and Russian. But she was still an outsider, and it was clear to her that she needed a protector. Liza received her new assignment: Trilisser sent her to Turkey to report directly to Blyumkin. This was good for her: Blyumkin was a shining star in Soviet foreign intelligence, one of the most adventurous—and lucky—operatives. Liza always recognized an opportunity when she saw it. She was a vivid and beautiful young woman, twenty-nine years old, with big, dark eyes and glossy black hair, and before long, Blyumkin had fallen in love with her.

In Constantinople, with Trilisser behind him and a woman he loved at his side, it looked like Blyumkin was on top of the world. But he made a mistake: he didn't give up on his affection for Trotsky.

On April 12, 1929, Blyumkin was wandering the Grand Rue de Péra, in the most fashionable district in the European part of Constantinople, two days after coming to the city. It was a sunny day, and spring was in full flower. Suddenly, he saw a familiar face—Blyumkin had run into Trotsky's twenty-three-year-old son. The young man invited Blyumkin to come and see his father. The Soviet operative readily accepted the invitation. Blyumkin had once worked as Trotsky's secretary, and he still adored him. They met four days later. At that meeting, they spoke for four hours. Blyumkin had several subsequent meetings with the exiled revolutionary's son, in which they discussed a wide range of topics, from Trotsky's chances of returning to Russia to how best to organize Trotsky's personal security detail.[2] It was a dangerous game for Blyumkin to play. Trotsky was Stalin's archenemy, and Blyumkin was on Stalin's payroll, his trusted spy.

Soon after these meetings, Trotsky made his move.

The vast majority of Russian refugees who fled Soviet Russia didn't want to settle abroad forever. They had every intention of going back home as soon as they saw the chance to change the political regime. Most never gave up that hope.

It is not surprising that by 1929, the Russian All-Military Union (ROVS), the military arm of the anti-Soviet émigré organization, counted more than sixty thousand members all over the world. Now led by General Alexander Kutepov, a tough anti-Bolshevik and a veteran of the civil war, the ROVS was actively preparing for the right moment to return to Russia and retake the country by force. The organization also launched a series of attacks on Soviet officials abroad, and in Russia, a number of officials were killed.[3]

While the ROVS's rank and file busied themselves with military training, the intelligentsia-in-exile launched anti-Soviet newspapers and journals, political clubs, and theaters. But instead of thinking of the future, the intelligentsia kept talking about the past. They seemed trapped in thousands of poignant what-ifs: What if World War I hadn't broken out, the tsar hadn't abdicated, Lenin was refused entry into the country, the allies hadn't betrayed the White Cause? Years, then decades, passed in conversations like these. They continued, endlessly, in kitchens and cafés, salons and meeting halls, from Harbin to Belgrade, Paris to Constantinople.

Dwelling on the past didn't answer any questions about the future, and it was a surefire way to lose touch with the realities of everyday life back in the Soviet Union. There, the Communists were changing the country rapidly. Indeed, the Soviet project interfered in just about every aspect of everyday life. The calendar was changed: the Bolsheviks dropped the Julian dates and adopted the Gregorian calendar and introduced new holidays while banning religious celebrations like Christmas and Easter. They reformed the Russian alphabet and got rid of some old Slavonic letters. The Communists even accelerated the pace of life as they encouraged the "overfulfillment" of plans for developing Soviet industry and promoted the cherished dream of catching up with the West. They taught their citizens to talk Soviet "newspeak," a bureaucratic and revolutionary argot studded with acronyms. The result was, well, the "Soviet people"—a new entity, barely recognizable to outsiders who still thought of themselves as Russian.

While Soviet Russia was undergoing these radical changes, the émigré community continued dressing their children in prerevolutionary uniforms and teaching them to sing "God Save the Tsar." They clung desperately to the (old) Russian way of life and wanted to keep it enshrined for the next generation. These political refugees believed that this was the way to keep the Russia they knew intact and uncontaminated by Bolshevism and to prepare for the glorious day when they could return to their homeland. It was touching, sentimental, and nostalgic—but if the émigrés wanted to have a say about Russia's future, this was not an effective way to go about it.

By 1929, whole neighborhoods on the European side of Constantinople were populated by Russian émigrés. The sighs of Russian romances issued from Russian restaurants. Outside of bookstores, old Russian books rescued from the barbaric Bolsheviks were prominently displayed. (Some are still there. Just a few years ago, we went to Istanbul and came upon an old bookstore in the European part of the city. In the narrow lane adjoining Istiklal, a modern name for Grande Rue de Péra, the shop window caught our eye, and we went in. Browsing, we found books left behind by the White Russians—including a nice copy of *Les Armes*, a French illustrated book about medieval weaponry published in Paris in 1890 with a book plate that read, "Librairie S. H. Weiss, successeur vis-à-vis le Consulat de Russie, Constantinople.")

Trotsky didn't live in the neighborhoods populated by the Russian exiles. Instead, he chose a district called Bomonti, in the Sisli—a large industrial area built around the city's first brewery—before settling in a villa on an island off the southern shore of the city in the Sea of Marmara. Unlike most émigrés, Trotsky had no interest in dwelling on the past. He was an experienced operative. When it came to underground resistance work, his know-how was extensive, and his organizational talents were truly impressive; after all, it was Trotsky who founded the Red army. Trotsky was nothing if not resourceful, and he already had a plan in mind. He had decided to launch a monthly publication, the *Bulletin of the Opposition*.

It was just a few sheets of cheap paper printed in Paris, but Stalin immediately understood its importance. He remembered what happened when public debate was banned under the tsar: Lenin established a sophisticated system of smuggling the prohibited *Iskra*, a party newspaper, into the country. Thanks to the *Iskra*, the revolutionaries soon learned an important lesson. Yes, the newspaper was a means of spreading propaganda, but it was more than that. Under the harsh conditions imposed by the tsarist secret police, the dissemination of the *Iskra* served to build and train an underground community of highly disciplined, determined operatives. After all, it takes a lot of trained people, well versed in all methods of *konspiratsiya*, to smuggle subversive literature into Russia and distribute it across the country without being caught. In the end, it was the *Iskra* that turned the social-democrats from a prosecuted and banned political party into a militant and highly efficient underground organization. Both Stalin and Trotsky understood that.

The first issue of Trotsky's *Bulletin* was printed in June 1929. The publication's stated goal was to "serve a practical struggle in the Soviet republic."[4] This message was ominous to Stalin's secret police: Trotsky had, in effect, just announced his plans to build an underground organization in Russia, directed from abroad.

The *Iskra*'s slogan had been "From a spark a fire will flare up." Stalin well remembered the spark that started the revolution that ultimately crushed the mighty and repressive tsarist regime. He didn't want to see something similar happen to him.

Blyumkin was in love, and one day he opened up to Liza about his contacts with Trotsky. All his adult life he had been a player, and now the stakes were higher than ever. He knew Liza and saw that she was a player too.

Liza, however, was terrified. Two Soviet stations and dozens of intelligence operatives in the city were dedicated to spying on Trotsky. Agents had been recruited from among his inner circle, and Trotsky's every move was under surveillance. Liza could not understand how Blyumkin could think his meetings with Trotsky and Trotsky's son had gone unnoticed. She was furious and tried to convince Blyumkin to report his contacts with Trotsky to his superiors. He refused.

In August, Blyumkin went back to Moscow. He brought several of Trotsky's letters, along with the first issue of the *Bulletin*.[5]

The dreaded purge was in full swing at Lubyanka, but Blyumkin, once again, got off lightly. Trilisser, although in trouble himself, was nevertheless a member of the party internal affairs commission tasked with ridding the agency of operatives that Stalin might consider insufficiently loyal, and he came to Blyumkin's aid: the commission found Blyumkin an "inspected and approved comrade."[6] Blyumkin's luck hadn't run out yet. Trilisser tried to send him abroad, but Blyumkin delayed his departure.

In the fall, Liza was suddenly recalled to Moscow. The official pretext was that her Austrian passport was reported to have been compromised by a careless Soviet intelligence officer in Vienna. But it was rumored that Eitingon, the chief of the legal rezidentura in Constantinople, was behind her recall. Liza was deeply worried.

In Moscow, Liza tried once again to speak with her lover about Trotsky. Once again, he could not be persuaded. When this effort failed, she didn't hesitate. She went straight to Trilisser and reported Blyumkin's contacts with Trotsky. She also went to Trilisser's deputy to make sure Trilisser would not flip and protect his protégé.

Blyumkin was expected to present himself to the chief, but his survival instinct told him it would be better not to. He failed to come to Lubyanka. Instead, he decided to flee the country. He was an experienced operative and knew how to outsmart the secret police. But he made one final call to Liza. Together, they went to the Kazansky railroad station in Moscow in the middle of the night;

he wanted to get on the train to Rostov. That train wasn't leaving until the morning, so they returned to the apartment. There, he was met by agents from Lubyanka. He got into their car and, as his last act of bravado, ordered the driver to take him to Lubyanka himself. "You have betrayed me, Liza," were his only words to her.[7]

Blyumkin was interrogated over and over again. Two weeks later, he was executed. Trilisser lost his job and was transferred out of Lubyanka.

Liza, however, survived. She even managed to get a new assignment—in Denmark. There, she went to work under a Soviet intelligence officer. His name was Vasily Zarubin.

Once again, Liza was in need of a defender. In fact, she needed one now more than ever, following the Central Committee's special request to the Soviet secret police to "establish the exact nature of Gorskaya's behavior."[8] After all, it was not entirely clear when exactly Gorskaya had learned of Blyumkin's involvement with Trotsky and how long she had kept the information to herself. Zarubin was a perfect candidate. And given his emotional, sentimental nature, her task was easy. Soon, Zarubin proposed to her.

Liza's fate was secure. The Moscow Center was happy; Liza Gorskaya was international, talented, easygoing, and fluent in three languages, while Vasily Zarubin was Russian, loyal, and disciplined. The two made a good pair of Soviet spies.

January 26, 1930. La rue Rousselet, a narrow street in the Seventh Arrondissement of Paris, was empty this Sunday morning, with the exception of two cars parked where the street met the rue Oudinot. The first—a large Alfa Romeo limousine with chrome headlights—was grayish green, the other a red Renault taxi.[9] A lonely French policeman stood on the corner.[10] Several men were in the cars, agents of Soviet intelligence, and they were nervous. Cadets from the École-Militaire next door could show up any minute and complicate things.

At 10:00 a.m., the street was still empty. The plan was still working.

Thirty minutes passed, and then the door at number 26—a shabby, four-story building cramped between similarly dilapidated buildings—finally opened. A tall, middle-aged man with a black beard and a long, black overcoat stepped outside. The man was well known to the men in the two cars. By now, in fact, Soviet intelligence knew almost everything about him. They knew that he lived with his wife and their five-year-old son in the small apartment on the third floor. They knew this man was powerful enough to always travel around the city in one of a dozen Parisian taxis that his organization had assigned to him. They knew that all of these taxis were driven by White Russian officers—thirty-three in all—and that these officers were experienced, well trained, and armed with revolvers.[11]

Every morning a taxi awaited the man's arrival. That was the routine. And routine was an important part of life for Alexander Kutepov, the forty-seven-year-old Russian general who was the leader of the ROVS, the military wing of the White Guard émigré community.

But this Sunday, there was no taxi waiting for Kutepov, and he'd emerged at 10:30 a.m. rather than 11:00 a.m. That meant he'd taken the bait, and the men in the two cars were still in the game.

The day before, Kutepov had received a letter from a friend. This friend had asked for a discreet meeting and promised that, although the meeting was important, it would not take much of Kutepov's time. They could meet at a tram stop on the corner of the Boulevard des Invalides, the friend suggested, right on Kutepov's route to the 11:30 a.m. memorial service for a mutual comrade-in-arms to be held at the Russian Church. But the "friend" had been recruited as a Soviet agent, and the men in the cars would be waiting. The plan was to "arrest" Kutepov and then take him somewhere far, far away from the French legal system. The agents held their breath.

The general headed to the meeting place. At the tram stop, he waited for his friend, in vain. Several minutes passed, and Kutepov, perplexed, started along the Boulevard des Invalides and then turned right, heading home. He was making a full circle. Luckily for Soviet intelligence, Kutepov had decided not to head to the church after his failed meeting but to return home by the tiny rue Oudinot, where the two cars were waiting for him.

The general walked in a brisk, military manner. As he neared the corner, two people suddenly emerged from the gray-green Alfa Romeo, turned to him, and one of them said something in French. Kutepov frowned, then stopped. Despite all his years in Paris, he didn't speak French. The plan to pretend to arrest Kutepov was falling apart because the stubborn general didn't understand commands in a foreign language.

The agents had to act, and fast. The two men twisted Kutepov and pushed him into the car. The general tried to fight back, but one of his assailants pacified him with chloroform. Now he was safely packed away. The policeman, a French Communist, jumped into the same vehicle.

The Alfa Romeo started off immediately, followed by the red taxi. An astonished cleaner at the hospital on the rue Oudinot caught a glance of the general in the car, and that was the last time anyone, apart from the Soviet secret police, saw Kutepov alive.[12]

His disappearance was part of a larger Soviet effort—a series of sophisticated deception operations with the goal of decapitating the White émigré movement either by luring its leaders into Russia or by abducting and assassinating them.

What happened after the group of Soviet operatives, known in Lubyanka as "the Administration for Special Tasks," snatched Kutepov from the street remains a mystery. Was chloroform immediately fatal due to the general's weak heart, or did Kutepov die on his way to Moscow? There was also a theory that he was brought safely to Moscow, to Lubyanka, and died there during interrogations. In any case, the operation was one of the most successful for the

Administration for Special Tasks, and the lesson was not missed by Soviet operatives, including Nahum Eitingon, who would become its deputy head that year. This was a new method of dealing with political opponents of the Kremlin who had left Russia. Seven years later, in September 1937, General Yevgeny Miller, who succeeded Kutepov as leader of ROVS, was also abducted in Paris and brought to Moscow, where he was killed.[13]

But it was another group of exiles—the generation of Soviet party officials who fled to the West—that truly worried the Kremlin. First among these exiles, of course, was Trotsky. The former leader of the revolution posed a real existential threat to Stalin's rule.

By the 1930s, the Kremlin urgently needed to do something about Trotsky.

CHAPTER 4

"THE HORSE"

W ell into the late 1930s, Soviet intelligence kept hunting down Stalin's archenemy Trotsky. Trotsky's archive was stolen in Paris; his son mysteriously died after what seemed like a rather simple surgery; his closest associate was kidnapped, and his body was later found in the Seine.[1] Moving from Turkey in 1933, first to France, then to Norway in 1936, Trotsky left Europe for Mexico.[2] When he did so, the city of New York suddenly became important for Lubyanka. After all, New York was an important center for Trotskyites' activities, and geographically it was closer to Latin America than other émigré centers. After giving the topic careful consideration, Soviet spymasters came to the conclusion that local activists could provide a point of access to Trotsky himself.

At a prewar co-op building in Greenwich Village, just two blocks south of Union Square, there was unusual, even feverish, activity: gloomy men from Moscow who called themselves Richard or Michael came and went frequently from the ninth floor. The ninth floor was home to the offices of Earl Browder, head of the Communist Party in the United States. What most New Yorkers didn't know was that the US Communist Party owned the entire building. And right now, the US Communist Party was in a state of mobilization.

The American names of the visitors with strong Russian accents didn't suit them very well. Everyone understood these gloomy men were coming straight from the Soviet secret police. And the Richards and Michaels brought urgent orders: US Communists were to gather information on Trotskyites.

Browder's deputy, Jacob Golos, was happy to help. Golos was a legend in the Comintern and Soviet intelligence.[3] A Russian Jew who belonged to the first generation of Bolsheviks, Golos had been banished by the tsar to Siberia for organizing an underground printing house but had escaped his Siberian exile and fled first to China and then to Japan before finally making it to the United States. In 1915, he became a naturalized US citizen.[4] With a prominent nose and curly hair, the energetic Golos—who never lost his heavy Russian accent—was a founding father of the Communist Party of the United States.

Golos had a God-given talent for recruitment. Few could compete with him. In New York, he ran several networks, each with dozens of agents. As an ardent Stalinist, infiltrating local Trotskyite organizations was at the top of his priority list. When the Moscow men asked for contacts, Golos knew just who they needed.

One meeting that would prove crucial was arranged between a gloomy Russian and Ruby Weil, a young American woman from Indiana. Then in her early thirties, Ruby was a secret Communist, trained in infiltration techniques. Her job was to penetrate international Trotskyite organizations, and she was good at it.[5]

The Russian knew that Ruby was on very friendly terms with Hilda Ageloff. Hilda was one of three young, sociable sisters who knew Trotsky personally. Indeed, two of the Ageloff sisters had done secretarial work for him.

At their meeting in New York, the Russian introduced himself to Ruby as John Rich.[6] He told Ruby he had plans for her: she was going to do an important job for her Soviet comrades. Ruby was handed a stack of cash. At first, Ruby was reluctant to take the money. She was a Communist out of conviction, not for material gain. But she was told it was important for her to be better dressed. She would also need the money to pay her phone bills. There was a plot against Stalin's life, she was told, and her help was needed. So she agreed.[7]

Her task, as outlined by the Russian, was not difficult: Ruby was to accompany one of the three Ageloff sisters—Sylvia, a twenty-eight-year-old Brooklyn social worker and occasional secretary to Trotsky—when Sylvia traveled to Paris to participate in a Trotskyite international congress. Bespectacled, shy, and slightly awkward, Sylvia was a polyglot, fluent in Spanish, French, and Russian (the sisters' mother was from Russia). In Paris, Ruby's job was to introduce Sylvia to a certain man who would make himself known to Ruby when they arrived.

Ruby got started right away. She was almost immediately lucky—Sylvia was more than happy to have a traveling companion and especially one who also believed in communism.

The trip across the ocean took many days but was pleasant, and the young women arrived in Paris in June 1938. While Sylvia stayed behind at their hotel, Ruby said she needed some fresh air. Once alone, she made her way to an address she had been given by John Rich to meet a comrade named Gertrude. It was this Gertrude who introduced her to Stalin's agent. The agent, a young and handsome man, said his name was Jacques Mornard. When Ruby saw him, she immediately grasped his role: that of a handsome lover for Sylvia.

Ruby took Jacques back to the hotel where she was staying with Sylvia and made introductions. Ruby's new acquaintance told Sylvia he was a Belgian businessman who was enjoying himself in France. He seemed completely disinterested in politics and had a great passion for theater and music. Sylvia quickly fell for Jacques, and they spent seven wonderful months together in Paris.

What Sylvia didn't know was that her Jacques was in fact a Spaniard named Ramon Mercader, a veteran of the Spanish Civil War. For now, his job was to cultivate this new relationship and wait.

In January 1939 Barcelona fell to the troops commanded by El Caudillo, the fascist dictator Francisco Franco. In March, Madrid surrendered. The civil war in Spain was over. The Republican forces, whose cause Moscow had supported, had lost, and Nahum Eitingon's chiefs at Lubyanka saw no reason for him to remain in the country where he had been stationed since 1936. His job there, as chief of the Soviet secret service's Spanish station, was done. Eitingon had safely ferried the country's high-ranking Republican officials and Communists to France and helped transfer Spain's gold to the Soviet Union. He had also made some promising recruits among the Trotskyites who fought there. It was time to go home.

But back in Moscow, Eitingon didn't like what he saw. The chief of foreign intelligence, a successor to Trilisser, was in prison, awaiting a verdict. For years, Trilisser's successor had fruitfully run a network of secret agents in Europe and had liquidated many enemies of the Soviet regime. But he had failed to kill Trotsky, and that failure had angered Stalin.

As a rule, if a high-ranking Soviet official fell, he did not fall alone. Instead, he brought his whole entourage down with him. Now Eitingon was being followed. Being the gifted spy that he was, it didn't take him long to spot the operatives trailing him down the streets wherever he went.

Eitingon made a phone call to his boss at Lubyanka. "It's been ten days since I arrived in Moscow," Eitingon began. "I am sure my phone is tapped . . . I'm under constant surveillance. Please report to your leadership: if they want to arrest me, let them do it now. They do not need to play children's games."[8]

His voice did not sound nervous or frightened. He seemed to convey that he was ready for whatever fate had in store for him.

But Eitingon was lucky once again: the man on the other end of the phone told him not to worry, that nobody was going to arrest him. The Communist Party needed him and his experience. Stalin still wanted Trotsky dead.

It had now been a decade since Trotsky left Russia, but people of Eitingon's age would never forget what a popular leader he had been. The founder of the Red army, Trotsky was second only to Lenin when it came to the people's love. Before his fall from power, he was nearly omnipresent: the Soviets named cities and streets after him. A submarine called *Trotsky* patrolled the Black Sea during the civil war. Air force planes protecting Moscow from its enemies took off from the military aerodrome named after him.

No wonder, then, that in the 1930s, Trotsky had been Russia's most prominent political exile. He had not had an easy time of it, traveling from one unwelcoming European country to another. Nonetheless, thousands of his supporters across Europe and in both Americas were still ready to die for him. The Soviet secret police had his closest followers in their crosshairs, and their secret agents had been infiltrating Trotsky's inner circle since he left Russia, but they had never managed to get him.

The task became even more complicated after Trotsky and his wife moved to Mexico. They settled in a beautiful and highly fortified villa in Mexico City's Coyoacán suburbs, where they hoped their lives would be safer than they had been in Europe.[9] But after two years there, Stalin wanted Trotsky dead even more than ever. The Russian leader believed that a huge war was on the horizon, and he needed his rival out of the way before it started. In 1939, he made it explicitly clear that he wanted Trotsky killed within the year.[10]

Eitingon was the man Stalin assigned to do it. The experienced intelligence officer agreed immediately and got to work. He knew the stakes and wanted to be certain of the result. He came up with two separate plans—one simple and cruel, the other sophisticated and complex. Both would be carried out by agents sent to Mexico who had never been used in operations against Trotsky or Trotsky-ites before. The two groups of assassins would have no idea about one another's existence. The newcomers all had to operate on their own and, just in case, keep their distance from the stations in both Mexico and New York.

Eitingon was given a free hand when it came to using Soviet intelligence resources. With all possible options at his fingertips, he decided to rely on the agents he had recruited in Spain and the contacts provided by Jacob Golos's network in New York.

To use people recruited during the civil war in Spain seemed like a reasonable idea. After all, they knew how to kill, and they hated Trotskyites, whom they considered competitors and enemies in the battle to institute the right kind of communism in the world. And because he had supported their cause in their country, they loved Stalin.

Indeed, the Mexican painter David Alfaro Siqueiros, who had fought in Spain, felt such a strong affinity for Stalin that when Eitingon asked, Siqueiros immediately agreed to lead a group of assassins in Mexico. Eitingon's choice was unorthodox. Although Siqueiros had battle experience in Spain, the idea of having a famous Mexican painter lead a group of armed people to attack Trotsky's well-guarded home appeared very risky. But then again, Eitingon had never hesitated to take risks.

He named the group led by Siqueiros "The Horse." This group was to launch the first assassination operation against Trotsky—a brutal frontal attack.

Trotsky's villa in Coyoacán was specially fortified to protect him and his family. The villa was equipped with a watchtower that overlooked the street, a high fence with electrified wires, and an automated alarm signal that was active at all times. Five Mexican police officers were on duty outside, and several guards watched the villa around the clock from the inside. In addition to Trotsky, the villa was home to Trotsky's wife, Natalia, and his teenage grandson, whose mother, a daughter of Trotsky from his first marriage, had committed suicide following her husband's imprisonment and execution in Russia as a Trotskyite.

Eitingon knew all of this. The Soviet secret police had an agent inside the fortress, and she provided Eitingon with a detailed plan of the villa before she was recalled to Moscow. She also provided all details of how Trotsky's bodyguards operated.

Among them were some passionate young American Trotskyites, recent college graduates who had not been given proper military training. For Trotsky, they were not the best option, but they were vigilant and available.

One of the Americans, a twenty-five-year-old named Robert Sheldon Harte, had fallen in love with Mexico and its exotic nature—so much so, in fact, that he bought several colorful birds and kept them in the garden. Once he was so engaged building a bird cage that he handed a gate key to the workers who were doing some renovations at the villa. "You might prove to be the first victim of your own carelessness," said Trotsky sadly.[11]

The Old Man, as Trotsky was known among Stalinists and Trotskyists, was still strong and full of energy, but all the catastrophes that had befallen his friends and family after his expulsion from Russia deprived him of sleep. The evening of May 23, 1940, was beautiful and warm, and he went to bed late. But he still couldn't fall asleep until he swallowed a sleeping pill.[12]

Trotsky's grandson, fourteen-year-old Seva, slept in the bedroom next to his grandparents. In the middle of the night, someone tried the door from the garden. The door scraped the floor, making a noise that woke Seva up. He suddenly saw a silhouette coming in and thought it was someone from the house, but the shooting started. He threw himself to the floor and hid under the bed.[13] The quiet night was engulfed by the sound of machine gun fire. Attackers in uniform smashed into Seva's room and fired through the bed where Seva was hiding, wounding his foot.[14] Then they rushed off.

On the other side of the wall, Trotsky and his wife were lying in a corner on the floor. They heard a loud scream: "Grandfather!" But they were under crossfire and couldn't move. Soon the shooting in the room stopped. "They have kidnapped him," whispered Trotsky. The sounds of gunfire moved on, to the patio. Then came silence. The intruders were gone. The attack had lasted no more than twenty minutes.

Everybody who lived in the house gathered in the patio. Seva was there too—a bullet had scratched his toe, but he was alive. Mysteriously, nobody was killed or seriously injured, but one man disappeared: young Robert Harte, who was on duty that night.

The follow-up investigation revealed that just before dawn, more than twenty men in police uniforms had disarmed and tied up the sentries outside the villa—without firing a shot. When they got to the gate, one of them talked to Harte, and he opened the doors. They ran into the courtyard and disarmed Trotsky's guards. The attackers then placed machine guns behind the trees opposite Trotsky's bedroom and opened fire. To be sure of their results, the raiders threw incendiary grenades into the house and a big bomb into the courtyard, which failed to go off. When they thought it was clear that Trotsky couldn't still be alive, they left. While leaving, the attackers kidnapped Robert Harte.

A month later, the Mexican secret police dug up Harte's body on a farm outside Mexico City—the same farm that had been rented by two Stalinist agents. When Siqueiros, who had led the attackers, was arrested, he did not deny his participation in the raid. But he maintained that they had never had any intention of killing Trotsky: he, for one, just wanted to protest Trotsky's presence in his country. Siqueiros also claimed that he organized the attack on his own. Later, he was released on bail.

Trotsky, however, understood all too well what had happened. "The author of the attack is Joseph Stalin, through the medium of the Soviet secret police," he told the Mexican police.[15] But he couldn't understand why Harte, whom he had loved so much, had opened the gates to the attackers.

Eitingon knew the answer. It was he, after all, who had ordered the Soviet agent who'd gotten Harte to open the gate to move from Europe to Mexico. There, on Eitingon's orders, he had befriended the curious young Harte, and later, when he knocked on the gates just before dawn, Harte opened them for his new friend. That was how the raiders broke in. Harte's mistake cost him his life—just as Trotsky had prophesied. Afterward, Harte was a liability, so the Soviet agents liquidated him. Trotsky—correctly—never believed Harte worked for the Soviet secret police. If he had, Harte's work as a guard would have given him plenty of opportunities to kill Trotsky silently and run away.

The botched attack was a spectacular failure for Eitingon. He had not participated in it himself and now regretted having kept his distance. He would have never allowed Trotsky to survive; those unprofessional peasants and miners led by a painter—they should have checked every room after they opened fire. Instead, they just ran away after shooting nearly two hundred bullets.

Eitingon sent an encrypted radio message about the disastrous outcome of the operation, but it failed to be delivered to Moscow in time.[16] Stalin learned about the attack from the Soviet news agency TASS. It seemed Eitingon's luck had run out.

Two days later, Eitingon asked Moscow to give him another chance. Stalin summoned Lubyanka's generals to the Kremlin. He asked only one question: How much of the Soviet intelligence network in New York was compromised? He was assured that Eitingon had followed instructions closely and hadn't used any agents from New York's spy ring.

Hearing this, Stalin agreed to give Eitingon a second chance.[17]

After the May attack, the house on Avenida Viena was further fortified. New watchtowers were erected, and steel shutters closed the windows. Now it was a real fortress—one that reminded Trotsky of the first prison in which he had been jailed in Russia.[18]

But Eitingon was not going to storm the villa again.

CHAPTER 5

"THE MOTHER"

Nahum Eitingon had a plan B—a second operation, already in the making. It was to be executed by a group of operatives he called "The Mother."

Ruthless and efficient, Eitingon decided to use the woman he had recruited in Spain; he was always good with women—and this one depended entirely on him.

The Mother consisted of only two people: Caridad and Ramon Mercader. Mother and son were both Spanish agents working for Soviet intelligence. Caridad was a fierce personality. Born in Cuba, she had been the respectable wife of a wealthy textile industrialist in a small town near Barcelona and mother of five children before she left her husband and family during the Spanish Civil War to become a fighter and propagandist for the Republican cause. Now she was an agent run by Eitingon and also his lover.[1]

Mother and son had been horrified by Franco's devastating victory over the Republicans—horrified at a safe distance, since by then Eitingon had helped resettle them in Paris. There, the handsome Ramon was engaged in playing the joyful, debonair, apolitical Jacques with his new love, Sylvia Ageloff, until Sylvia regretfully took leave of Jacques in February 1939 and returned to New York.

The following month, when Eitingon received Stalin's order to organize the assassination of Leon Trotsky, he thought at once of the Mercaders. To Eitingon's experienced eye, Sylvia's lover was the best candidate for the job. Sylvia, another woman in the plot, would provide access to Trotsky, while Caridad would ensure that Ramon would not flinch and do the job of killing Stalin's archenemy.

Nonetheless, Eitingon decided to go ahead with plans for "The Horse" as well.

Eitingon trained the two groups concurrently, with both The Mother and The Horse based in Paris. The summer was spent in preparations. Although the two groups were training within blocks of each other, according to the rules of *konspiratsiya*, neither had any idea the other existed.

Before the first—ultimately unsuccessful—strike, a high-ranking secret service official was sent from Lubyanka to Paris. He met with the two groups separately to determine whether they were operational. Apparently, he was satisfied.

The amount of time that all this preparation took almost torpedoed the operation. September came, and, as Stalin expected and abetted, Germany invaded Poland. France entered the war on the side of Poland, and Eitingon's fake Polish passport, issued by Soviet intelligence, became a liability. There was a very real chance Eitingon could be drafted into the French army as a Polish citizen. If he refused to join the army, his movement could be restricted—he would be singled out as a "suspicious person" and put under surveillance or worse.

The situation needed to be resolved quickly. To buy time, the chief of the Soviet intelligence section in Paris hid Eitingon in a psychiatric clinic run by a Russian émigré, disguising him as a mentally ill Syrian Jew—a trick that successfully kept him out of view of the French authorities. But Eitingon had yet to find a way to get to the United States to set the plot in motion.

In the meantime, The Mother was getting closer to its target. While Eitingon was stuck in hiding in France, his agents Ramon and Caridad Mercader boarded a ship bound for New York.[2]

When they landed, Ramon promptly called Sylvia. He explained to her that when the war broke out, he had been drafted into the Belgian army, but apolitical Jacques did not want to fight and left the country with a fake Canadian passport.[3] That explanation provided a perfect cover for his trip to the United States.

Back in Europe, Eitingon was finally issued an Iraqi passport, a French residency permit, and an American visa, thanks to the help of a Soviet agent in Switzerland. The most crucial part of the operation now began: Eitingon crossed the Atlantic in October and arrived in New York. He rented offices in Brooklyn and registered an export-import company there.[4]

This became his operational base, as he shuttled between Mexico and New York. Now forty years old, Eitingon had lost some hair and gained a bit of weight. He also limped slightly—a consequence of a wound he'd received in 1921 during the Russian Civil War.[5]

Ramon regularly dropped by the offices of Eitingon's cover company, looking for instructions and money. Time was of the essence, and Eitingon moved quickly. At the end of the month, he ordered Ramon to move to Mexico. As Ramon/Jacques explained to Sylvia, his mother had arranged a job for him in a trading company there. Sylvia followed him to Mexico City in January 1940. Meanwhile, Eitingon and Caridad continued to travel between Mexico and New York.

Caridad's main task was to support and reassure Ramon. Anxiety over his double life and impending mission had pushed her son to the brink of a nervous breakdown. Things didn't improve when he read in the local Mexican newspaper about the failed attempt on Trotsky's life by Siqueros's group.

In Mexico, Ramon was also faced with an unexpected obstacle. Sylvia, as Trotsky's former secretary, was invited to Trotsky's villa right away and continued to visit frequently, but she never suggested that Jacques come with her. It seemed he was not on the guest list. He offered to drive his lover to see her friends and thus developed a routine: he drove Sylvia there, then parked his Buick and waited for her outside, chatting with the guards.

After several months, Sylvia's friend Jacques had become a familiar face to the inhabitants of the villa. They liked him: Ramon was
handsome, polite, and obliging. When he offered Trotsky's guests at
the villa a ride to the port of Vera Cruz, they agreed. The morning
Ramon came to pick them up, they invited him into the courtyard.
Less than a week had passed since Siqueiros's attack, and Ramon
felt he was making progress.

When he went inside, the first thing Ramon saw was Trotsky
feeding his rabbits in their hutches. Ramon was introduced, and
Trotsky shook his hand. But rather than trying to talk with the Old
Man, Ramon walked over to Seva's room and gave Trotsky's grandson a toy glider. It may not have been a very sophisticated move,
but it worked: Ramon was invited to breakfast with the family.

Mercader was off to New York for a few weeks, but when he
came back, the Trotskys invited Ramon and Sylvia for tea. Ramon
was in—and he spent more than an hour with the Old Man. A few
more visits were enough for him to learn all he needed to know to
carry out his plan.[6]

Eitingon thought they couldn't wait any longer, and Caridad
gave her blessings. Now they had to decide how to kill Trotsky.
Ramon, drawing from his wartime experience, offered various
options: he could shoot Trotsky, stab him, or hit him in the head.
Finally, after a long debate, Eitingon and Caridad chose an ice axe
and a knife. These could be easily hidden under Ramon's clothes
and, unlike a gun, would not make much noise.

On August 20, Ramon knocked on the gate of the villa. It was
a sunny day, but he had on his hat and raincoat. He was alone. The
guards let him in. Ramon asked Trotsky to read the updated draft of
his article on the politics of the Left, which Trotsky had previously
found "confused and full of banal phrases."[7] Trotsky agreed, and they
went to a study. Ramon put his overcoat on a chair. While Trotsky was
reading, the assassin reached for his overcoat and pulled out his ice axe.

* * *

Outside the villa, two cars were waiting. One was Ramon's Buick. Eitingon and Caridad sat in the other car, holding their breath. This time, Eitingon wanted to stay close to the events. Police cars began arriving at the villa. Something had happened. But what? Soon it became clear that Ramon had been caught.[8] "They made me do it . . . They've got my mother!" he cried out when the guards knocked him to the ground.

In an instant, Eitingon and Caridad were gone. They had a long way ahead, first to Cuba, then to New York, across the United States and sailing to China, and finally reaching the Soviet Union.

It was officially announced the next day that Trotsky was dead. Eitingon sent another encrypted cable to Moscow. Once again, his message came too late. Stalin learned the news from a news report, but this time the news was pleasing to him: the job was done.

By then, World War II had been tearing Europe apart for almost a year. The Soviet Union was already mired in it, with Soviet soldiers occupying part of Poland. Russia was a belligerent power, even if not yet officially so—and the leader of the country kept wasting the precious resources of his intelligence services, its most able and capable operatives, in the hunt for their exiled compatriots scattered all over the world. Stalin made Ramon, now in Mexican jail, a Hero of the Soviet Union, the highest national award his secret order could confer. Stalin bestowed Eitingon and Caridad with the Order of Lenin—a clear indication to others in Soviet intelligence of what was expected of them. Stalin also honored the Soviet vice consul in New York who supervised Jacob Golos and John Rich.[9]

In decades to come, Russian exiles would continue to be at the top of the priority list for the country's intelligence services. Meanwhile, thanks to Eitingon's prowess, Jacob Golos's spy networks in New York were also safe and fully operational. They would continue to be ready and waiting for the moment when they would be most needed.

CHAPTER 6

OPERATIONS AREA: UNITED STATES

Soviet intelligence entered World War II with a unique advantage—an edge that, in fact, no other intelligence service had ever had. Approaching potential agents of other nationalities is always risky and uncertain. In any country, spying for another country is an act of treason, and very few people are ready to cross this line. But the Communist cause was different. Thousands of committed Germans, French, Spaniards, and Britons were happy to help Moscow. In some countries, particularly the United States, recent Russian emigrants who had fled the insane tsarist policy of encouraging pogroms were also sympathetic to the Soviet cause.

Lubyanka took advantage of this pan-national goodwill, using every dirty trick in the book. In the 1920s and 1930s, it was the Comintern—an international organization of revolutionaries—that did the heavy lifting. The Comintern, whose aspiration was to set the world ablaze with revolution, was responsible for recruiting and training supporters of the Communist cause across the world. A truly global organization, the Comintern's working language was German, and its headquarters were in Moscow. But it was exactly this Moscow headquarters that ultimately made the organization vulnerable: in the late 1930s, Stalin ruthlessly purged the

Comintern leadership. Comintern workers, stripped of their leaders, were co-opted by the Soviet intelligence services.

What the Soviet intelligence services wanted to do with the Comintern was problematic. It was one thing to plot a revolution—and few could object to working with comrades from abroad who shared a common idea of the future. It was quite another, even for a committed Communist, to provide classified information for the government of another country.

And there was a more serious problem. Stalin had remade the Soviet secret police in his own image: paranoid, suspicious, and constantly on the hunt for traitors. This organization was uniquely ill suited to the challenge of running horizontal networks of comrades, none of whom were used to practicing unconditional obedience or subordination.

On June 1, 1940, Muscovites crowded around the city's newsstands. Hitler's Germany was winning—Holland had capitulated in May, followed by Belgium, and now France was falling to pieces in the face of the unstoppable German blitzkrieg. This was what the people wanted to read about. But the top Soviet newspaper, *Pravda*, instead devoted its front page to an article about the need to improve the party's propaganda and a report from the latest session of the Soviet Supreme Council.

News about the war was banished to page 5 and was restricted to cheerful communiqués like, "The chief of the First French army taken prisoner." On page 6, a short news item about a national convention of the Communist Party of the United States held in New York read, "General Secretary Earl Browder laid out a new platform for the upcoming presidential election: The United States must be prevented from entering the war. This is the task which requires [the US Communist Party's] most intense struggle."[1]

In northeast Moscow, the news about the war filled the corridors of the newly built Comintern rectangular headquarters with anxiety. There, a small community of political exiles who had fled the Nazi and fascist regimes—pale-faced, middle-aged men and women—gathered in small groups and talked about the rumors. Their voices were low so as not to echo.

Many of these people's comrades had disappeared in the Great Purge, having been accused of being Trotskyites. Then, just a year earlier, Stalin had made the alliance that shocked Communists all over the world: he came to terms with Hitler and signed the Molotov-Ribbentrop Pact. When Germany and Soviet Russia jointly invaded Poland, a terrible rumor spread among the small community of émigrés in Moscow—that the Soviet secret police had started handing over German and Austrian Communists to the Gestapo. (While you wouldn't find it printed in any newspaper, the rumor was true.) Now the exiles whispering in the hallways of the Comintern's two-year-old building wondered if they would live to see the autumn leaves change.

But it was the Americans that the Soviet secret services came after next. Isaiah Oggins, an American member of the Comintern, was arrested in Moscow and sentenced to eight years in the gulag— "for spreading anti-Soviet propaganda." He was promptly sent to Norilsk, eighteen hundred miles from Moscow, just above the Arctic Circle. There was also a rumor that the Center, as the Soviet intelligence headquarters in Moscow was called, tried to recall Jacob Golos, but he refused to come to Moscow, fearing repression. Starting in 1940, Lubyanka began to turn its attention not just to American Communists in Russia but toward America itself.

One reason was the war. As a high-ranking intelligence general put it, "Now we realized we needed to know American intentions because America's participation in the war against Hitler would be decisive."[2]

Beyond the war, Moscow still focused on getting rid of any Trotskyites who might be hiding out in the United States plotting revenge. In January 1941, the Moscow Center sent a secret cable to the chief of the Soviet intelligence station in New York: "We agree with you regarding the need to intensify the struggle against the Trotskyites by making use of the disarray among the Trotskyites since the death of the 'Old Man,' the departure of many of them and the uncertainty and disillusionment among them."[3]

Even as the United States came into focus as the Soviet secret service's most important target, the Moscow Center seemed to be anything but sure-footed in its approach. In another private communiqué sent in 1941, a note of hysteria can be heard in Moscow's reprimand of the New York station's chief: "We have repeatedly written you regarding the need to seriously address the cultivation of White and nationalist organizations, but to date we don't have any reports or specific suggestions from you."[4] The Soviets could not forget their old enemies.

As World War II gathered pace, Stalin ordered his secret services to step up their activities in the United States. Moscow's spymasters badly needed people on the spot.

Then in June 1941, the Germans attacked Russia. Eitingon was given an assignment that was particularly well suited to him: organizing diversionary activities at the rear of the German troops. In other words, the master spy was to supervise a savage guerilla war in the occupied territories.

In October, when Moscow was under siege by the Germans, the chief of foreign intelligence telephoned Zarubin. The two men were to report to Stalin that evening, Zarubin was informed. They hastened to the Kremlin. There, Stalin instructed Zarubin to take over political intelligence collection in the United States. The career spy was the new chief of the legal Soviet intelligence station in the United States.

Zarubin and his wife, Liza Gorskaya, departed Moscow on October 20. They traveled by train to Uzbekistan, then across China by air to Hong Kong. From there they went to Manila, where they boarded an American liner bound for San Francisco. They arrived in California on Christmas day 1941. From there, the spy couple crossed the country to the East Coast, ready to meet the new year of 1942 fully operational in the United States.[5]

June 13, 1942, dawned bright and sunny in New York City. Beginning in the early morning, hundreds of thousands of people gathered, waving paper flags. They lined both sides of Fifth Avenue, from Washington Square Park to Seventy-Ninth Street, as the parade began. Army servicemen in green uniforms, nurses in white, policemen in black marched past, along with a dragon the size of a dinosaur on a float that read, "Hitler The Axis War Monster," decorated with the flags of Germany, Italy, and Japan. By the end of the day, half a million people had marched for eleven straight hours in what would be the largest military parade ever held to support the US war effort.[6]

By now, 1942, the United States and the Soviet Union were military allies. Still, on that beautiful June day, most New Yorkers would have been surprised to learn that their patriotic parade was marching through an area dense with Soviet spies. The rectangle between Twelfth Street and the south end of Central Park housed, among others, the office of the Communist Party of the United States; Trotsky's *Bulletin of the Opposition* offices (which had moved to New York from Paris in 1939 because of the war); and, in the high-rise on the corner of Fifth Avenue and Twenty-Ninth Street, the offices of Amtorg—the Soviet trade organization that had traditionally provided cover for spies. Finally, at the southern end of Central Park, a fancy four-story villa was leased to the Soviet Consulate-General. This building was, unsurprisingly, packed with smaller and larger offices frequented by Soviet agents.

These Soviet agents had been in New York for more than twenty years. After the Russian Revolution, US president Woodrow Wilson had been reluctant to formally recognize the Bolshevik government—nor was he ready to hand them the property of the Russian embassy in Washington. Instead, he agreed to let the Soviets open an official office in New York, at the World Tower building on Fortieth Street—a Gothic high-rise in the middle of midtown. (There was some irony in this: during World War I, the World Tower had been used by film companies to produce patriotic movies.) In early 1919, the Soviet Government Bureau rented out the third and fourth floors, with a mission, ostensibly, to promote the new Bolshevik state. The office had been operational for only a few months when the police raided it in search of illegal seditious activity, sent the boss packing for Russia, and shut the bureau. This unimpressive start nonetheless helped launch a number of pro-Soviet organizations in New York with activities that ranged from collecting donations to establishing commercial contacts, providing assistance to those who decided to re-emigrate to Soviet Russia, and publishing propaganda magazines. And, of course, these pro-Soviet organizations were a good way to give cover to spies.

Thus, by the early 1940s, New York was already home to a large network of Soviet agents. This had been accomplished thanks to a very effective scheme: First, Earl Browder, head of the Communist Party in the United States, talent-spotted would-be assets. Then his deputy, Comintern veteran Jacob Golos, would recruit and handle them.

For more than a decade, Golos ran the World Tourists agency. It was a good cover for sending American volunteers to Spain, but the agency also helped Soviet spies get legitimate American passports. Golos had figured out a way to obtain genuine birth and naturalization certificates.

The Soviets were thinking big. Golos's offices were located in the iconic Flatiron building—that tall, rectangular high-rise that, even today, seems to cut through Fifth Avenue and Broadway like a boat through waves. His network consisted of dozens of agents, many of them remarkably well placed. Golos had people on the US Board of Economic Warfare, which coordinated the operations undermining the Third Reich's economic capabilities; on the staff of a chief of the Army Air Forces; and in the US Treasury Department, to name just a few. These people had the potential to make serious impacts on the course of history. Take the radio engineer who ran one of Golos's groups of agents, Julius Rosenberg: ten years later, Rosenberg would be a household name when he was sent to an electric chair along with his wife for passing the secrets of the atomic bomb to the Soviets. Many of these agents were idealists; some thought they worked for the US Communist Party. They had no idea they were actually working for Soviet intelligence.

Golos still had agents in Trotsky's Socialist Workers Party, too. Ruby Weil, the operative who had helped bring about the assassination of Trotsky, was just one of them.

With the war in Russia raging against the Germans, the savvy spy runner saw an opportunity. Golos approached the White émigré community. Calling on their patriotism, he successfully recruited agents there. He told them—truthfully—that he had sent his wife and son to live in Moscow in 1936, and when the war started, his son, at his urging, had joined the Red army (he was wounded defending Leningrad). Now, as Golos made the rounds in New York, he worked on persuading some White émigrés to take their sons back to Russia to join the army. It was a new, nationalistic tactic. The White émigrés were told that it didn't matter anymore whether they were enemies of the revolution; they were first of all Russians, and only that mattered. Some White émigrés responded, actually following through on Golos's suggestion to take their sons back to Russia—and Soviet intelligence got its hands on more hostages.[7]

Golos's was just one of several Soviet spy networks in New York. Some, like his, were successful, and others less so. Around the corner from the World Tourists office, in the building where Golos had his apartment, was a small company called Raven Electric. The company's owner, another Russian emigrant, had a habit of dropping by Golos's office.[8]

George Koval, a Raven Electric employee, was born in Iowa. Twenty-six years old and good-looking, George settled easily into his life in New York. A modest engineer, a thin man with high cheekbones and delicate features in round glasses, he was a fan of Walt Whitman, good at tennis, and liked by women. What George's new acquaintances in New York didn't know was that in 1932, he and his entire family—his mother, father, and two brothers—had moved from Iowa to the Soviet Union, lured by the IKOR (Idishe Kolonizatsie Organizatsie in Rusland), the Organization for Jewish Colonization in Russia. George, in his early twenties at the time, continued his studies in Moscow and in 1939 earned a degree in chemistry with an eye to a career in academia. But Soviet intelligence urgently desired access to a US military poison program. They couldn't pass up the prospect of using a genuine American citizen to do the job—one with chemical training to boot. Koval was recruited, not that he had much of a choice: the secret police had compromising material on young Koval's wife that could have landed her in jail.[9] Koval was given intensive training and sent back to the United States. He left his wife and family behind—as perfect hostages.

Now, though, nothing was happening. Soviet military intelligence patiently waited for Koval to deliver, but the US military apparently didn't have the chemical poisons program Koval had been sent to spy on. Koval was idling aimlessly in New York.

As had been the case in Constantinople, there were not one but two Soviet intelligence stations, or *rezidenturas*, in the United States—one legal and one illegal. Vasily Zarubin ran the legal station based in the New York Soviet consulate. His wife, Liza Gorskaya, helped him run the station. One of their tasks was to reactivate contacts with agents who had fallen off the radar or stopped collaborating. Gorskaya was particularly good at bumping into people on the streets, getting invited to lunch, and then firmly reminding them that it was time to get back to work for Soviet intelligence.

In the beginning of 1943, Stalin initiated a major change to the Soviet uniforms, replacing the futuristic Communist cubes on the collars with the golden epaulets of the tsar's Russian army. In May, these golden epaulets were also introduced for Soviet diplomats— and soon Zarubin, too, sported a gold-framed tunic at receptions. The country's ideology was rapidly moving from a vision of a universal Communist future to a dream of the Russian empire's glorious past. Nationalism was deemed more inspirational to soldiers fighting the horrible war with Germany.

The uniforms were not the only thing that changed. Soviet intelligence also started to change the rules. From now on, Moscow Center wanted full, top-down control over all recruited agents. Thus, it set out to abolish all roles played by Communist Party intermediaries. The horizontal networks of agents—a vibrant mix of determined operatives, fantasists, and idealists—were to be replaced with a hierarchy. Information would be compartmentalized and subordination strict. As in the Soviet Union, unquestioning obedience was top priority. Obedience, after all, was seen as the best guarantee of security.

Golos was the first to fall. He was efficient, yes, but he ran his extensive network largely on his own and on his own terms. It fell to Zarubin, ever the disciplinarian, to enforce Moscow's wishes. He was chosen to force Golos to hand over his agents to Russian officers to control. Moscow's—and thus Zarubin's—argument was that Golos might be under FBI surveillance. After all, he had already been investigated during the Spanish Civil War for helping American volunteers travel to Spain to fight for the Republican side. Golos had even been arrested, but he paid a fine of $500 and was quickly set free. Zarubin informed Golos that he was a security risk and must step down.

Golos refused. He was adamant: the inexperienced Soviet officers Moscow had begun sending to work in Zarubin's station didn't understand the American mentality. The new Russian operatives were "young and inexperienced, didn't work hard, and were not careful," Golos complained to his colleague.[10] Indeed, many didn't even have a basic command of English. Golos explained that some of his agents didn't realize they spied for the Soviets, rather than Browder's party, and the revelation that they worked for a foreign country would come as a shock. This, he said, would be dangerous.

Zarubin was not one to be swayed by argument when he had his orders. He was also aware of two important events from Golos's past that made him potentially dangerous. First, Golos had known Trotsky; the two men met in New York during World War I. Second, at the height of the Great Purge, Golos had enjoyed the backing of the then-chief of foreign intelligence.[11] But when the chief fell out of favor, he was summoned to Lubyanka and injected with potassium cyanide. Golos lost his protector and remained tainted by the association.

So Zarubin kept pushing. In April 1943, Moscow's chief of foreign intelligence sent Golos a personal letter urging him to give up his network. Again, Golos refused.

The same month, George Koval was drafted into the US Army. Uncle Sam needed young men with engineering training. Koval's youngest brother, Gabriel, who had enlisted in the Red army, had just been killed in Russia.

---------------- CHAPTER 7 ----------------

THE TIDE TURNS

That very month, in April 1943, the FBI recorded a conversation that took place at the house of a US Communist Party activist in Oakland, California. Steve Nelson, a veteran of the Abraham Lincoln Brigade in Spain, was under FBI observation, as he had long been suspected of running an underground Communist Party cell within the Berkeley Radiation Laboratory. Because his work was involved with the atomic bomb project, Nelson's phone and house had been wiretapped for months.

On April 10, Nelson hosted an unusual guest at his home at 3720 Grove Street.[1] The man arrived at Nelson's modest Berkeley residence in a chauffeur-driven car with a license plate from the Soviet Consulate in San Francisco. The guest introduced himself as Cooper.[2]

There was something odd about Cooper from the beginning of the conversation. "By the way, I don't know if you really imagine my position, who I am and so on? I'm about five heads up over people you know nothing about," said Cooper, for starters.[3] To FBI agents listening to the conversation, it soon became apparent that Cooper was indeed a high-ranking Soviet diplomat. Cooper produced a thick stack of money, counted it out, and handed it over to Nelson. They then spoke at length about Soviet intelligence operations in the United States. Nelson, like Golos, argued that it was better to keep using Communist Party intermediaries to run agents, but the unnamed Soviet official was adamant: Soviet intelligence didn't want to do that anymore. The agents' names were stated and the role played by Browder discussed in detail. In short, the conversation amounted to a full disclosure of espionage activity in the United States, recorded in its entirety by astonished FBI agents.

The FBI typed up a complete transcript and quickly identified the diplomat. It was Vasily Zarubin. He had just made one of the biggest mistakes of his life.

Naturally, the FBI embarked on a thorough investigation. Ironically, it was Zarubin, not Golos, who posed the real security risk. His meeting with Nelson awakened the FBI for the very first time to the threat of Soviet spies on American soil.

On May 7, FBI chief J. Edgar Hoover sent a letter to Harry Hopkins, Roosevelt's foreign policy adviser, at the White House.

> Personal and Confidential
> by special messenger
>
> Dear Harry:
>
> Through a highly confidential and reliable source it has been determined that on April 10, 1943, a Russian who is an agent of the Communist International paid a sum of money to Steve Nelson, National Committeeman of the Communist Party, USA, at the latter's home in Oakland, California.
>
> The money was reportedly paid to Nelson for the purpose of placing Communist Party members and Comintern agents in industries engaged in secret war production for the United States Government so that information could be obtained for transmittal to the Soviet Union.[4]

In the letter, Hoover fully identified Zarubin as "a Russian agent" and the third secretary of the Soviet embassy.[5]

Hoover at once launched two intelligence investigations. More than fifty FBI agents in New York and fifty more in Washington were tasked with tracking Soviet spies.

A week later, the Kremlin declared the complete dissolution of the Comintern. The timing of the move was hardly a coincidence; the White House had briefed the Soviet ambassador about Hoover's letter. When the Moscow correspondent for Reuters asked Stalin about the reason for disbanding the Comintern, Stalin answered that the Comintern's dissolution was "proper" for several reasons, the first two being:

(a) It exposes the lie of the Hitlerites to the effect that "Moscow" allegedly intends to intervene in the life of other nations and to "Bolshevize" them. From now on, an end is put to this lie.

(b) It exposes the calumny of the adversaries of Communism within the Labour movement to the effect that Communist Parties in various countries are allegedly acting not in the interests of their people but on orders from outside.[6]

Stalin had many reasons to dissolve the Comintern, but it was clear he especially wanted to downplay the ties between American Communists and Soviet intelligence. With the war raging, Russia's relationship with its most important ally was not something Stalin wanted to jeopardize. Any day now, the Soviet army anticipated a big German offensive near Kursk—and American tanks supplied by lend-lease were part of the Soviet defensive effort.

But things kept falling apart. On August 7, an anonymous letter addressed to Mr. Hoover arrived at FBI headquarters in Washington. It exposed Zarubin as "the so-called director of the Soviet Intelligence in this country" and named Zarubin's nine "closest associates," including his wife, Liza, who "directs political intelligence here, has a vast network of agents in almost all ministries including the State Department."[7] The letter was sent by Zarubin's deputy—who considered Zarubin too arrogant.

The White House briefed the Soviet ambassador about the letter, but Zarubin was undeterred. Zarubin kept pushing Golos, to no avail. Then he changed tactics and approached Golos's deputy, Elizabeth Bentley. If he wanted to bypass Golos, he greatly miscalculated; Bentley was Golos's lover, and she immediately reported her contact with Zarubin.

On November 26, 1943, Zarubin and Golos held a meeting to clear up the mess. A fierce argument ensued, but Golos was adamant and firmly refused to give up his network. The next day was Thanksgiving. Golos took Bentley to dinner and then to a movie. After the movie, he went to Bentley's home in the West Village and spent the night.[8] The next morning, Golos was dead, apparently of a heart attack. Whether Zarubin had anything to do with his death remains unclear to this day.

Bentley inherited Golos's contacts, and she also refused to give them up to Zarubin's people. She was already convinced that the Soviets had killed her lover. Zarubin put her under the same pressure he used with Golos, but instead of turning over the contacts, she went to the FBI. Meanwhile, Earl Browder's Soviet bosses removed him from his longtime position as chairman of the US Communist Party. It looked as if everything Jacob Golos, a Communist idealist and a shrewd secret operative, had worked to build for twenty years was turning to ashes because of Soviet intelligence's paranoia and obsession with control.

Meanwhile, Zarubin kept wreaking havoc. After his visit to Nelson's home in Berkley, the FBI followed his every step, identifying people on the way. Zarubin was contaminating everybody he spoke to.

But some of Golos's Americans-turned-Soviet-spies were still out there. As it turned out, these agents were the ones who helped Stalin get the bomb—the biggest Soviet intelligence coup ever, bar none.

The war was still on, but the era of recruitment on anti-Nazi grounds was ending. Golos, a Comintern veteran, had been able to reach out to a wide variety of people: Americans with Communist leanings, German refugees, and European scientists who had fled from Hitler, to name a few. He could win them all over, using different strategies, to spy for a cause. Under the new scheme, where any new agents had to work directly for Soviet intelligence, this approach was all but impossible.

In August 1944, Washington had enough of Zarubin and requested his removal. Zarubin was summoned back to Moscow. There, he had to face accusations of being careless in running New York's station. Worse, he was suspected of being a double agent for the FBI. Stalin, in the depths of his paranoia, started a new purge in the secret services.

It was almost surreal. While the FBI was working hard to crack the spy rings built by Golos and his comrades in the United States, in Moscow, Stalin began attacking the very operatives who ran these successful networks. The first to fall were the Jews.

In addition to sheer luck, surviving a pogrom requires two qualities: One is boldness. The other is an ability to build horizontal networks through relatives, friends, and other contacts. Anyone who masters these skills makes for a perfect spy—something the Soviet secret service had understood since the civil war. But the ability to benefit from unauthorized connections fell out of fashion in light of Stalin's paranoid state.

Zarubin survived the purge. He had made serious mistakes (to put it mildly); among the accusations he faced were that he had addressed his subordinates by their code names in the presence of diplomats and settled "illegal" agents in the apartments of "legal" officers.[9] Despite all this, he was not punished. In fact, he was rewarded and made a major general of state security.[10] But his wife, Liza Gorskaya, then just forty-six years old and the brains behind the couple, was forced into retirement. She was a Jew, which had now become a problem.

*   *   *

There was one intelligence function for which Stalin still needed tough, brutal, old-school spies like Nahum Eitingon: assassinations. With the war nearing an end, Eitingon was tasked with building a new department dedicated to assassinating enemies.[11] Stalin still valued the skills of the killer of his archenemy, Trotsky. So Eitingon, too, was lucky again. In his department, Eitingon was joined by his stepdaughter, Zoya Zarubina, the child of Vasily Zarubin. By now, Eitingon already defined a large part of Zoya's life.[12]

Zarubina had once been that nine-year-old girl who smuggled Eitingon's gun out of the Soviet Consulate in Harbin in 1929. Later, it was Eitingon, her beloved stepfather, who brought her to Moscow. At school she excelled in languages and became an athletics champion. Just before the war, Zarubin, visiting Moscow, talked her out of following his and Eitingon's path into the secret service, so she chose a career in linguistics. But when the war started, she was immediately enlisted in the special forces division OMSDON, tasked with terrorizing the German rearguard and supervised by Eitingon. She became an experienced saboteur. Later, because of her family connections and her command of foreign languages, she was put in charge of translating the atom bomb documents that Stalin's agents stole from the Manhattan Project.

Eitingon's new department immediately began carrying out assassinations. Victims included a prominent priest of the Ukrainian Church, a Polish engineer, and a Ukrainian activist. All were injected with a poison developed by the Soviet secret police's laboratory.

The list of victims also included an American, former Comintern agent Isaiah Oggins, who in 1939 had been sentenced to eight years in the gulag for supposed "anti-Soviet propaganda" (in reality, he was yet another victim of Stalin's paranoia). Oggins had spent the war years freezing in Norilsk, imprisoned in a gulag camp. In the middle of the war his case became public, and for years the US authorities had demanded his release. In 1947, after the series of Soviet intelligence failures in the United States, the Kremlin feared that releasing Oggins would attract more unwanted public attention to their American operations. Stalin ordered Eitingon to get rid of the American instead. The orders were that Oggins's death should appear to be due to natural causes. Eitingon promptly had Oggins transferred from Siberia to Moscow, where he was also poisoned.[13]

In 1947, Eitingon's department occupied the Comintern's spectacular rectangular headquarters in the east of Moscow, the former assortment of European refugees having long since been expelled from the building. But he could not evade the changing political winds forever. In 1951, when the anti-Semitic campaign was in full swing in the Soviet Union, Eitingon was accused of being part of the Zionist plot against the Soviet government, along with other prominent Jews. He was sent to jail. That same year, his stepdaughter, Zarubina, left the service for good. Soviet intelligence was becoming a truly nationalist, purely Russian agency.

In the meantime, Soviet intelligence unexpectedly scored a huge success. In 1943, George Koval had so pleased his officers in the US Army with his mathematical skills that he was sent to an Army Specialized Training Program at the College of New York. In August 1944, he was transferred to the Manhattan Engineers District at Oak Ridge, Tennessee. Instead of an imaginary poisons program, Koval now had direct access to the atomic bomb project. He immediately began sending intelligence to Moscow (among other things, he got access to the neutron initiator, the trigger of the bomb).[14] In this, he added to the efforts of the Rosenbergs, who had also been recruited by Golos, and other spies seeking atomic secrets. Despite the efforts of Moscow Center to dismantle Golos's networks, the networks still delivered.

This incredible development in Koval's spy career came about not because of his efforts, nor the efforts of Soviet military intelligence. Rather, George Koval got lucky—not the least important factor in espionage. In Oak Ridge, Koval had access to information regarding the production of plutonium and polonium. In 1948, this most unconventional Soviet émigré spy, an American citizen who went back and forth between Russia and the United States for twenty years, left the United States for good. He was not compromised; rather, Soviet military intelligence had recalled him. The paranoid controllers in Moscow hadn't liked it when Koval asked that they let his mother write to him—he was suspected of a lack of loyalty. Anti-Semitism played its part, too. When Koval got to Moscow, he was given the lowest military rank of a private and thrown out of military intelligence.[15]

Sixty years later, when Russian president Vladimir Putin visited the new headquarters of the Russian military intelligence GRU, he described Koval as "the only Soviet intelligence officer" to penetrate the Manhattan Project.[16]

Before and during World War II, Moscow's spymasters outsmarted the Americans. They accomplished this despite several failures, caused largely by Stalin's paranoia and the serious incompetence of individual Soviet operators. They also found a way to use Russian emigrants to penetrate areas vital to US interests.

After the war, the Americans became more focused. They decided to change the game and fight back.

CHAPTER 8

WARRING NARRATIVES

Six years after the Allies defeated Hitler's Germany, the Cold War between the Soviet Union and the West was in full swing. The US government believed a hot war was inevitable too and started looking for a politically minded group of Russian émigrés who would, when the time came, be able to replace the political regime in Russia.

In summer 1951, America entered its second year of war in Korea. There, in the first direct military confrontation between the world's two superpowers, US and Soviet pilots downed each other. Meanwhile, in Sing-Sing Prison on the Hudson River in Ossining, New York, Julius and Ethel Rosenberg awaited execution. They had been sentenced to death that April for passing atomic bomb secrets to the Soviets. The pair, once part of Jacob Golos's wide network, had been convicted of spying, but they were also convicted of having caused the deaths of Americans in Korea. In pronouncing sentence—the death penalty—federal judge Irving Kaufman stated his opinion that the Rosenbergs' "conduct in putting into the hands of the Russians the A-Bomb years before our best scientists predicted Russia would perfect the bomb has already caused . . . the Communist aggression in Korea."

In July, *The Catcher in the Rye* hit New York's bookstores, and the story of an alienated adolescent became an immediate bestseller. But a different book published that same month prompted heated discussions first in the offices of Kremlinologists in New York and then in the offices of Central Intelligence Agency (CIA) officials in Washington. The book was a thin volume, just 103 pages long, with the unassuming title *Russian Émigré Politics*. It consisted of a preface, four chapters, an appendix, and an index, all compiled and edited by one George Fischer, a twenty-eight-year-old former US Army captain. Only two hundred copies had been printed.

As it happened, Russian émigré politics was something the CIA had been trying to understand for years, with little success. Fischer's book outlined the current situation better than any other sources had been able to.

The CIA knew that Paris was no longer the capital of Russian emigration. Rather, the new wave of emigrants was centered in Germany—Munich, in particular. But mass Russian migration to New York City made it look as if it would soon take over Paris's role as the center of anti-Soviet activity.[1]

On July 2, 1951, William H. Jackson, deputy director of the CIA, wrote to George Kennan, Fischer's boss and the most prominent US expert on Soviet affairs: "Dear George: thank you for sending us copies. . . . A hasty glance indicates it will make interesting reading and will be a valuable contribution to our library."[2] Kennan was the author of the famous "Long Telegram," which he had sent to the secretary of state in 1946, while he was serving as chargé d'affairs in Moscow. In the Long Telegram, Kennan raised the alarm about Kremlin intentions, which led the United States to adopt a policy of containment. A few months later, President Harry S. Truman made him the US ambassador to Russia. When it came to Russia, Kennan's opinion counted.

On July 10, James M. Andrews, who ran the CIA's Office of Collection and Dissemination, sent an internal note to the CIA's general counsel: "Herewith the volume we spoke of over the phone. General Wyman feels that everyone in OSO [the CIA's Office of Special Operations] should read it, and I believe it should be widely read in OPC [Office of Policy Coordination]. I should like to make 50 to 100 copies by photo offset. Will you advise me as to copyright etc?"[3]

Major General Willard G. Wyman, the man mentioned in the letter, ran the OSO.[4] The OPC was the US covert psychological/political warfare unit. These CIA departments were the most active in dealing with the Soviet Union. The next day, Andrews was duly advised on copyright issues. His department received fifty copies of the book.

A week later, no less a personage than Director of Central Intelligence Walter B. Smith sent a personal note to the book's author, George Fischer, saying in part, "I'm hoping . . . to see Mr. Kennan next time he is in Washington and would be very glad to see you at the same time, if that is satisfactory to both of you."

Finally, it seemed, there was someone who could help the CIA navigate this mess.

Fischer, a tall, bespectacled young man, fluent in both German and Russian, certainly knew a thing or two about Soviet Russia. His father was the prominent American journalist Louis Fischer, a longtime authority on Soviet affairs. In the 1920s and 1930s, Louis had sympathized with the Bolsheviks, and they had trusted him. That meant he had extraordinary access to the leaders of the Soviet state—a group photograph dated 1922 shows him standing next to Vladimir Lenin. Louis was married to Berta Mark, a Russian Jewish pianist who had worked as an interpreter for not one but two Soviet foreign ministers. They had met during World War I when Berta was living in New York.

In the late 1920s, Louis moved from Germany to Moscow and brought Berta and their two sons with him. As a foreign correspondent for *The Nation*, Louis covered European affairs and reported from Spain as a member of the International Brigade. He mostly followed the Soviet line; Trotsky had called him a "Stalinist agent."[5]

By the early 1930s, harsh living conditions in Moscow prompted the Fischers to send their sons to Berlin to live with family friends—sociologist Paul Massing, of the famous Frankfurt School of Marxist theorists, and his wife, Hede. While Massing stayed largely in Berlin, Hede shuttled between Berlin and New York. A naturalized American citizen, Hede was also a Soviet agent, supervised by the resourceful Soviet spy Liza Gorskaya.

When Hitler became chancellor and the Reichstag was burned down, Fischer was forced to bring his boys back to Moscow. This move came in the nick of time, as the Gestapo came after Massing just a few days later. They interned him at the Sachsenhausen concentration camp, where he suffered five months of solitary confinement. After Massing was freed, he and Hede managed to escape Germany, and Moscow Center ultimately sent them both to the United States, to New York.

In Moscow, George Fischer was placed at the prestigious school N32, along with the children of the party fat cats. The school, organized as a Communist commune with teachers chosen personally by Lenin's wife, was just a stone's throw from the famous House on the Embankment—an imposing, physically enormous, luxury apartment complex built along the river Moskva for the Soviet elite.[6] George thrived there. He made friends. His two best buddies were Konrad and Markus Wolf, the sons of a famous German Communist writer.

For almost seven years, George and his friends led the lives of the offspring of the Soviet elite. Summers were spent between Peredelkino, a village populated by Soviet writers, and a pioneer camp named after Ernst Thälmann, a leader of the German Communists. Autumns were devoted to preparation for the parade on Red Square, in which the children played a part. Surrounded by Comintern members and their children, George, an American/ Soviet dual citizen, was duly indoctrinated. As a matter of course, he joined Komsomol, the Young Communists organization. All in all, he was well prepared to become a Soviet spy.

And then Stalin started the Great Purge. Right away, some of Louis's friends—and George's friends' fathers—were sent to the gulag. Louis Fischer didn't like what he saw. While on assignment abroad, he decided not to return to the Soviet Union—even though his family was still in Moscow.[7]

Louis also learned that Liza Gorskaya had lured his friends the Massings from New York to Moscow in 1937, as the purge was gaining momentum. Hede and Paul were placed in the Metropole Hotel and subjected to a series of exhausting questioning sessions: Gorskaya and Vasily Zarubin had been assigned to test their loyalty. Interrogations were mixed with parties, which were almost equally exhausting. On several of these occasions, with the alcohol flowing, Zarubin would sit in the center of the room playing the balalaika and singing Russian folk and Red army songs.[8] This series of "conversations" lasted for months, and Zarubin told the Massings at one point that if they decided to give up their work for Soviet intelligence, it could end very badly for them.

Now two American families—the Massings and the Fischers— felt trapped in Moscow, their futures uncertain. Finally, both leveraged their American citizenship: the Massings threatened to contact the American embassy, and Fischer asked First Lady Eleanor Roosevelt to intervene on his family's behalf. On the eve of World War II, the Soviet government let the two families leave for New York. They were now united by their fear and loathing of Stalin.

Over the years, George remained close to Paul Massing, who he considered a mentor. George enrolled at the University of

Wisconsin, but during World War II, he was drafted into the US Army and promptly sent back to Russia as a US liaison officer. George ended the war in Germany as an officer on General Dwight D. Eisenhower's staff. By that time, he had become even more critical of Stalin's regime.

In Berlin, in May 1945, George met up again with friends from his Moscow days, Markus and Konrad Wolf, who were now Soviet officers in the occupation forces. George spent several days and nights with them arguing about the Soviet Union's harsh approach to dealing with the Communist opposition in Berlin. Finally, they parted ways; the brothers stayed in Berlin while George returned to the United States to finish his education. (Konrad would become a prominent film director in East Germany, while Markus—known as Misha among his Soviet colleagues—would found the foreign intelligence branch of the Stasi, East Germany's brutal secret service. Misha Wolf would lead the Stasi's foreign intelligence branch for three decades.)

Back in America, George Fischer didn't break with Russia entirely; he decided to study Russian liberal movements in tsarist Russia. He was accepted to Harvard, where his classmates included Zbigniew Brzezinski and Henry Kissinger. Meanwhile, the book *The God That Failed*, an emotional denouncement of communism coauthored by George's father, Louis Fischer, along with Andre Gide, Arthur Koestler, and other prominent writers—all former Communists—set the intellectual stage for the Cold War.

As George began his research, he learned how Russia's liberal movements had been routinely squeezed out of Russia by the tsar's secret police. In exile, they flourished, founding networks, newspapers, and journals. Change in Russia had come about from the West, from the time of Alexander Herzen to that of Vladimir Lenin. An idealist, George believed he, too, could have a say about the future of Russia.

*   *   *

Meanwhile, in Washington, DC, the US government tried to bring structure—or, at the very least, some modicum of order—to the Russian political émigré community. War with Stalin was inevitable, they thought, and coming soon. Desperate to find out more about this bellicose regime, the American government invited all kinds of people and entities, from American intelligence officers to private foundations to academic intellectuals, to contribute ideas and information.

When the Soviet Union tested its first atom bomb in August 1949, Washington quickened the pace of war preparations, calculating that within a decade the United States would become vulnerable to a Soviet attack.[9] Very few in the United States thought it would be a contained regional conflict—Washington planners imagined all-out war. And this conflict, they believed, would inevitably result in the collapse of the Soviet regime.

The question, then, was, Who would govern a defeated Russia? Washington initially took the view formulated by George Kennan, then chief policy planner at the State Department, that the US government would help all émigré organizations return to Russia to try their luck. The American government didn't want to take the responsibility of "sponsoring entirely" a specific group.[10]

This plan sounded democratic, but it was not very practical. The United States could not win a war with Russia and then just trust its governance to chance; after all, Russia was the country with two hundred million people and atomic weapons. For a start, it made sense to study the list of probable leaders. Kennan then suggested that while the Americans waited for all-out war to break out, they could concurrently begin using political refugees, organized into "liberation committees," to foment resistance behind the Iron Curtain.[11]

Before implementing this new strategy, the CIA prepared a report on existing Russian émigré organizations. It was dispiriting. The agency praised the ROVS, the military wing of the White emigration, as being—still—the most capable of the Russian organizations. CIA analysts admitted, however, that these Russian Civil War veterans were aging. After all, thirty years had passed since their exodus from Russia. It was unrealistic to think these elderly officers would be able to go back to Russia and lead the country when the time came.

Next the CIA assessed a new generation of Soviet citizens living in the West for leadership potential. This group, located largely in Germany, had come to the West as displaced persons or prisoners of war during World War II and stayed. Nevertheless, the CIA concluded they were equally useless: this group "had even less capable and recognized leaders than its predecessor."[12]

The more they searched for future leaders in exile, the clearer it became to the US government that they knew almost nothing about the society of the country they were planning to fight and conquer. The Soviet borders were sealed, its national media printed and broadcast only propaganda, and Soviet citizens were discouraged from having any contact with foreigners. Some high-ranking American officials came to believe that only the behavioral sciences—a combination of sociology, social psychology, and cultural anthropology—could help the United States understand what made its enemy tick.

But the United States couldn't study its subject in Russia. The largest source of data that was readily available came from the Soviet citizens who had been captured by the German army and transported to the Reich to serve as forced labor in the factories and fields. There were also the Red army prisoners who found themselves in the American zone in Germany after the war ended. Now these men and women were living in displaced persons camps in Bavaria, near Munich. Many, fearing Stalin's camps, didn't want to return home.

In 1950, American researchers from Harvard, which was sponsoring a special project with funding from the US Air Force, traveled to Munich. They sat down to talk with hundreds of displaced Soviet citizens to develop a more sophisticated understanding of Soviet society. Interviewers asked displaced Soviets about everything from their individual life stories to the way Soviet society was organized. These interviews were very detailed, touching on specifics like the role of the secret police in controlling Russian factories.

One of the people who had been invited to run the project in Munich was George Fischer, then a Harvard doctoral student. While researching his thesis, George had already come into contact with some White Russian émigrés in the United States. When he heard about the newest generation of Russian émigrés—the thousands of Soviet soldiers and citizens held by the Allied powers in western Germany—he naturally felt their experiences would be very important to his work. Harvard offered to send him to Munich, and he readily accepted. As an added benefit, George's mother was already there; the former translator was working for the Allies, helping Soviet citizens in refugee camps.[13]

After a good deal of lobbying from George Kennan, the American Committee for the Liberation for the Peoples of Russia was launched that same year. There was also the National Committee for a Free Europe, an American-based group whose goal was to mobilize political exiles from Eastern Europe. To kick off these efforts, the CIA gathered Russian exile leaders together at an inn in the Bavarian town of Fussen. But the meeting was a failure. The White émigrés didn't trust the social democrats; the Ukrainians accused the Russians of trying to reinstate the Russian empire's 1914 borders; groups who were not invited complained bitterly. One group even staged a protest walkout.[14]

The Russian émigré community proved very difficult to deal with at all, let alone to direct from the outside. The British—America's best ally in Cold War secret adventures—didn't help. They preferred to spend their limited funds on acquiring defectors.[15]

Toward the end of 1950, a powerful new player appeared: the Ford Foundation. In the 1930s and 1940s, the Ford Foundation had operated as a small, not very significant fund. Then, in 1950, it began receiving tens of millions of dollars in dividends from the huge endowment of stock bequeathed to it by Henry and Edsel Ford.[16] With $417 million at its disposal, the Ford Foundation became almost overnight the country's largest philanthropic organization, and it decided to set a more ambitious international agenda for itself. To help accomplish this, the foundation elected Paul G. Hoffman, an automobile executive, as its president. Hoffman, who after the war had served as the first administrator of the Marshall Plan, turned to Kennan. Kennan, in turn, reached out to George Fischer in Munich.

George Fischer jumped at the opportunity to advise the foundation. He proposed the launch of the Free Russia Fund. He envisaged three objectives for it: to help refugees integrate into American society, to support political refugees in case of a change in the Soviet system, and to fund research on the USSR.

Fischer worked feverishly trying to get on paper how the fund would achieve these objectives. He soon came to a damning conclusion that echoed the CIA assessment: Soviet refugees were "so inexperienced in organization, so lacking vitality, and so unable to think outside the framework of totalitarian schemes, that they should be excluded from any management positions within the fund."[17]

Still, he didn't give up. The Free Russia Fund was launched in March, headquartered in New York. Fischer was the fund's director and Kennan its president.

The publication of *Russian Émigré Politics*, George Fischer's book, was the fund's first achievement.

The book used the research George had done for Harvard in Munich to analyze the post–World War II Russian refugees. Fischer argued that this generation of Russian refugees—consisting mostly of people with military experience—could be useful as rank-and-file soldiers, should there be a war with the Soviet Union. He called them "fervent and equally invaluable allies in Freedom's resistance against Soviet imperialism."[18] Fischer outlined his belief that once the war started, the Soviet military itself would likely become a hotbed of dissent. To support this theory, Fischer cited what had happened during World War II, when a huge—indeed, unprecedented—number of soldiers had deserted the Soviet army and switched sides to join the German army.

The CIA liked Fischer's book. If Hitler's army—which had committed horrible atrocities against the Russian population—was nonetheless joined by so many Red army soldiers, why shouldn't the United States expect Soviet military personnel to defect in large numbers in the case of war with the United States? The idea was appealing. (The most common mistake generals make is to prepare fully for the previous war, and this hypothesis clearly seems to be an example).[19] However, the question of émigré leadership remained unsettled.

The CIA decided on a compromise. Because the first émigré generation of Russian Whites was too old and the Soviet postwar generation too disorganized, the CIA chose to support an organization that was more or less in the middle. The CIA's pick was the National Labor Union, or NTS (*Narodno-Trudovoy Soyuz*), a group composed mainly of the sons and other younger relatives of the Whites.

The agency listed three specific reasons for this choice. First, the NTS had developed relatively popular media outlets in the United States and Germany, such as the *Posev* (Seeding) publishing house, which had been launched in a displaced persons camp near the German city of Kassel. Second, the NTS headquarters were in the United States. Finally, the CIA reported that President Truman had granted an audience to the NTS chairman in the fall of 1948, which meant the group was recognized in Washington.[20] Furthermore, the NTS was also known to have cooperated with Red army turncoats during the World War II. As such, it seemed well suited to the role envisaged by Fischer—namely, that of embracing Soviet military defectors when the war started.

As it happened, the hot war between the United States and the Soviet Union never started. Thus it came about that in the 1950s, the CIA used NTS members extensively to conduct covert operations behind the Iron Curtain. It was from the ranks of the NTS that the CIA recruited secret agents to send back into Russia. NTS also launched giant weather balloons—20 meters in diameter, made of transparent plastic—to carry leaflets and false bank notes over the Iron Curtain.[21]

For all the Sturm und Drang surrounding these NTS actions, they were mostly useless. Straightforward covert actions didn't work behind the Iron Curtain. Most operatives were caught before they made contact with any resistance operation inside the Soviet Union, real or imaginary, and none of the balloons ever reached the Soviet mainland—the wind too often blew them out back to Western Europe.

Other measures met with equally modest results. In the 1950s, Kennan's "liberation committees" set up a number of radio stations, such as Radio Free Europe and Radio Liberty, targeted at audiences in Eastern Europe and Russia. However, because of jamming, very few people in the Soviet Union could listen to them even if they wanted to. In that early period, secret agents, balloons, and radio broadcasts had a minimal impact on society in the Soviet Union.

The Iron Curtain worked pretty well in both directions: it didn't let Russians out, and it didn't let Western agents or subversive ideas in.

CHAPTER 9

STALIN'S DAUGHTER

Like the United States, the Soviet Union was also readying itself for an all-out war. Soviet intelligence agencies fully comprehended that large numbers of their compatriots had opted to stay in the West rather than return to the Soviet Union, and they directed a massive effort against this group. A series of assassinations took the leaders of resistance groups, one after another. The NTS was constantly in the crosshairs. Radio broadcasting targeted Soviet refugees in Germany, urging them to return or intimidating them into not taking part in any kind of anti-Soviet activity.

Still, times changed. When Stalin died, some rules were relaxed, if very slightly. The secret police began failing to prevent defections.

Arguably, some of the most important defectors to the West were not the generals and officers envisaged by Fischer but rather something that looked, on the surface, rather innocuous: books.

Stalin died in March 1953, and Zarubin, Gorskaya, and Eitingon found themselves suddenly and unexpectedly back in business. Lavrentiy Beria, the head of the secret services, called Zarubin and Gorskaya out of retirement and released Eitingon from jail. He gave them, along with another officer involved in Trotsky's assassination,[1] a new assignment: they were to form a special operations brigade to blow up American air bases in Europe if things got hot between the Soviets and the Americans. It was probably the only time when all of them worked together.

Once Eitingon felt securely established at Lubyanka, he invited his stepdaughter, Zoya Zarubina, back too. But this time, she said no. She was already forging a career at the Institute of Foreign Languages. This turned out to be a smart decision on her part, probably saving her from prison when, a few months later, Beria was ousted, crushed, and killed in a coup.

Eitingon was sent to jail again, this time for eleven years, for being Beria's accomplice. He was convicted, along with his superior, of "heading a special group tasked to develop plans of assassination and beating up of Soviet citizens." Eitingon's "direct involvement in killing people by injecting poison was established," read his sentence.[2]

After his arrest, the Soviet secret services went about their business as usual. They responded to Western covert warfare with a string of killings abroad. Germany, and Munich in particular, became a hunting ground for Soviet secret services: In 1957, a Soviet agent killed a Ukrainian émigré activist and writer with a poison vapor gun. A leader of the Ukrainian émigré community was poisoned by cyanide in 1959.[3] An NTS chairman was about to be poisoned in 1954, but his would-be assassin defected to the West. Three years later, the defector himself barely survived a poisoning by thallium. Poison, indeed, never went out of fashion.

The Munich area was also targeted by Russian radio propaganda. One station, run from East Berlin by the Soviet Repatriation Committee, had Soviet citizens call on their husbands, sons, nephews, or old friends to return via personal letters read aloud on air. Even if the radio show did not tempt exiles to go back, it surely made emigrants think twice about taking part in any anti-Kremlin activity, in that it provided evidence that Soviet forces were keeping close watch on their relatives back home.[4]

In the mid-1950s, this sort of blackmail tactic expanded to the United States. Countess Alexandra Tolstoy, Leo Tolstoy's daughter, had fled the Soviet Union in 1929 and in two years had moved to the United States. She was living on a farm in upstate New York and working to provide help to refugees coming to America. The countess testified to the Senate that, in her experience, many Soviet exiles were targeted by Soviet agents. Exiles received mail "addressed to them under their original Russian names at the addresses in which they are living under false identities," she said.[5] The message was clear: the secret services had traced them in the United States, despite their new names.

Meanwhile, George Fischer's ambitious plans for the Free Russia Fund hadn't worked out. The fund had failed to find any high-profile political fugitives to support. There was, it seemed, no new Trotsky waiting in the wings—no one, anyway, who had any real chance of changing the Soviet system. No breakthrough research on the Soviet system was produced by emigrants that the fund could help promote either.[6]

The US military found a more practical and focused use for Russian émigrés: it set up a Russian institute in the Bavarian Alps, in the small mountain resort town of Garmisch, Germany, not far from Munich. From the 1950s on, American diplomats, military staff, and spies about to be stationed in the Soviet Union were sent to a yearlong military training program there, conducted entirely in Russian and taught by Russian émigrés from both the first and second waves.[7]

Fischer's Free Russia Fund was more successful helping to resettle Soviet refugees in the United States, giving grants to the Tolstoy Foundation, run by Alexandra Tolstoy, among other organizations.

It was becoming clear that the Americans couldn't expect any big breakthroughs until someone with a large following at home—a writer, a scientist, or an artist—defected to the West.

On April 26, 1967, the luxurious Plaza Hotel on the corner of Fifth Avenue and Central Park in New York hosted a large press conference. The Plaza—a monumental building, nineteen stories high and framed with towers, intended by its developers to call to mind a beefed-up French chateau—was crowded that morning with reporters.

Stalin's only daughter, forty-one-year-old Svetlana Alliluyeva, had been in New York for a week. Her defection, on board a Swissair plane, made headlines all over the world. Alliluyeva had fallen in love with an Indian Communist, but her father's old comrades refused to let her marry him. Within a year, she watched her lover die in Moscow. She was reluctantly allowed to take his ashes to India to pour into the Ganges River. From there, she walked into the US embassy in New Delhi, presented her passport, and requested political asylum.[8]

Now she walked into the Plaza's grand reception hall. Red-haired, like her father, Svetlana was dressed in a modest deep-blue outfit. She took a seat at a long table, in front of a microphone. To her right stood George Kennan, watching her with pride.

This was a big moment for the former diplomat. When the US embassy in New Delhi sent a cable about Svetlana's defection to Washington, the State Department had reached out to Kennan, now in retirement. At Svetlana's request, they asked Kennan to fly to Geneva to meet her. Svetlana had likely asked specifically for him as the two knew each other from Kennan's days as the US ambassador to Moscow. Kennan jumped on a plane immediately. He liked Svetlana. More important, her defection was just what he and George Fischer had been looking for, until now in vain: a high-profile Soviet defector who could sway American public opinion regarding the Soviet Union.

At the press conference, Svetlana started by answering reporters' written questions in English that was hesitant but clear. She first addressed one posed by a reporter from NBC: "What is your political philosophy?" Alliluyeva said she didn't have any political philosophy and explained that the young Soviet generation had become more critical, but to her, the religion made a big change. Svetlana conceded then that it was her relationship with Mr. Singh that changed her perspective on the Soviet Union. But, she added, this was not the only problem she had with her former homeland:

> Among other events, I can mention also the trial of Sinyavsky and Daniel, which produced a horrible impression on all intellectuals in Russia and on me, also. I can say that I lost hope which I had before that we are going to become liberal, somehow. The way the two writers were treated and sentenced made me absolutely disbelieve in justice.[9]

Andrei Sinyavsky and Yuli Daniel were two prominent Soviet writers who had been convicted of anti-Soviet propaganda in 1966, after they published their satirical writings in France. They were sent to labor camps. Svetlana stressed that she was also a writer. In fact, she had already completed a book and had it smuggled out of Russia. "I hope you will read my book this autumn," she said.[10]

Svetlana's book, *Twenty Letters to a Friend*, was a personal memoir structured as a series of letters. It was indeed published but not in the fall; after the press conference, Harper & Row sped up the publication date, and the book was available in June. An instant national sensation, it became a *New York Times* bestseller.

Kennan helped arrange the book deal. He also helped Svetlana settle in, lending her his farm. It was located near a small town in Pennsylvania called, of all things, East Berlin.[11]

Svetlana's was not the first book published by a Soviet defector in the West, but the others had been written by spies—unknown in the wider world and talked of only within the relatively small circles of counterintelligence and intelligence operatives. Stalin's daughter's memoir, for obvious reasons, was different. And it was also a very good book.

With Svetlana, Kennan finally got what he and George Fischer had dreamed of more than fifteen years earlier: a Soviet émigré of huge political significance who could reach a large American audience.

Kennan remained a loyal friend to Svetlana for years to come. Always supportive, he helped her settle in at Princeton, where he lived. For him, she was a new Trotsky. Because he believed she was in real danger of being kidnapped by the KGB, he enlisted his family to look after her as well.[12] So loyal was he that he stood behind her even when Svetlana, always emotional, behaved foolishly—for example, when she fell in love with her neighbor, Louis Fischer. George's father was then seventy years old. The affair was passionate but didn't end well. One day Svetlana smashed in one of the glass-paneled doors at Fischer's house, demanding that he return the letters she had sent him.[13]

In the meantime, Louis's son George was going through a traumatic experience. He had become very critical of the Vietnam war. After all, the protesters modeled much of their thought on the ideas of the New Left, propounded by George's old tutor Paul Massing and his colleagues in the Frankfurt School. In spring 1968, when antiwar student protests broke out at Columbia University, Fischer—by then a forty-five-year-old associate professor of sociology and a staff member of the Russian Institute at Columbia— sided with the students.

After he added his signature to the statement, published in the *Columbia Spectator*, asking that "all civil and criminal complaints against those arrested during the recent demonstrations be dropped,"[14] he was forced to leave Columbia University. With that, he gave up Kremlinology altogether. There is no evidence that he was ever in touch with Kennan after that.

Svetlana Alliluyeva remained a unique and personal case for Kennan. But it was a success amid failure. None of the émigré organizations Kennan helped launch in the early 1950s ultimately played any role in the success of Svetlana's book. More important, she refused to become a new Trotsky—a mobilizing and organizing figure for the Russian émigré community. Nor did she want to advise US foreign policy makers. She stuck to the promise she made at her press conference at the Plaza Hotel: "I'll preach neither for communism nor against it."[15]

Svetlana may have refused to play the role of a cold warrior, but her escape had serious repercussions in the Soviet Union.

Three weeks after Stalin's daughter held her press conference at the Plaza, KGB chairman Vladimir Semichastny was called to the Kremlin. The Soviet leader Leonid Brezhnev had gathered a conference of the Politburo and announced to Semichastny in its presence that he was dismissed. The reason? He had failed to prevent Stalin's daughter from fleeing to the West.[16] In a way, Kennan's operation had caused the fall of an all-powerful chief of the omnipotent KGB—a remarkable achievement for a retired diplomat, a forty-one-year-old woman, and her 272-page book.

By the end of the 1960s, though, some of Kennan's other ideas finally began to bear some fruit. In April 1968, in the kitchens of Moscow's freethinking intelligentsia, people were talking in low voices about the launch of the Soviet Union's first uncensored underground human rights newsletter, the *Chronicle of Current Events*. The newsletter took as its epigraph Article Nineteen of the 1948 Universal Declaration of Human Rights: "Everyone has the right to freedom of opinion and expression; this right includes freedom to hold opinions without interference and to seek, receive and impart information and ideas through any media and regardless of frontiers." The *Chronicle of Current Events* would continue to report arrests and the prosecution of dissidents in the country for fifteen years and became the longest-running *samizdat* publication in the country.[17]

In August 1968, Soviet troops invaded Czechoslovakia. Eight people, including the editor of the *Chronicle*, walked to Red Square, where they unfolded homemade protest posters. In just a few minutes, all of them were arrested. The *Chronicle* reported on their trial. From the first issue, the *Chronicle* was routinely smuggled to the West, reprinted, and read aloud on Radio Liberty—one of the stations that had been launched thanks to Kennan's efforts. And thousands of Russians, having figured out a way around the Soviet authorities' jamming, now listened to broadcasts (dubbed by the Kremlin "the voices of the enemy") from Radio Liberty and other Western stations.

In December another Russian book hit bookstores in the United States: Harper & Row published *The First Circle*, by Alexander Solzhenitsyn. The novel was based on Solzhenitsyn's experiences in a secret research facility that used gulag inmates as workers. The book had been refused publication in Moscow and then was smuggled to the West. Soon the flow from the Soviet Union of manuscripts critical of the Kremlin regime became unstoppable. A new era had begun.

CHAPTER 10

NOW IT'S OFFICIAL

The crushing defeats of democratic upsurges, first in Hungary in 1956, then in Czechoslovakia in 1968, were expensive and sobering lessons for the Western powers. Kennan's dream of the impending liberation of the peoples of Eastern Europe from Communist control faded away. But there was still something that could be done for those trapped behind the Iron Curtain.

Hundreds of thousands of people wanted out. If the lands themselves couldn't be wrested from the Communist grip, went the thinking in the West, then at least some individuals could be rescued.

However, this was easier said than done. The Socialist camp, as people living behind the Iron Curtain referred to their nations, made a point of not letting people go. The borders were sealed.

This began to change in the late 1960s and early 1970s. The Soviet Jews became the most active in fighting for the right to emigrate. After the Six-Day War in 1967, which was followed by a break in diplomatic relations between the Soviet Union and Israel, the Soviet Union's long-running campaign of anti-Semitism worsened significantly. The Soviet Jews had been attacked again and again, in wave after wave. Now they called for help from the outside.

That call did not go unheard. Numerous rallies in support of Soviet Jews were held in New York and Washington, DC. Advocacy organizations leveraged support from Jewish institutions and from allied advocates of religious freedom all over the country. The United States raised the issue at the United Nations.

But the Nixon administration was reluctant to officially back the cause of the Soviet Jews. Both Nixon and Brezhnev wanted to improve relations. The Soviet Union had its eye on a new status— that of a Most Favored Nation trading partner of the United States. Nixon, for his part, was ready to grant that.

Rather than champion the rights of Soviet Jews to emigrate, the White House preferred to privately hand Soviet officials lists of Jews refused exit visas from time to time. Sometimes, on an ad hoc basis, the USSR let the people on these lists go.

Then things got worse for Soviet Jews. In August 1972, three months after Nixon's visit to Moscow, the Soviet authorities instituted a fee for Jews who applied for exit visas. This fee was exorbitant, ranging from 4,500 to 12,000 rubles—then roughly the cost of three cars. The logic for the fee, which some in the West called a "ransom," was the same as that used to justify anti-Semitic Soviet restrictions on Jews enrolling in universities: "We don't want to provide costly education to people who are about to leave for Israel." The introduction of the fee, an overt sign of the state's hostility, resulted in more applications.

In response, some congressmen and activists in New York came up with the idea of introducing legislation that would make the Soviet Union's access to Most Favored Nation trade benefits dependent on its allowing for the free emigration of Soviet Jews. Senator Henry Jackson drafted the amendment, which would require all countries of the Communist bloc to comply with a set of free emigration requirements. He and Congressman Charles Vanik cosponsored the amendment. By spring 1973, Jackson and Vanik were determined to get their amendment passed. That didn't suit Nixon at all.

On March 1, Nixon met with Israeli prime minister Golda Meir in the Oval Office of the White House. Three Israelis and three Americans were in the room, but the conversation took place mostly among Meir, Nixon, and Henry Kissinger, Nixon's secretary of state. They had talked for an hour, mostly about arms shipments and the prospects for peace with Egypt, when Meir raised the emigration issue.

"One other point. The Soviet Union is bad. They have people in prison just because they want to go to Israel. This ransom is terrible. If they would only let them leave. Anyone who applies for emigration loses his job, and usually goes to prison," said Meir.

"I know about anti-Semitism in the Soviet Union," Nixon responded.

Meir interrupted him. "Now it's official."

Nixon was now on the defensive. "What do we do? We have talked to them, Henry and I, and we will continue—but privately. We could do it publicly—like Congress—but what good would that do?"

Kissinger came to the president's aid and asked Meir not to interfere. Nixon quickly added, "We can't face down the Soviet Union any more—it would mean mutual suicide. We have a dialogue."[1]

Moments after the Israelis left, however, Henry Kissinger turned to Nixon. "The emigration of Jews from the Soviet Union is not an objective of American foreign policy," Kissinger said. "And if they put Jews into gas chambers in the Soviet Union, it is not an American concern. Maybe a humanitarian concern."[2]

Nixon had his own deeply anti-Semitic theories about Jews—who he believed shared a common trait of needing to compensate for an insecurity complex.[3] Not surprisingly, then, the US president's policy toward Jews wanting to leave the Soviet Union was quite clear. "I know," Nixon replied to Kissinger's comment. "We can't blow up the world because of it."[4]

Two weeks later, on March 16, Jackson reintroduced his amendment in Congress. This caused a hysterical reaction at the Kremlin, which was busy with preparations for Leonid Brezhnev's first official visit to Washington in June.

Angry and confused, Brezhnev summoned a session of the Politburo. The Politburo, he said, had agreed to suspend the collection of the fee. Why had that not happened? Brezhnev stopped just short of accusing the Interior Ministry and the KGB of sabotage. "My instructions were not met," he said. "It worries me."[5]

Yuri Andropov, the KGB's chief, stepped forward and took responsibility for the delay, but he backtracked immediately: "Only 13 percent of them are people who pay."

Angry, Brezhnev snapped back: "Excuse me, but I have this information before me. I'm reading it: In the first two months of 1973, 3,318 people left, including 393 people with education, and they paid 1,561,375 rubles." Then Brezhnev asked sharply, "So why do we need this million?"

Undeterred, Andropov evoked the threat of a brain drain. "Off go the physicians, engineers, et cetera," said the KGB chief. "We've begun getting applications from academicians. I presented you the list."

But Brezhnev was adamant. He wanted a good trade deal with the United States, and he did not want this issue to get in the way. He had his own peculiar solution to the problem, as revealed in his quarrel with Andropov: "When I reflected on these things, I asked myself . . . Why not give them a small theater with five hundred seats, which would work under our censorship, and keep the repertoire under our supervision? Let Aunt Sonya sing Jewish wedding songs there." He seemed genuinely certain that giving Jews a theater would make the problem of Jewish emigration go away.

Finally, the fee was quietly abandoned. But the change that the conflict over Jewish emigration had set in motion—the slow dissolution of the impermeable Iron Curtain—would prove irreversible. Even in the absence of the fee, Jackson and Vanik's cause steadily gained support, both at home and abroad. In September 1974, Andrei Sakharov, a leading dissident from the Soviet Union, sent an open letter to the US Congress voicing his support for the amendment. It was published in the *Washington Post*, entirely in capitalized letters.[6]

In December, Congress approved the amendment. Under the new law, countries that denied their citizens the right to emigrate forfeited both credit and investment guarantees.[7] It was Sakharov's letter that was credited with having persuaded the American congressmen to vote the way they did.[8] President Ford signed a trade agreement with the Soviet Union in January 1975 with the Jackson-Vanik amendment, although he expressed his reservations about "the wisdom of legislative language."[9]

The new amendment failed to help Soviet Jews immediately, though. Jewish departures declined sharply, from thirty-five thousand in 1973 to just thirteen thousand in 1975.[10] The amendment was meant to be punishment for breaking international obligations—the United States clearly articulated what it wanted the Soviet Union to do to look like a civilized country.[11] Instead it became, as the *New York Times* put it, the "very symbol of a cold war turning colder."[12]

CHAPTER 11

BEAR IN THE WEST

Throughout the 1970s, Soviet people kept trying to find ways to leave the country. Some Russians were allowed to travel abroad. It was not surprising, then, that a visit to any capitalist country became seen—by the KGB and by Soviet citizens of all stripes—as an opportunity to defect.

Most of those granted the precious privilege of being allowed to travel were the crème de la crème of Soviet society, foot soldiers in the cultural Cold War with the West, like dancers of the Bolshoi Ballet and classical musicians. But by the 1970s, the Kremlin was clearly losing the battle, as the Soviet Union's cultural warriors kept defecting to the enemy.

In Moscow and Leningrad, everyone knew *Mishka na Severe*, meaning "Bear in the North." It was one of the country's most beloved chocolate candies, with an easily recognizable paper wrapper featuring a huge white polar bear standing on an ice floe. In 1974, a new joke started circulating in Leningrad: *Mishka na Zapade*, meaning "Bear in the West." People laughed because they all knew the anti-Soviet story behind the twist of phrase: In June 1974,

Russia's most famous ballet dancer, twenty-six-year-old Mikhail Baryshnikov, had defected while on tour in Canada (Mishka is diminutive for Mikhail).[1] A popular artist, loved by everyone, Baryshnikov was a once-in-a-lifetime talent, someone who could make the most difficult and complicated ballet jump look as effortless as his leap over the Iron Curtain appeared to be. With his good looks—big blue eyes and fair hair—Baryshnikov is an icon. He would later become known to many Americans when he played Carrie Bradshaw's charming but self-centered Russian lover in the TV show *Sex and the City*.

By Soviet standards, Baryshnikov was already a successful and prosperous young man before his defection. A star of the Kirov Ballet in Leningrad, his career was skyrocketing. He had a comfortable apartment in Leningrad and a car—the roomy Volga, named after the great Russian river, that usually only Soviet bureaucrats could afford to drive.

But Baryshnikov felt constrained in his art. He was not happy with the extremely conservative style of Leningrad's former Imperial Russian Ballet, which was still performing mostly classical works. To the young dancer, this repertoire felt outdated. He yearned to explore more contemporary forms of dance. After all, the sexual revolution had reached the Soviet Union too, and as Baryshnikov would say later, he could not dance as if nothing in the world had happened since the premiere of *Swan Lake* one hundred years earlier.

Then there was the KGB. The Soviet secret police had agents and informants everywhere, and the Kirov Ballet was no exception. Dancers and singers grew accustomed to being under constant surveillance—it was considered a sort of tax to pay—but sometimes, as Baryshnikov learned, the KGB turned to blackmail. After his return from a tour in London, the KGB informed the dancer that they had a record of everything he had done abroad—including the romantic relationship he had struck up with an American girl.[2] "It was during this period that I really began to take stock of my life and realize how uneasy I was feeling most of the time," he remembered later.[3]

Despite these gloomy thoughts, Baryshnikov had no plans for escape when, in May 1974, he and a group of dancers from the Bolshoi Theater embarked on a tour headed first to Canada and then to South America.[4]

John Fraser, a young dance critic for the *Globe and Mail*, saw Baryshnikov's performance at the O'Keefe Centre in Toronto and was deeply impressed by the Russian dancer's talent. Fraser got to the office to write a review of the show and saw a note marked "urgent" on his typewriter. It was from an acquaintance, the wife of another critic. Intrigued, he called back. She asked Fraser to do her a favor. Her instructions were mysterious: The journalist was to approach Baryshnikov in the theater and pass on a phone number. Fraser was instructed to tell the dancer that his friends were waiting for his call. "Remember these names: *Dina, Tina,* and *Sasha*. Have you got them? *Dina, Tina,* and *Sasha*," she told him.[5]

Time was short. The woman insisted that Fraser had to find a way to meet Baryshnikov that night or the next. Fraser didn't have to think twice. He adored Baryshnikov and agreed to help. He finished writing his review, then hastened back to the O'Keefe Centre. Fraser hoped to find Baryshnikov at the gala dinner held after the performance.

Fraser wanted to be very cautious, as instructed, so he hid the scrap of paper with the phone number beneath his wedding ring. He made his way through the crowd at the gala dinner and spotted Baryshnikov. Now Fraser just had to catch him alone. Finally, the moment presented itself. Fraser approached the dancer and tried to pull the scrap of paper out from under his wedding ring—but in his haste, he tore it. Baryshnikov burst into laughter and took his notebook out of his pocket. Confused but determined to accomplish his task, Fraser scribbled the number and the names.

Dina, Tina, and Sasha—Baryshnikov decrypted this message immediately. Dina and Sasha were his friends from Russia, and

Tina was the American girl he had met in London. They wanted him to escape.

There was one last performance left to do at the O'Keefe Centre in Toronto, and Baryshnikov did not want to let his colleagues down. He decided to escape the next day. It was a risk, but he decided to take it.

The night of June 29, however, everything went wrong. The curtain failed to lift, so the performance started fifteen minutes late. The anxiety made Baryshnikov's hands shake as he elevated a ballerina. But the public noticed nothing, and the spectators were thrilled by his role in *Don Quixote*—which meant that the ovation lasted much longer than usual. Baryshnikov had one curtain call after another.

According to plan, Baryshnikov's friends were waiting for him in a car not far from the theater. After the show, Baryshnikov was supposed to duck out of the O'Keefe Centre's stage door, run to the waiting car, and jump in. They would drive away, and he would be free—far from the Soviet Union and out of reach of his KGB handlers and the annoying Communist Party, which he was being pressured to join.[6]

With all the delays, Baryshnikov was late. He knew his friends would be getting increasingly nervous. He made it out the theater door only to encounter the next problem: a crowd of his admirers waiting for him in front of the bus that was supposed to drive him and the other artists to a mandatory closing reception. There was no doubt that Baryshnikov's KGB handlers would also be at the reception: they had to keep tabs on each and every artist to make sure all the Soviet dancers returned safely to the Soviet Union. This was not an easy task nor one they took lightly. After all, Baryshnikov's colleague, the Kirov ballerina Natalia Makarova, had fled during their London tour only four years ago.

Baryshnikov stopped to sign autographs. Then, thinking quickly, he slipped into the crowd of his fans. Voices called from the bus, "Where are you going?"

It was his last chance. He started off, away across the parking lot, with the crowd following him. Baryshnikov was already thirty minutes late, and the getaway car's driver was walking over to the O'Keefe Centre to see what was going on. Then he spotted Misha, running across the parking lot. He ran back to the car and hustled the dancer into the back seat. Misha had nothing but the clothes on his back, but he was free.

It was a major failure for the KGB. Baryshnikov had slipped through a network of overseers—he and other dancers had been under the watch of agents assigned to the troupe by the Fifth (Ideological) Department of the KGB and probably other agents as well—that had kept close watch on them since they left the Soviet Union.[7] The KGB saw the Soviet ballet troupes touring the West not only as a security and public relations challenge but as an opportunity to keep tabs on the old enemy—the émigré groups. Semen Kaufman, a dancer with the Bolshoi Theater, had traveled abroad with the troupe frequently since the 1960s. He was also an agent of KGB foreign intelligence, tasked with gaining access to émigré circles abroad, including Russian personnel at the Voice of America and Radio Free Europe radio stations and at Russian publishing houses, mostly in the United States and France. He had been spying for the KGB for twenty years.[8]

News of Baryshnikov's escape reached Moscow just as KGB chairman Yuri Andropov was finalizing his plans to change the ways in which the secret service dealt with the people who left the country for political reasons and the negative ideas about life in the Soviet Union that they took with them.

CHAPTER 12

THE KGB THINKS BIG

I n 1974, KGB chairman Yuri Andropov was at the height of his
powers. A tall, reserved man with sparse gray hair combed back
off his forehead and thick, square glasses, he had headed the
Soviet secret police for seven years. He was only sixty years old,
and as a present on his birthday, Brezhnev made him a Hero of
Socialist Labor, the highest Soviet award. With his position secure,
Andropov felt it was the right moment to update the KGB hand-
book when it came to dealing with Russians abroad. But first
Andropov needed to get rid of a thorn in his side: a Russian writer
named Solzhenitsyn.

Monday, January 7, 1974, was frosty in Moscow. The streets looked
deserted.

Perhaps nowhere was emptier than Red Square. Even in better
days, it had never been a real town square. Now that the old city
had largely been paved over by the modern, Communist one, Red
Square was so far from most Muscovites' daily paths that few ven-
tured there. Usually you would find only tourists stumbling over
the cobblestones.

This day was cold even for tourists. The gloomy rectangle of Lenin's tomb and a bright green dome with a red flag peeping up from behind the high wall of the Kremlin underscored the square's official function and its emptiness. The dome was part of the ornate, neoclassical Senate building inside the Kremlin—not visible from the square—that housed Leonid Brezhnev's offices on the third floor. Next to it was the Politburo's conference hall. Today, as an icy wind swept through the streets of Moscow, fourteen elderly men—members of the Politburo—had gathered there. Brezhnev had summoned them to a closed session on this new year's day.

The Soviet head of state was angry. He called the meeting to talk about a book: "In France and the United States, our agencies reported, a new book by Solzhenitsyn is coming out soon. It's called *The Gulag Archipelago*. No one has read it yet, but the content is already known—and it's a cruel anti-Soviet libel! We have all the grounds we need to send him to jail." He turned to his comrades, "So what are we to do about him?"[1]

Andropov, the chairman of the KGB, had an idea ready. He wanted to throw Solzhenitsyn out of the country. Why not send Solzhenitsyn into involuntary exile? "Just like we kicked out Trotsky back then," he said.

The ghost of Stalin's archenemy seemed to appear in the hall as Andropov went on: "He [Solzhenitsyn] is trying to build up an organization inside the Soviet Union, hammered together from ex-Gulag prisoners." Furthermore, Andropov added ominously, "*The Gulag Archipelago* is not a book; it's a political document. And it is dangerous."

Andropov believed that Solzhenitsyn (unlike Trotsky) would pose no serious threat from abroad. For several weeks, as the KGB and the Politburo exchanged notes on Solzhenitsyn, the KGB kept insisting that exile was the best option.

On February 13, it was finally done: Solzhenitsyn was put on a plane bound for West Germany. From there, he moved to Zurich, where he rented a house. The writer's expulsion caused a major political scandal, but Andropov remained optimistic. He thought everything was under control. As had been the case with Trotsky forty years earlier, Solzhenitsyn's inner circle had been penetrated by Soviet spies: in Zurich, Solzhenitsyn was surrounded by no fewer than four Czech intelligence agents who reported the writer's every move to the KGB.[2]

Solzhenitsyn managed to alienate the Western media almost immediately on his arrival in the West, thanks to his arrogant manner and harsh criticism of the West. Six months after sending Solzhenitsyn into exile, Andropov proudly reported to the Politburo that "all available information indicates that after Solzhenitsyn's deportation abroad, interest in him in the West is steadily on the decline."

Andropov was both right and wrong. He was right because Solzhenitsyn, who soon moved from Zurich to the United States (he established himself in remote Vermont), failed to become a mobilizing figure for the Russian émigré community. Neither did he become an adviser to the White House on Kremlin affairs.[3] Much like Stalin's daughter, Svetlana, before him, the writer instead became a recluse on his isolated farm in the American Northeast.

But Andropov was also wrong. *The Gulag Archipelago* became a phenomenal success. The book—a detailed, compelling, and damning depiction of the huge network of Stalin's concentration camps, which ranged all over the northern and eastern parts of Russia—reached far beyond the traditional audience for Soviet-themed books. Mainstream Western readers were fascinated. They weren't the only ones. Copies of the book were also smuggled back into the Soviet Union, as the Soviet intelligentsia was eager to read it. The book was endlessly copied and disseminated through dissident channels.

Andropov was looking only for Solzhenitsyn's (nonexistent) subversive organization; when he failed to find any traces of it, he thought he had won. But in the West, Solzhenitsyn's presence was also seen as a huge win. *The Gulag Archipelago* confirmed Westerners' very worst suspicions about the behavior of the Soviet government.

In the years to come, the KGB would continue putting dissidents in jail, finding inventive ways to lock them up for years. They also began imprisoning political dissidents in psychiatric clinics. But they didn't entirely end the practice of throwing troublemakers out of the country. Starting with Solzhenitsyn, Andropov returned with a vengeance to a practice that had been all but abandoned after Trotsky's exile. From 1974 to 1988, dozens of people from the Soviet intelligentsia—writers, artists, and dissidents—were kicked out of the country and stripped of Soviet citizenship.[4]

It was a major shift in the Soviet secret services' strategy, one that indicated flagging institutional health. "It was a sign of weakness, not strength," Nikita Petrov, a leading Russian historian on the KGB and Stalin's secret services, told us. "They simply couldn't afford any more to do what they had done in the 1930 and 1940s, which was kill people at will."[5]

With more politically active people out of the country, Andropov needed to expand the KGB surveillance of the exiled. He wanted to keep tabs on political activity beyond Soviet borders. But he had another, very ambitious goal: he hoped to exploit any and all spying potential offered by the Russian émigré community, especially in the United States.

Andropov was briefed on the issue of émigré communities by someone he trusted deeply: his close associate and protégé Vladimir Kryuchkov, a small, nondescript man with receding gray hair and distinctly Slavic features. Now deputy head of the KGB's foreign intelligence branch, Kryuchkov had no intelligence background. Just like Andropov, he was a Communist Party man born to a working-class family and had followed Andropov in all his career moves.

The previous autumn, in 1973, Andropov had sent Kryuchkov to America following the FBI's arrest of a Soviet intelligence officer in Washington, DC.[6] Kryuchkov flew to New York, where he spent almost a month. He also traveled to Washington and San Francisco and made a point of meeting with every KGB officer working in the field.[7] All of this was very unusual for such a high-ranking KGB officer.

Kryuchkov came back to Moscow with an idea, which he presented to Andropov in December 1974. His big idea was to streamline the large, complex, and unwieldy system of KGB departments dealing with emigrants.

In the 1970s Soviet Union, the KGB was truly omnipresent. As in a crazy bureaucrat's dream, every time a new ideological threat presented itself, the KGB formed a unit to deal with it. Everything from rock-n-roll fans to hippies generated new KGB departments dedicated to keeping these subcultures in check. This policy had been going on for decades. As a result, by the 1970s, the KGB had special units to deal with almost everything, including Jews, unruly youth, athletes, and so on.

The KGB empire also had incredible reach. It spread across every corner of the country, and each region had its own KGB department.

The challenge of Russians abroad was one the Kremlin had been facing from day one. For more than fifty years, the Soviet secret police had being launching departments and units to deal with this threat from every angle imaginable, both inside and outside the country.

By the 1970s, this scheme was complicated, to put it mildly. It looked like this:

The Fifth Directorate of the KGB, which dealt with ideological subversion, spied on dissidents. It collected compromising materials on them to use in case a dissident moved to the West, and it checked the effects of émigré publications in dissident circles. It also had officers assigned to Soviet artists, such as Baryshnikov, traveling abroad.

Within the country, the Soviet Republics departments of the KGB recruited visiting foreigners as spies and reported on the activities of prominent émigrés from their respective republics, obtained through their agents in organizations like the Society for the Development of Cultural Ties with Estonians Abroad.

For foreign operations, the First Chief Directorate of the KGB also had several units dealing with emigrants.[8] Service A, in charge of spreading disinformation abroad, made up news about prominent exiles—something they called "active measures." Department K's role was to run external counterintelligence, meaning addressing all kinds of threats to Soviet intelligence operations abroad, including preventing defections and unauthorized contacts with Russians abroad (the dancer Semen Kaufman was recruited by this department). The Fourth Section of Department K helped plant fake news in Western émigré magazines and newspapers, since the department ran agents embedded in émigré organizations abroad, including radio stations like Voice of America, Radio Liberty, and Free Europe. To help on the spot in foreign countries, the KGB stations in the Soviet embassies—rezidenturas—had several officers whose job was to watch emigrants. They were attached to Line EM—"line" meaning area of operations, and "EM" meaning emigration—whereas gathering political intelligence was Line PR, industrial espionage was Line X, and so on.[9]

In the United States, the picture was a bit different. Emigration was such a top priority that all political intelligence officers working at the Soviet embassy were tasked with spying on émigrés.

It worked like this: In 1966, a Soviet sailor jumped off a Soviet reconnaissance warship twelve miles off the coast of California and successfully made his escape to freedom. The US Army's Russian institute in Garmisch, Germany—always hungry for fresh refugees from the Soviet Union to supply its students (themselves diplomats and spies) with the latest information from behind the Iron

Curtain—hired him as an instructor. Radio Liberty, conveniently located in nearby Munich, made him a radio host. By that time, it should be noted, Radio Liberty, Voice of America, and the Russian Service of the BBC had become much more popular in the Soviet Union and were turning into a real threat to the Kremlin's information monopoly.

But the defector turned out to be a KGB agent run by the Fourth Section of Department K. He gathered intel on the personnel at Radio Liberty and personal details about the US diplomats and spies trained in Garmisch.[10] When the sailor ran away again—this time back to the Soviet Union—he publicly denounced his American hosts in Germany. This part of the operation was supervised by the Fifth Directorate (ideology) and Service A (active measures).[11]

As with every complex bureaucracy, the question was how best to coordinate all these units.

Inside Russia, the KGB had already formed a special unit, the Tenth Section in the Fifth Directorate (ideology), charged with dealing with "the centers of ideological subversion abroad," to be a contact point between all KGB units in the Soviet Union and all units engaged with émigré groups at the First Chief Directorate (foreign intelligence).[12]

After his trip to America, Kryuchkov suggested forming a contact unit in the First Chief Directorate to mirror the domestic one. He needed a coordination point for all the anti-émigré activities outside the Soviet Union.

Andropov gave it a green light and made Kryuchkov the head of the entire foreign intelligence branch of the KGB. Kryuchkov promptly set up a unit he called the Nineteenth Section, staffed with more than thirty intelligence officers.

The KGB's preferred method was brutally simple: exploit paranoia among émigrés. The KGB spread rumors that either the close friends of a prominent emigrant were KGB agents or that the emigrant was a KGB agent recruited years ago back in the Soviet Union. The KGB tried this on Solzhenitsyn, too, planting disinformation that he had been recruited by the KGB in the gulag. Few believed it. Still, these tactics were considered the most effective for creating and maintaining "an atmosphere of distrust and suspicion."[13]

"There is no other business like it," said Leonid Nikitenko, a former chief of the KGB's Nineteenth Section, later the head of Department K, to his counterpart in the CIA many years later.[14] "We are politicians. We are soldiers. And, above all, we are actors on a wonderful stage."

Following the official "de-Stalinization" of the late 1950s, the KGB claimed to have broken completely with Stalin's secret police tradition of mass repression. Moreover, Lubyanka hastened to claim to be the first victim of Stalin's purges, citing the high number of its operatives killed and imprisoned in the gulag.

But were the KGB's methods for dealing with émigrés any different from what had been practiced from the 1920s through the 1940s? The KGB still employed and was still listening to Stalin's top spies, people like Vasily Zarubin. Indeed, Zarubin remained a respected authority for the KGB, giving lectures for the new recruits well into his retirement. When he died in 1972, Zarubin was given a state funeral, and memorial services were held inside Lubyanka at the KGB's Central club. An honor guard was posted near his coffin, and Andropov came to pay his respects. At the funeral, Andropov walked up to Zoya, Zarubin's daughter, and told her that the country had lost a great intelligence officer.

But what about the brutal methods perfected by Nahum Eitingon in the 1930s and 1940s, namely, assassinations and abductions? Did they fall out of fashion within the KGB? Eitingon himself was alive and well and in 1965, when he was finally released from jail, landed a job in a publishing house that translated and published foreign books. He got the job thanks to his stepdaughter, Zoya Zarubina (she was always fond of him and even tried to call Eitingon Dad, but he reminded her that she already had a father,

Zarubin). But he was legitimately qualified for it; among Eitingon's many talents was his command of many languages.

When the KGB lured a defected naval officer named Arta-monov to Austria in December 1975, he was abducted on a Vienna street by KGB agents, injected with a sedative, and driven to the Austrian-Czech border.[15] He died there suddenly. Some said it was a heart attack; some said poison. His fate was strikingly reminiscent of what happened to General Kutepov in 1930.

Three years later, the Bulgarian political émigré Georgi Markov was poisoned on the streets of London after a stranger pricked him with an umbrella. Perhaps unsurprisingly, the KGB provided the poison. Both operations—abducting Artamonov and sup-plying the Bulgarian secret services with the poison for Markov's assassination—were arranged by Department K, a part of the vast collection of the KGB units tasked to deal with the Russians abroad.[16]

Eitingon's old tricks were still reliably effective in the right situation.

Andropov remained convinced that forcing prominent trouble-makers out of the country was a good option. In 1976 he agreed to an unusual swap. One of the founders of the Soviet dissident movement, thirty-four-year-old Vladimir Bukovsky, had exposed the KGB's extensive practice of using psychiatric clinics to imprison critics of the regime. As a result, Bukovsky was put in a prison camp. Now Andropov had him put on a plane to Zurich—in handcuffs all the way. In Zurich, Bukovsky was exchanged for the leader of the Communist Party of Chile. But if the KGB and Andropov believed that Bukovsky would cause them less trouble outside Soviet borders than he had within them, they greatly miscalculated.

CHAPTER 13

MOVING PEOPLE

A ndropov's KGB had been throwing Soviet dissidents out of the country for so many years that by the beginning of the 1980s, there was a substantial community of third-generation Russian political exiles in the West. This group was very different from their predecessors. Unlike the first wave of White Russians, who understood close to nothing about the political circumstances in Soviet Russia, the third generation knew the Soviet regime inside out. They also differed from the second wave of postwar emigrants—who stayed in the West out of fear of repressions—in that they had emigrated largely because of their political convictions.

The new wave of Soviet emigrants included a lot of people who had protested the regime while they were in the Soviet Union. That was the reason they were thrown out of the country or escaped to the West (sometimes via very unorthodox methods, like the hijacking of planes). Now the most prominent among them set out to build organizations in the West with the goal of changing the political regime in their home country. Here, finally, was the generation Kennan had long hoped to see.

No matter how brave they were, this generation of emigrants faced a formidable challenge: their underground experience in the highly restricted climate of the Soviet Union hindered rather than helped them when it came to building effective political organizations in the open society of the West.

In May 1984, journalist Masha Slonim got a phone call at her studio in Bush House, the time-honored London headquarters of the BBC. Lord Nicolas Bethell, an old friend of hers, had a tantalizing offer: Did she want to fly to Pakistan and bring back two Soviet soldiers who had recently defected from the Soviet army barracks in Afghanistan? Bethell, who had opposed the 1979 Soviet invasion of Afghanistan from the very beginning, was involved with many projects providing help to Afghan mujahedeen. As a result, he knew a lot of people on the other side of the Afghan border.

Masha couldn't resist the temptation. The idea was, above all, interesting. And it touched a personal chord: Masha was part of a remarkable family, from the highest echelons of Soviet elite-turned-dissident. Her grandfather had been Stalin's foreign minister Maxim Litvinov, and her cousin Pavel Litvinov was one of the eight people who had gone to Red Square to protest the Soviet invasion of Czechoslovakia in 1968. Masha herself had left the Soviet Union for good a few years earlier. In London she stayed in touch with Soviet dissidents in exile who tried to organize a resistance to the Soviet invasion of Afghanistan—an effort of which Lord Bethell was a part.

Masha took three days off and flew to Islamabad. She didn't say anything about her trip to her BBC bosses. When she arrived, she spent a night at the British ambassador's residence before her meeting with the soldiers. A fragile, delicate young woman, Masha was nervous. Bethell had explained that the soldiers were junkies, and she wasn't quite sure how she should talk to them. The ambassador gave her a bottle of vodka, saying, "These guys haven't seen it for months; they'll love that!" Then she was driven to the airport where the meeting was to take place. Finally, a minibus dropped off two skinny boys whose names were Oleg Khlan and Igor Rykov.

Masha had never seen withdrawal symptoms before, but on the plane back to London she could hardly fail to recognize them. The boys moaned continuously and wandered aimlessly around the plane. A steward threatened to kick them off at a layover in Damascus. Masha gave them the ambassador's bottle of vodka; they drank it immediately, but it didn't quite do the job. When the plane landed in London, the boys could hardly stand.

In London, Bethell arranged for them to stay in a safe house, but the withdrawal symptoms got worse. Oleg and Igor demanded that they be brought back to Peshawar or to the Soviet embassy—at least there must be some vodka there. They drank all the aftershave they found in the house. Frightened, Masha called a psychiatrist. He forbade her to give them any alcohol. At dawn, Masha packed the boys in a car and brought them to a private clinic. There, every night, flying severed heads haunted Oleg in his room, and he hid from them under his bed.

The two boys spent almost a month in the clinic. When they were discharged, only a bit better off, nobody knew what to do with them. Masha put them up at her house while they waited for their big moment.[1] It came in late June.

On June 27, a press conference titled "Soviet defectors to the West tell their story" was organized in London. Lord Nicolas Bethell hosted the event, where the surprise guests were Rykov and Khlan. Thin and pale, both dressed in blue jeans and seersucker jackets, the two told the journalists of atrocities committed by Soviet troops in Afghanistan, including a mass killing of civilians in an Afghan village. Although it was no more than hearsay—neither of them had been present in the village—journalists were impressed. It was the very first time Soviet army deserters appeared in person in the West, and the press conference was reported by the world press, including the *International Herald Tribune*.[2] Masha was not there.

Her BBC bosses knew nothing about her role, and she wanted to keep it that way.

For Bethell, the event was deeply emotional. He was a fierce critic of the Western powers' treatment of Soviet prisoners of war after World War II, and he wanted to help a new generation of Soviet army deserters. He was not alone in his beliefs. When hosting the press conference, Bethell identified himself as a representative of an organization called Resistance International.

The day after the press conference, an American diamond trader based in Paris picked up his copy of the *Tribune*. The front-page story about two Soviet defectors caught his eye. When Bert Jolis read that the conference was "arranged by Lord Bethell and Resistance International, a group that supports the Afghan insurgents," it piqued his curiosity.

Who was behind it? He asked friends in Paris, who replied, "Oh, don't you know? It's Vladimir Bukovsky, the Soviet dissident." Jolis smiled. He had been waiting to hear something like this for a very long time. The diamond trader knew Bukovsky by reputation and believed he was just the kind of man of action needed.

Jolis was a successful if not very scrupulous diamond dealer active in Africa (where he was trading with the Central African dictator Bokassa). But he was also a veteran of OSS—the Office of Strategic Service, the predecessor of the CIA. Jolis had learned to hate communism when, as an American officer fighting in France during World War II, he witnessed the desperation with which Soviet soldiers tried to escape forcible repatriation. After the war, Jolis stayed in touch with his former colleagues at OSS, who were now serving in the CIA. He also kept thinking of the Russian deserters he had known.

Jolis considered himself an expert in this field and remembered how in 1951, the CIA's legendary director Allen Dulles had asked him to write a report about how to encourage Soviet bloc defections. The topic was close to Jolis's heart, and he was happy to oblige. In his opinion, the US government should take a more active stance. He envisaged the defectors' program in place at the time evolving from a small-scale covert exercise in psychological warfare into a "major weapon in our hands."[3] Jolis had carefully saved Dulles's thank-you note.

Jolis set out to meet Bukovsky. "Right now," Jolis was told, "he is in Palo Alto, doing scientific research." Bukovsky was on a fellowship at Stanford University finishing his master's degree in neurophysiology; in the Soviet Union, he had never had a chance to complete his education, since he was in and out of jail constantly from the age of twenty.[4] At the first opportunity, Jolis flew to the West Coast and met Bukovsky, "a pleasant stocky man with a broad Slavic face, in his early forties, with an air of the street-smart intellectual about him."[5]

Walking across the Stanford quad, in the Californian sunshine, Bukovsky told Jolis that Resistance International had started in Paris a year earlier when he and a group of former political prisoners and exiled dissidents formed L'Internationale de la Resistance. An umbrella organization, it embraced a broad spectrum of political, religious, and social movements around the world, united by a common commitment to fighting Communist oppression. Bukovsky was president, and Armando Valladares, a Cuban poet who had spent twenty-two years in prison, was vice president.

Bukovsky told Jolis about some of the activities they carried out—for instance, how they printed a dummy mock-up special edition of the Soviet army newspaper, *Krasnaya Zvezda* (Red Star), in January 1984 urging Soviet troops to "Stop the War and Go Home." At first glance, he said, it looked like the genuine issue of *Krasnaya Zvezda*. Afghans posted the paper on public walls in the streets of Kabul. The new organization also cooperated with Radio Free Kabul, launched by Lord Nicolas Bethell. Among other things, they broadcast ten-minute prerecorded tapes in Russian by prominent dissidents aimed at provoking opposition among the Soviet troops.

"I'd like to help," Jolis said.

"There is only one thing we need," Bukovsky told him. "Money!"

"I'm sorry," Jolis answered. "I'm not rich enough for that. But maybe I can help you raise some. I'm not a professional fund-raiser, but one can always try. Give me a little time to think this over. I'll get back to you as soon as I can."

Indeed, Jolis got back to Bukovsky very quickly. A month after Bethell's press conference, the American Foundation for Resistance International was incorporated. Vladimir Bukovsky was president, and Albert Jolis served as executive director. Bukovsky was already well connected in Reagan's Washington; he was in touch with the senior Soviet specialist at the State Department and the director of European and Soviet affairs at the National Security Council, among others. George Kennan, however, who was now in academia, was a disappointment: "He was getting more and more pro-Kremlin, promoting the improving of relations with the Soviet Union," Bukovsky told us.

Bukovsky wanted something else from Jolis: "I needed a treasurer," he recalled in an interview with us. "For this sort of organization, it's essential to have a rich treasurer, from a rich family. . . . For any of us it would be uncomfortable to ask for money. We are émigrés; we don't have our own money. But Jolis was already very rich."[6]

Jolis was, indeed, ideal: he was well connected and turned out to be very good at raising money, eventually raising several million dollars for Resistance International from politically conservative American foundations.

The war in Afghanistan was the top topic in the world. It had already done the Soviets a good deal of political damage, not the least of which was the Western boycott of Moscow's Olympic Games. What's more, the Soviet army was not winning. With every year that passed, the situation in Afghanistan looked more and more like the one the Americans had gotten themselves into in Vietnam. And as had been the case with Vietnam, a military disaster in Afghanistan ran the risk of huge political consequences at home.

Bukovsky had a specific goal in mind: "We argued with the Americans that if we can make defections in masses—we thought of several hundred—it would force the Kremlin to limit the Soviet army's involvement in combat missions, leaving the fighting to the Afghan army, which was already unreliable. And that would be a big help."

Thanks to Jolis's intervention, Resistance International—seven people in a three-room apartment on the third floor of a Belle Époque building on the fashionable Champs-Élysées in Paris—was soon thriving. At its peak, it coordinated the efforts of forty-nine anticommunist organizations, from Polish's Solidarnost to Czechoslovakian Charter 77.[7]

But how effective was it?

January's mock-up *Red Star* issue turned out to be a one-time adventure. It was an odd bit of propaganda. On the front page it featured such a nasty cartoon of a Soviet soldier that no soldier would associate himself with it. It also had a language problem. Using outdated slang gave the impression that the paper had been printed during World War II. Mock-up newspapers and radio broadcasts all had a whiff of the CIA's 1950s-era tool kit. The Radio Free Kabul stunt was also useless. The station was used as a communications tool by Afghans, but it was not at all popular among Soviet troops, who preferred to use the Japanese cassette recorders they bought at Afghan markets to record and play songs by popular Russian bards. It is perhaps not surprising that Resistance International failed to become an organization with significant influence in the propaganda war in Afghanistan. It also failed Russian political émigrés in the West.

Bukovsky, an inspiring figure but hardly a good manager, soon busied himself with other projects, and clashes began in the three rooms of the Belle Époque apartment on the Champs-Élysées. Like many another Russian émigré organization, this one was also falling apart.

The restricted character of Soviet society affected those opposing the regime. With the government having effectively banned any kind of independent organization, and with no room for political debate outside of people's kitchens, Soviet dissidents simply didn't have the experience needed to build effective political organizations. This was the curse that had haunted the second wave of the Russian emigration, and now it haunted the third.

As the summer of 1984 progressed, Oleg Khlan and Igor Rykov were growing more and more desperate in London. Lord Bethell had housed them with a Ukrainian woman (both boys were born in Ukraine) and arranged for them to apply for Canadian visas so they could join the large Ukrainian diaspora there. But they couldn't give up narcotics. One of them sent a letter home to his mother and revealed his address in London.

They started frequenting a Russian restaurant called Balalaika in Richmond, a suburb in southwest London, and there they met Boris. He said he was from a Soviet trade mission. Meanwhile, the Canadians set out conditions for issuing them visas—Oleg and Igor had to agree to surprise drug tests. The first test showed signs of LSD. Two weeks later the second test showed the same result. The Canadians refused to grant them asylum.

In November, Igor got a letter from his mother with a photo of a three-year-old girl in it, signed by his former fiancée (she had broken up with him while he was in the army). "Your daughter and I are waiting for you at home!" it read. The next day, Oleg and Igor went to the Soviet embassy.[8]

On November 11, the two maverick Soviet soldiers, Oleg Khlan and Igor Rykov, were driven to Heathrow Airport in a Soviet embassy car. "Both soldiers could be seen smiling through the car's rear window," reported the Associated Press. Soviet officials put them on a Leningrad-bound flight. "The return of the two soldiers came a week after Svetlana Alliluyeva, Stalin's daughter, secretly returned to Moscow from Britain after seventeen years in the West," the agency added.[9] In the Soviet Union, Alliluyeva was granted Soviet citizenship, but Oleg and Igor were at once sent to camps.

They fell victim to a typical KGB ploy: they were lured back and then punished mercilessly.

Dissidents' propaganda completely failed to affect the mind-set of Soviet soldiers and officers in Afghanistan. But books found their way to soldiers, and they worked.

In June 1985, Valeri Shiryaev, a military interpreter stationed on the outskirts of Kabul, headed to a local market. He wanted to buy something that was impossible to find in the Soviet Union: a *Penthouse* magazine. He'd heard it was even better than *Playboy*. He located a shop with stacks of old magazines, picked out an issue of *Penthouse*, and started the long but necessary bargaining process with the tradesman. When they finally came to an agreement, the tradesman gave him something that looked like a thick pack of Marlboro cigarettes along with his dirty magazine, as a gift.

Shiryaev took it and saw it was a book—*The Gulag Archipelago*, printed in very small font, with no margins at all. On the first page, there was a description—"a novel." Well, so be it, thought Shiryaev, and he brought the book with him to the dormitory in the fourth district of Kabul where all the military interpreters lived. In the next few weeks, he read it under his blanket at night, thankful for his very good eyesight. He soon understood it was not a proper novel, but he read the book to the end.[10]

The copy Shiryaev picked up by accident had traveled a long way to Afghanistan. It had originally been shipped from a warehouse in

Paris, near the Opéra, from a tiny apartment filled with thousands of copies of *The Gulag Archipelago* and Orwell's *1984*. The warehouse was run by a couple who were both veterans of the Russian émigré organization NTS—that old enemy of the Soviet regime that the CIA had supported since the 1950s.[11]

But the war could have lasted for another ten years if not for the arrival of a new Soviet leader, Mikhail Gorbachev. Gorbachev had taken over the top position in the Communist Party in March, two months before Shiryaev picked up his copy of *The Gulag Archipelago*.

Gorbachev started slowly opening Soviet borders, and the number of Soviet émigrés, especially to the United States, kept growing. And the next year, in February 1986, Gorbachev made a statement at the party congress: the Soviet Union was planning to pull its troops out of Afghanistan.

Resistance International was quietly disbanded. "Our funding just stopped. Probably our American sponsors decided that there was no longer any need to undermine the Soviet Union; it undermined itself," said Galina Ackerman, who was a member. "At the end of the day, our joint efforts helped to move sixteen defectors from Afghanistan to the West," said Bukovsky.

The country was falling apart. While Gorbachev's policy of *perestroika*—a set of political and economic democratizing reforms in the Soviet Union—was gaining momentum, all kinds of disasters hit the Soviet Union, including the nuclear catastrophe in Chernobyl. It looked like everything the Soviet government was involved in had started to collapse. And in May 1987 it became clear that this included the performance of the army and air forces: a single-engine Cessna aircraft rented by an eighteen-year-old amateur German pilot flew from Helsinki to Moscow and landed right on Red Square. Nobody stopped him.

That month, Liza Gorskaya, age eighty-seven, was hit by a bus and killed. Though she had outlived Zarubin by fifteen years, she succumbed to a violent death.

Four months later, in the United States, the Permanent Sub-committee on Investigations of the Senate Committee on Governmental Affairs called on the director of the National Security Agency (NSA), William E. Odom, to testify on the topic of Soviet émigrés. That the director of the NSA, essentially an electronic intelligence agency, would be addressing the subject of Russian émigrés might sound odd, but Odom was known as an intellectual who was deeply knowledgeable about Russian culture. He had made his own contribution to the Cold War effort: while serving at the US embassy in Moscow in the 1970s, he smuggled out a large portion of Solzhenitsyn's archive.[12]

Odom started his testimony by evoking the tradition that had begun with Alexander Herzen and Mikhail Bakunin, Lenin and Trotsky. "A very large community of Russian intelligentsia . . . found it necessary to come to the West, if they were going to carry on the intellectual and political activities they desired," he said. Odom went on, describing the difference between the three generations of émigrés to the United States and focused on the third wave, "which includes very sophisticated and well-educated people":

> They are not victims of war and upheaval, but people who have tried to change the USSR from within, people who have begun to rethink the basic and age-old questions facing their former country: What is Russia's purpose? Whither the USSR? Can a totalitarian regime evolve toward a liberal and humane regime? They have come West not merely to survive Stalin and the fate of war, as did the second wave; they have come from relative privilege in many cases, from positions of status, with keen and energetic minds. They have come with basically different aims, hopes and purposes than did their predecessors. They are more akin to their nineteenth century predecessors than to the first and second waves.[13]

It looked like emigration had come full circle.

Among the people Odom mentioned as the most prominent voices of Russian dissent was Alexander Solzhenitsyn—"I listen to him for what he knows about the Soviet Union, not the US," he said. Books still worked.

The next year, Gorbachev granted amnesty to Soviet soldiers who had defected in Afghanistan. He also signed a decree that returned Soviet citizenship to twenty-three people who had been stripped of it by previous Soviet authorities.[14]

Three years later, by December 1991, the Soviet Union would officially be no more: all Soviet republics proclaimed themselves independent of Moscow's control. And the year after that, Boris Yeltsin's government would invite Bukovsky to testify at the trial of the Communist Party. This trial was held in the Constitutional Court of Russia—a country born out of the ashes of the Soviet Union. To prepare for his testimony, Bukovsky requested and was granted access to the Soviet archives. He brought a small handheld scanner and a laptop computer with him to Moscow, and he managed to secretly scan many documents—including highly sensitive KGB reports to the Central Committee and transcripts of Politburo sessions. (This is how we know about the heated argument between Brezhnev and Andropov over the fate of Soviet Jews.) As Bukovsky later told us, he managed to scan these documents only because archive officials didn't know what the scanner was. Bukovsky's efforts resulted in his 1993 book *Judgment in Moscow*, which documented extensive behind-the-scenes cooperation between Western politicians and the Soviet Union throughout the Cold War. But this book, unlike Bukovsky's other books, was never published in English. Bukovsky believed that he was subjected to Western censorship.[15]

Bukovsky himself, a man of action and the most familiar name among dissidents to the Russian populace, would not return to Moscow. Many believed he could have been a strong competitor to

Yeltsin in the presidential election—many, but not Bukovsky. He chose to stay in Cambridge in the United Kingdom. In fact, nobody from the resistance decided to move back after the fall of the Soviet Union. The once-legendary organizations from the first generation of Russian political emigration—the NTS, the ROVS—tried to find a foothold in the rapidly changing country. They opened offices in Russia, but they failed to win popular support.

The dream George Kennan articulated in 1948 in the National Security Council's memo, "US Objectives with Respect to Russia," was that when the time came, he hoped to get "all the exiled elements to return to Russia as rapidly as possible and to see to it, in so far as this depends on us, that they are all given roughly equal opportunity to establish their bids for power." The time had come, and the dream went unfulfilled.

The US government, foreign policy makers, and the intelligence community quietly forgot about the Russian émigré community. William E. Odom was the last US top-level official to address the subject of the Russian Americans. The next time Congress would address the issue would be in the mid-1990s, and then the topic would be the Russian mafia. "The Russians in the US fall in the category of lessened interest," Rolf Mowatt-Larssen, who served in Moscow's CIA station in the 1980s and 1990s, told us.

The time came—and passed by.

CHAPTER 14

THE OTHER RUSSIA[1]

n 1990, although the Iron Curtain had fallen, the Soviet Union was alive and well. Boris Yeltsin, Gorbachev's main rival, wanted to enlist the help of the émigrés to create a new and better country. The country he envisaged was a democratic place, free of Communist Party control. On the New Year's Eve that ushered in 1991, Yeltsin, then head of the Supreme Council (Russian parliament), delivered a speech. It was immediately picked up by the country's newspapers. Yeltsin's speech was very unusual in one way: he addressed neither the deputies nor his constituents but "Russian compatriots" abroad. He evoked Solzhenitsyn's name and said that he understood the bitterness of those who had been forced to leave their homeland. There was a hope now, he said, that "today, the government's war against its citizens, which has been going on for decades in Russia, has been put to an end. . . . A dead wall, that for so long separated the Russians abroad from their native land, has begun to collapse. And it will be destroyed forever!"[2]

This was a calculated political move. The author of Yeltsin's address was Mikhail Tolstoy, a member of Yeltsin's Supreme Council whose attitude toward the compatriots abroad had been shaped by his personal history. A physicist from St. Petersburg and a distant relation of Leo Tolstoy, he was also the grandson of the prominent Soviet writer Aleksey Tolstoy, nicknamed the Red Count, a nobleman who had served in the propaganda section of the chief commander of the Whites during the civil war. The Red Count had fled Russia along with the White army but returned a few years later and became one of Stalin's top propagandists. Stalin, in turn, let him live in a grand style, in a big house with an old family servant who still addressed him as "your excellency"— thus his nickname.[3] Among other things, the Red Count wrote a novel called *The Emigrants* that exposed the White émigrés' plot to kill Soviet officials—given its timing, the book could have been a Soviet response to the scandal around General Kutepov's abduction in Paris.[4] Forty-nine years old, with expressive eyes, a prominent nose, and full lips, Mikhail, who bore a striking resemblance to his grandfather, had inherited his interest in the history of the Russian White emigration.

Tolstoy talked to Yeltsin, and the two developed an ambitious plan for the émigré community. Yeltsin needed a new national idea for Russia—one that could replace the old, compromised communism and help build a new national identity. For that, he needed the support of the "other Russia"—the Russian diaspora, those who had fled the Soviets. Mikhail Tolstoy thought he could help with this.

To enlist the other Russia's support, Yeltsin and Tolstoy needed to find a way around the paranoid KGB, whose members were still deeply suspicious of Russians abroad.

Tolstoy drew on the vocabulary of Soviet propaganda, according to which "emigrant" was synonymous with "enemy, defector, anti-Soviet element, traitor, renegade."[5] In Soviet lingo, people loyal to the Soviet authorities, in contrast, were always described using another word: "compatriot." Thanks to this carefully chosen wording, Yeltsin seemed in his speech to be addressing the pro-Soviet sort of émigrés.[6]

Tolstoy's big plan kicked off when the Supreme Council decided to gather the first Congress of Compatriots in Moscow and began inviting Russian émigrés from all over the world. On August 17 and 18, 1991, seven hundred delegates were brought to the Rossiya Hotel, the massive brutalist rectangle that was Europe's largest hotel and that loomed over Red Square, right between the Kremlin and the Moskva River. Yeltsin and Tolstoy wanted the congress to be a very big event; it was supposed to last for twelve days and include several trips around the country.

On August 19, the participants were woken up by the sound of tanks rolling through Moscow's streets. In the early morning, armored columns had taken up positions right outside the hotel's windows, in the center of the Russian capital. The compatriots who had come to see the new Russia were suddenly front-row witnesses to the country's first coup d'état since the Russian Revolution.

The horrified delegates turned to the chief organizer, Mikhail Tolstoy. Understandably, the émigrés felt trapped. Tolstoy shared their feelings of dismay: to him, it now looked as if the KGB had eased entry restrictions for many invitees in order to trap them. He felt terrible. He assumed the KGB must have decided to lure them back into the country thinking it would be easier to deal with them in Russia than abroad.[7]

He knew that the coup was organized by the KGB and the military. Unhappy with Gorbachev's reforms, they wanted to roll back history and reinstall the Soviet rules. They started by locking up Gorbachev in Crimea, introducing censorship, and placing tanks on the streets.

In the gloomy Rossiya lobby, some emigrants were nearly hysterical. They sought out Tolstoy and told him that what they were witnessing was exactly the kind of revolution their ancestors had fled from. Some rushed to the airport.[8]

The congress's opening ceremony was scheduled for that evening; there was still time to decide what to do. Tolstoy hurried to the Russian parliament's White House, but people there had more urgent things to do than worry about the congress. They were busy trying to erect barricades around the building, which Yeltsin had turned into the center of the resistance.

Left to themselves, the emigrants went out into the streets. Many headed to the White House, while others cautiously approached the officers and soldiers in the tanks. From what they saw, it didn't look like the soldiers had any desire to fight.

Evening came and Tolstoy returned to the hotel. He had decided to proceed with opening the congress. In the large hall of the Tchaikovsky Concert Hall, with the great organ behind him, Tolstoy took his position at the lectern. He began to read Yeltsin's call to resist the coup. And the audience applauded.

Two days later, the coup collapsed—and Boris Yeltsin won.

On August 27, Yeltsin signed a decree granting the Russian Service of Radio Liberty permission to open a bureau in Moscow. With that, the very same "subversive center of emigration" the KGB had fought for so long was officially welcomed into the heart of the Russian capital.[9]

The next day, a victorious Yeltsin attended the congress's closing ceremony. In his speech, he directly addressed the emigrants present, inviting them to help build a new, democratic Russia. "The most important goal of the congress is to start a permanent dialogue with the Russians abroad to overcome the deep internal disunity of the Russian people," he said from the stage. "The disruption of party-state organizations, including the most ominous, like the KGB, is already under way," he added cheerfully.[10]

The Soviet Union collapsed three months later. The Kremlin, now under Yeltsin's command, was already busy dealing with galloping inflation and ethnic conflicts. The role of Russian émigrés was nowhere near the top of their to-do list.

Still, Tolstoy managed to host two more congresses. One was attended by St. Petersburg's deputy mayor, a man by the name of Vladimir Putin.

The Russian emigrant community had now dramatically expanded to include millions of ethnic Russians living in the former Soviet Union republics, now independent from Moscow. But Yeltsin simply didn't have the resources to deal with them, and he probably was not very interested in doing so. His search for a new national idea was achieved when, in 1991, Russia adopted a new flag. White, blue, and red, it was the tricolor of pre-Bolshevik Russia used by the Whites during the civil war.

The Russian émigrés, then, were left to themselves—until a new leader came to the Kremlin.

PART II

MARKET FORCES

CHAPTER 15

MOVING THE MONEY

By the late 1970s, the Soviet Union had been restricting people's movement for decades, but the Kremlin always needed to be able to move something else in and out of the country: money. Extremely sophisticated schemes were developed to channel hard currency and all kinds of untraceable commodities, from gold to diamonds, to the West. And these schemes were operational right until the collapse of the Soviet Union—and a bit after.

Life gives everyone one big chance. In June 1978, Stan Rifkin, a chubby-cheeked, thirty-two-year-old engineer who ran a computer consulting firm out of his apartment in California's San Fernando Valley, experienced this firsthand.

Rifkin's firm had been contracted to install a new computer system for the Security Pacific Bank in Los Angeles. This system would automate the bank's wire room, which handled transfers between accounts and electronic payments in the event of a failure in the primary transfer system. Essentially, Rifkin's company was supposed to build a security system backup.[1]

As part of his assignment, Rifkin learned about the bank's money transfer procedures. The bank used a daily code—four digits that changed every morning—that a bank clerk wrote down by hand and kept on display in the wire room. The bank gave Rifkin access to this room while he was building their backup system. Before long, Rifkin figured out that now he too could transfer money out of the bank.

Rifkin wasn't a fool. He could get the money out of the bank, but he also knew he would have to come up with a way to pick up the money after the transfer without being caught. So Rifkin contacted a lawyer, an acquaintance, and explained that he wanted advice on a sensitive issue. He said he was working for a large corporation, and his boss needed to find an untraceable commodity he could use in his dealings with another corporation.

"Diamonds," was the answer.

"OK," said Rifkin. "Do you know anyone who knows a thing or two about diamonds?"

The lawyer put him in touch with one Lon Stein, a well-respected diamond broker in Los Angeles. Rifkin invited Stein to lunch at the fancy French restaurant La Serre on Ventura Boulevard in Encino.[2] At lunch, Rifkin explained that he represented a large corporation he couldn't name and that his boss wanted to purchase $10 million worth of diamonds. From the beginning, Rifkin was thinking big. "Impossible," said Stein.

But Rifkin didn't give up. For the next four months, Rifkin came back to Stein every week with ideas. (Stein was convinced that Rifkin was legitimate.) He was determined to figure out a way to make his plan possible and squeezed every imaginable option out of the dealer. By October, the two decided they had found a way to accomplish the deal that Rifkin's boss supposedly wanted done. Rifkin gave Stein a small advance—$700—for a short trip to Geneva, Switzerland. The trip went well, and three weeks later, it was time for Rifkin to take action.

On Wednesday, October 25, Rifkin walked into the fifty-five-story Security Pacific Bank building on South Hope Street in downtown Los Angeles. With its spacious lobby lined in flamed granite walls, the stone-and-glass tower was a true embodiment of the international corporate style.

Once inside, Rifkin took the elevator, descended to level D, and went straight to the wire room. When a clerk asked what he was doing there, Rifkin said he was conducting a study. It was almost 4:30 p.m., a time when the wire room employees were relaxed. The code was there in plain view. He wrote it down and walked out to the street to a pay-phone booth. He phoned the wire room and said he was Mike Hanson, from the international department of Security Pacific, and he wanted to make a transfer.

"Ten million two hundred thousand dollars exactly to the Irving Trust Company in New York, for credit of the Wozchod Handels-bank of Zurich, Switzerland," he said, calmly—after all, he had long since decided on the sum of $10 million for himself. And $200,000 was the amount he had promised Lon Stein. A numbers guy, Rifkin didn't want to ruin his nice round sum with the dealer's commission—so he simply made it $10.2 million. And besides, he thought, that number looked less like a lottery winning and more like bank business.

A young woman on the other end of the phone asked for the code.

"Four-seven-eight-nine," Rifkin said.[3]

And that was it. It was done. The woman thanked him and hung up.

The next day Rifkin flew to Geneva. Once there, he phoned Alexander Malinin, managing director of Russalmaz. Russalmaz was a relatively new company, established only two years earlier. It had a single mission: Russalmaz was in charge of selling Soviet diamonds abroad. Rifkin asked if Malinin had received the $8 million he had transferred (the other $2 million Rifkin put aside in his savings account). There was some delay, but a few hours later, the money duly arrived—wired from Security Pacific in Los Angeles via the Irving Trust in New York to the Wozchod in Zurich, where it was deposited in the Russalmaz account.

It was time for Rifkin to head over to Russalmaz's Geneva offices and pick up a Swissair baggage claim ticket for a piece of luggage. As Rifkin had explained to Russalmaz, it was his desire to export the stones; therefore, he could not take delivery of the diamonds at their office. Russalmaz had a simple solution: Rifkin could pick them up instead at duty-free in the Geneva airport.

The next morning, Rifkin presented the baggage claim ticket to Swissair. The airline employee assured him the bag would be on his flight. Rifkin flew to Luxembourg. He retrieved his bag there, checked into a hotel, and opened the bag. For the first time, he saw his diamonds—a sparkling 8,639.84 carats.

He repacked them in a piece of luggage designed to carry folded dress shirts and flew back to the United States—where he was caught a few days later. Rifkin made a visit to his lawyer in Los Angeles and showed him, out of the blue, a $1 million cache of diamonds. The astonished lawyer immediately reported him to the FBI.

Rifkin's heist made it into the Guinness Book of World Records under the category of "biggest computer fraud," and the legendary hacker Kevin Mitnick started his own book with a description of the heist.[4] But because the first part of the scam—the transfer of more than $10 million from a telephone booth on the street—was so spectacular, few people paid attention to anything other than that.

In fact, the smoothness with which an American from Los Angeles could fly to Switzerland and pick up a suitcase of Soviet diamonds worth $8 million at the local airport's duty-free desk— right in the middle of the Cold War—was perhaps even more remarkable. Indeed, the ease with which this was accomplished speaks volumes about the nearly perfect system built by the Soviet

Union for transferring commodities like diamonds smoothly from the East to the West.

Lon Stein, for example, was no stranger to Moscow. Later, Malinin, who handled the transaction for Russalmaz, would say that when his firm received a Telex message from L. Stein expressing interest in buying $8 million worth of diamonds, Russalmaz followed up with an inquiry.[5] "I phoned Moscow," Malinin said. "They told us they knew this person (Stein). He had been to Moscow several times." Taking this as a go-ahead, Russalmaz agreed to the scheme and waited for the money to be deposited in its account at the Wozchod bank.

The Wozchod bank, however, was by no means a conventional Swiss bank. Rather, it was part of a large archipelago of Soviet banks abroad (Wozchod means "sunrise" in Russian) that extended from London to Singapore to Tehran to Paris to Zurich. Some of the banks were launched in the 1920s; others, like the one in Zurich, started up in the late 1960s.

All of them were created with one mission: to help the Soviet Union buy, sell, and borrow in hard Western currency. Starting in the 1960s, the Kremlin had another requirement for these banks: to operate in a way that was untraceable by the United States. The new requirement was prompted by one 1959 lawsuit—a Russian émigré in the United States, Elena Weilamann, sued the Soviet Union in a New York court, accusing Soviet authorities of failing to make payments on their obligations to two English corporations with concessions in the Soviet Union. Weilamann was one of the holders of these obligations. She also brought a suit against Chase Manhattan Bank for transferring money from the accounts of Soviet banks at Chase. That so scared Soviet bankers that they moved all their accounts in dollars to Soviet banks abroad—in Paris and London.[6] The goal, a high-ranking Russian banker explained to us, was "to make Soviet dollar transactions impenetrable for the US government." And that was why there was no Soviet bank in the United States.

Even among this archipelago of banks, the Wozchod was remarkable. Located in a nondescript five-story building at Number 1, Schutzengasse, in the heart of fairy-tale Zurich, the Soviet government tasked the bank with very sensitive missions indeed.

One of them, exclusive to the Wozchod bank, was the sale of Soviet gold. It worked like this: Soviet gold was transported to Zurich by ordinary Soviet passenger aircraft, five to seven tons of gold per flight. Standard ingots of 12.5 kilograms were distributed evenly throughout the plane under the passenger seats—the gold was heavy, and the aircraft had to be carefully balanced.

The Wozchod bank also helped sell diamonds, another of the Soviet Union's precious commodities. Russalmaz was the exclusive exporter of Soviet diamonds, and it had an account with Wozchod.

Furthermore, the Soviet government put the Wozchod in charge of working with American banks, one of which was the Irving Trust—the bank so cleverly used by Rifkin to transfer his more than $10 million out of Security Pacific.

But was Rifkin actually so clever? On the American side, his ingenuity allowed him to exploit a breach in bank security. But once his plan reached international waters, Rifkin simply tapped into an existing scheme, one designed by very smart people in Moscow to transfer much-needed US dollars smoothly and untraceably from the United States to the Soviet Union. "I had nothing to do with the selection of Russalmaz: it was completely under the control of the broker. I had not heard of them before or since," Rifkin told us in an email exchange.[7]

Even after Rifkin's arrest, the Los Angeles bank's money was still in Moscow. As a Soviet magazine gleefully remarked in 1980, "The ending of this story is awesome. There are no victims in it." The magazine then added, "The Swiss company made an excellent deal, selling diamonds for eight million dollars."[8] We must point out that the company—Russalmaz—was not Swiss but Soviet.

The fact that Rifkin was caught did not hurt Malinin—he enjoyed a long and successful career in the gem industry, and in the 2000s he became head of Brillianty ALROSA, the cutting and polishing division of the world's largest diamond mining company, ALROSA.[9] Neither did it affect the Soviet Union's banking operations in any way. The scheme was a very good scheme, after all, and it had been operational for decades.

But just ten years later, in the late 1980s, as the Soviet government began to liberalize its economy, a new, pressing question emerged: Was it possible to use the same scheme to channel money in the reverse direction—out of Russia and into the United States?

Over the next few years, many people would set to work answering this question. Nobody was better equipped to find a solution than people who knew both sides of the coin: the Western and Eastern worlds, the Russian Americans in the US banks. And so in the 1990s, the very same bank Rifkin had used to channel his spoils out of the United States began to play a new role. Russia's new money launderers used it to move large amounts of dollars out of Russia and into the United States, causing the largest bank scandal of the decade between the two countries.

CHAPTER 16

THE SCHEME DEVISED

Generally speaking, there was no love lost between the aristocratically minded, deeply Russian Orthodox descendants of the first wave of Russian emigration and the third, mostly Jewish wave of Soviet emigrants that began pouring into the United States in the 1970s. History, family background, and prejudices played a part in the divide. But as the Soviet Union liberalized, the emerging opportunity to make money in the homeland brought individuals from these two groups together. The results of this unexpected teamwork would be far reaching, with deep consequences for both Russia and the United States.

In 1988, after what the *New York Times* described as "one of the biggest, longest-running, and most hostile takeover battles in the United States,"[1] the Bank of New York—America's oldest bank—succeeded in taking over Irving Trust, one of the biggest.[2]

Thanks to the merger, the Bank of New York got everything the Irving Bank had, including its handsome, Art Deco–style building at One Wall Street. It also got the department dealing with Russian transactions.

Before the merger, Irving Trust had been running an extensive business with Soviet banks. This business was supervised by a Russian émigré named Natasha Gurfinkel. A Soviet Jew who had moved to the United States, Natasha was one of those lucky enough to have had their applications approved by Brezhnev's government in 1979. In 1986, Natasha got a job with Irving Trust, where she dealt with the lucrative trade with Soviet banks.

Over at the Bank of New York, Soviet banks were handled by a Russian aristocrat from the highest echelons of tsarist society, a Russian prince named Vladimir Galitzine. When the two banks merged, Gurfinkel and Galitzine teamed up, sharing an office on the ninth floor of One Wall Street.

This was the moment when two different waves of Russian emigration to the United States finally came together. These two groups, who had never quite been able to find a way to cooperate politically, finally found some common ground when it came to making money.

With their very different backgrounds, the newly minted banking partners began working together.

Natasha, a nice-looking, outgoing woman, grew up in Leningrad. Her parents sent her to an elite school, the first in the city to teach English. The education was indeed good: the English department was run by the son of a former Russian emigrant who had returned to the Soviet Union from England, along with his father, in the 1930s.[3] After high school, Natasha enrolled at Leningrad University, where she specialized in Eastern studies—her field was ancient Assyria, Babylon, and Sumer.[4] In 1979 her family made a tough decision: Natasha, along with her first husband, her sister, and their mother, moved to the United States while their father stayed in Leningrad. In the United States, the new emigrants settled in Louisville, Kentucky, where a vibrant Jewish community dated to the beginning of the twentieth century. From there, Natasha entered Princeton University, where she earned a master's degree in Near Eastern studies. In 1986 she landed a job with Irving Trust, which put her through a yearlong course in commercial banking.

The thin-mustachioed prince Vladimir Galitzine, nicknamed Mickey, on the other hand, had the "countenance of a silent-screen actor."[5] Natasha was always teasing him for his archaic Russian vocabulary. The Galitzines were, in fact, nobler than the Romanovs—indeed, if it hadn't been for the fact that the head of the family was stuck in Polish captivity in the sixteenth century, it could well have been the Galitzines rather than the Romanovs on the throne in 1917.[6] Despite having lost their sixteenth-century bid, the Galitzines nonetheless remained important in the Russian empire for the next three hundred years.

All that was destroyed when the Bolsheviks killed the tsar. Fleeing the revolution, the Galitzine clan spread all over Europe. Vladimir's parents, newly married, settled in Belgrade, where he was born. In the midst of World War II, the family moved to Germany, where, after Hitler's defeat, they found themselves in a displaced persons camp in Munich.

They became lost there in the huge crowd of a second wave of exiles from the Soviet Union—the captured Red army soldiers and Soviet displaced persons studied with such assiduity by the American Russia watchers George Fischer and George Kennan.

In 1951 the Galitzines made it to New York, where they settled in the Brownsville neighborhood of Brooklyn. Vladimir's aristocratic father worked as a hospital orderly, and his mother toiled in a match factory. They were poor, but Vladimir's mother made sure to send young Galitzine to a good school. In 1960, at eighteen years old, he joined the Bank of New York as a junior clerk.

In the late 1980s, Mickey Galitzine worked his way up from an accounting position to the International Department. His timing couldn't have been better. This was the very moment when, driven by the pressing need for hard currency in the face of an impending economic catastrophe, the Soviet Union was opening up its financial market.

By the time of the takeover, this process was well under way in the Soviet Union. Gurfinkel and Galitzine didn't want to miss out.

Before the Irving Trust takeover, Galitzine had made several trips to Moscow, but he didn't understand the people he met in his family's native land, nor did he feel any urge to return to Russia for good. "The United States continues to be my home," he said at the time. "The opportunity to visit the places we've been hearing about all these years is all very attractive. But my career is here. My home is here."[7]

After the bank merger, Galitzine's closest ally at the bank, Natasha Gurfinkel, stepped up and began making most of the trips to Russia. Thanks to her work at Irving Trust, she already knew all the big shots in the Soviet banks abroad, so her existing network was very good.

Natasha was a real go-getter and very good at developing new contacts. In September 1989, a rising Soviet political star named Boris Yeltsin was stuck in Moscow's airport with a group of American bankers. Yeltsin was on his way to the United States to give a series of lectures. At the airport, he was suddenly surrounded by Americans, but he didn't understand a word of English. Natasha volunteered to help with translation. The two got along swimmingly, and the gentlemanly Yeltsin even carried Natasha's suitcase to the plane.[8]

Thanks to the dynamic duo of Garfunkel and Galitzine, by the time the Soviet Union collapsed, the Bank of New York was leaps and bounds ahead of all the American banks suddenly interested in the Russian market. The bank took steps to solidify its lead and promptly formed a new unit within the bank: the Eastern Europe division. It was led by Natasha, with Galitzine happily serving as her right-hand man. Together they were in charge of fifteen people on the ninth floor of the One Wall Street building.

As part of their work, Natasha brought Galitzine to Moscow to meet some people who were big shots, both then and now. "I was on friendly terms with Natasha, and she brought [Galitzine] to

us. It was like going to a museum," remembered Mikhail Khodorkovsky, the richest and most powerful tycoon of the first generation of Russian oligarchs, whose businesses had accounts with the
Bank of New York in the 1990s. "Natasha was special," he went
on to explain. "The problem with émigrés—they compensated for
their low social status [in the United States] by trying to make the
impression in Russia that they were great professionals. They spoke
in Russian with a deliberate American accent, all that. That's why
we always treated them with a great deal of humor." It was different
with Natasha: "She was normal, and everybody connected with her
very quickly."[9]

When the Moscow stock exchange opened an account at the
Bank of New York in the mid-1990s, the bank became the undis-
puted leader in the transfer of money between Russia and the
United States. "BoNY [as the Bank of New York was known] took
over most of the clearing [operations]. They also opened a bunch
of corresponding accounts with Russian banks within Russia,"
remembered Khodorkovsky. Soon more than 80 percent of all Russian transfers in US dollars came through BoNY.

Very soon, however, the steady stream of dollars flowing from
Russia to the United States became muddy.

CHAPTER 17

MUDDYING THE WATERS

I n New York, Gurfinkel and Galitzine's Eastern Europe division was expanding. In need of more personnel to handle traffic, they hired another recent Russian émigré, Lucy Edwards, in 1992.

"We were looking for people speaking Russian and found Lucy doing something in another department. She was very talented, so we hired her," Natasha told us. Then thirty-six years old, Lucy Edwards was a resourceful woman. She was also extremely energetic: while others in similar positions at the bank would see four or five clients a day, she saw ten to twelve.[1]

Nobody at the bank was concerned about Lucy's background, which was colorful. She had moved to the United States in the late 1970s by marrying a nineteen-year-old US merchant seaman she met in a Leningrad nightclub—a not-uncommon way for an attractive young woman to escape the Soviet Union. In the United States, she and her husband moved to Colorado, where Lucy started working as a bank teller, then as a waitress. After her marriage fell apart, she moved to New York in 1988. There, she landed an entry-level job handling commercial accounts at the Bank of New York.

Four years later, she joined Natasha and Galitzine in the bank's new Eastern Europe division. Soon Lucy became a loan officer, moving into the executive ranks for the first time.[2] In 1994 she was promoted to vice president of BoNY's Eastern Europe division.

Her record, however, had certain red flags. In the early 1990s, she was caught stealing more than $1,400 worth of clothing from a Nordstrom's department store in Edison, New Jersey. Two years later she was caught shoplifting at a Bloomingdale's store in Hackensack, New Jersey. She pleaded guilty both times. (Lucy remarried in 1992. She and her new husband, a Russian emigrant named Peter Berlin, were apparently soul mates: he was also arrested for shoplifting in Fairview, New Jersey, when he tried to steal sinus medicine from a local A&P.[3]) The bank later claimed it knew nothing of Lucy's criminal record.

Regardless, for most of the 1990s, the Eastern Europe division was run in the following manner. In New York, Natasha held the highest position, as senior vice president and head of the division, and Galitzine was vice president. As of 1996, Lucy Edwards was seconded to the bank's London office.

Lucy and her husband, Peter, were getting rich, and they frequently spent weekends in Italy. They also bought a new spacious apartment in central London—a striking contrast to the very modest home the couple had shared in upstate New York. They enrolled Lucy's daughter in an expensive private school.

And no wonder they were getting rich: money was flowing out of Russia to the tune of billions of dollars a year, and BoNY provided a secure and respectable channel for that flow. "To have an account at BoNY back then was like having a badge of honor; it meant you were important," a Russian banker who worked with BoNY in the mid-1990s told us.

But that flow of dollars from Russia had begun to attract the attention of law enforcement agencies in not one but several countries. Still, nothing happened to disrupt the channel. Despite warnings from the British authorities alerting the FBI that the money filling BoNY's coffers could be connected with Russian money laundering or organized crime, the system continued to function without a hiccup for years.[4]

That changed suddenly in the summer of 1998.

In June of that year, a successful, young Russian lawyer was kidnapped in the center of Moscow. Bandits put a gun to his head when he left home and ushered him into a Mercedes, which drove him to the suburbs. This kind of thing was not unusual in Moscow in the late 1990s—in fact, it happened quite a lot. What was unusual was that a few hours later, the captive lawyer phoned a friend in San Francisco and asked her to transfer $300,000 to his abductors' account.

The rules of such business in Moscow held that a ransom always had to be delivered in cash, but apparently not this time. The friend in San Francisco duly complied, and the lawyer was released as soon as the money showed up in the kidnappers' account—which happened to be at BoNY.

The Russian Interior Ministry launched an investigation. They sent a request to the FBI asking for help tracing the ransom. This prompted the FBI to launch its own inquiry. The abductors' account turned out to belong to a company set up by Lucy Edwards's husband. Lucy and her husband were put under surveillance, and their phone was tapped.

On August 18, 1999, Natasha's phone rang in her office on the ninth floor of One Wall Street. It was a correspondent from the *New York Times* asking her about a particular company account. Natasha explained that her department didn't have access to companies' accounts, as they only dealt with other banks. A minute later, a handyman came to Natasha's office to install a lock. She was surprised; they had never locked their offices before. She asked the handyman, who happened also to be a Russian emigrant, why a lock was being installed. He said he didn't know; he was just following orders. Then her phone rang again. Natasha was called up to the tenth floor—BoNY's executive level. There she was informed that she was now suspended because of an investigation launched by the district attorney's office. She was then escorted out of the building, and her colleagues were told not to contact her. Natasha would never see her office again.[5]

The next day the world learned that something was rotten at BoNY when the *New York Times* ran a front-page story under the headline, "Activity at Bank Raises Suspicions of Russia Mob Tie."[6] "Billions of dollars have been channeled through the Bank of New York in the last year in what is believed to be a major money laundering operation by Russian organized crime," reported the *Times*. The two persons who had surfaced in the investigation, the paper reported, were both senior officers with the bank's Eastern Europe division. Both had emigrated to the United States from Russia, and both were married to Russian businessmen. The paper named them: Natasha Gurfinkel (the *Times* claimed "the accounts have been handled" by her) and Lucy Edwards.

FBI investigators had discovered that Lucy's husband, Peter, had set up several companies whose bank accounts were at BoNY. These accounts were used for transferring billions of dollars from Russia to the United States. One account, registered to a company called Benex, was linked to a notorious mafia boss from the former Soviet Union, a man wanted by both US and British authorities. According to the *Times*'s story, British intelligence reported that "some of the money from the account went to pay contract killers and some went to drug barons."[7]

The scandal gathered momentum, and more accusations followed. US media outlets published more stories; $7.5 billion was said to have been moved out of Russia through the accounts controlled by Lucy's husband in just three years via BoNY.[8] American newspapers began naming various Russian oligarchs as well as, among others, Boris Yeltsin's son-in-law.[9] Moscow decided to run its own investigation.

Things got hotter in September 1999 when the US House of Representatives' Committee on Banking and Financial Services launched hearings on Russian money laundering. The BoNY investigation became even more important when Yeltsin vetoed Russia's ratification of the International Anti-Money Laundering Convention.

"I was summoned by Yeltsin," remembered Khodorkovsky, who, by late 1999, was one of Russia's top oil tycoons. "He told me that the FBI complained about me because of the scandal. I said I knew nothing about it. Yeltsin said, 'Then go and get it sorted out.' So I came back to my office, we prepared all documents, and I phoned the US embassy in Moscow and asked to talk to the FBI people. I gave them our documents, went back to Yeltsin, told him that I spoke to these guys and that everything was OK."[10]

What Khodorkovsky failed to mention was that he had been invited to testify before the American congressional committee on Russian money laundering and had declined to come.[11] The congressional committee also invited Natasha Gurfinkel and Lucy Edwards to testify, but they also failed to come. Instead, the bank sent its chairman and CEO, Thomas A. Renyi, a Vietnam veteran. It was Renyi who had supervised the integration of the Irving Trust and BoNY. On the witness stand, Renyi admitted that allowing the suspect accounts "to remain open and active without sufficient questioning was a lapse on the part of the bank."

Before long, many financiers in Russia and the United States came to see the BoNY case as an anti-Russian witch hunt. As the Russian presidential election of 2000 approached, fighting among different power groups intensified. The country was recovering slowly from the devastating economic crisis of 1998 when Russia defaulted on its national debt. Now politicians tried to capitalize on emerging feelings of inflamed patriotism combined with a sense of grievance against the West for its failure to rush in and help the Russian economy. Even liberal Russian newspapers treated the BoNY scandal as a manifestation of anti-Russian bias.[12]

The scandal had started with a bang. But after just a few months, it became clear that little would change. Too many interests had too much at stake to stop the hemorrhaging of Russian money. US law enforcement never accused either Galitzine or Gurfinkel of any crime. Natasha, for her part, was angry that BoNY had done nothing to protect her. She spent a month and a half in New York waiting to be questioned about BONY, but nobody was interested in talking to her. Eventually, she resigned and moved to London. Her lawyers in Moscow subsequently sued BoNY, and in the end, the bank agreed to unfreeze her money, benefits, and bonuses—all in all, over a million dollars. But she never got another job.

Still, she didn't hold a grudge against Lucy. "Lucy was just a fool. She traveled to Russia a lot, saw this crazy amount of money coming and going, and couldn't resist the temptation," Natasha told us.[13] Then she admitted, "Well, it was our mistake, mine and Galitzine's—we didn't watch her."

After a year and a half of investigation, US federal agents took Lucy Edwards and her husband, Peter Berlin, to District Court in Manhattan. The couple told a federal judge that they helped create a money-laundering scheme that successfully moved billions of dollars out of Russia through a network of front company accounts at the Bank of New York that were controlled by Lucy's husband. From there, the money went to offshore accounts. The scheme was designed by "a group of small but politically well-connected Russian banks."[14]

The couple said the scheme had three main goals: to avoid Russian customs duties on imports, to evade Russian taxes, and to wash the profits of criminal groups through legitimate banks—including the ransom for the young Russian lawyer kidnapped in Moscow. Lucy and her husband admitted that they earned nearly $2 million in due course.

This was evidence of wide-scale state plundering. Yet, ultimately, it had little or no effect on how business between the two countries was done.

Lucy and her husband cooperated with the investigation and pleaded guilty. In 2006 they were sentenced to five years' probation.[15] A year before that, the Bank of New York agreed to pay $38 million in penalties and victim compensation arising from the case of money laundering and fraud.[16]

In Russia, the scandal ended with a whimper. No one in Moscow was accused of any wrongdoing whatsoever. In 1999 Vladimir Putin, then prime minister, said that Russian law enforcement agencies had investigated the case and could not confirm that Russian money had been laundered through the Bank of New York. As Putin rather cynically explained, "Our senior law enforcement officers met with their American counterparts. But, unfortunately, or fortunately for us, the information that was in the media was never confirmed."[17]

In the end, only two people were held responsible for the scheme.

Once the Russian émigrés had pried the door to the American financial market open for Russians, their main concern was to keep that door open. Abiding by the rules, on the other hand, was never a top priority.

It took a good decade for US policy makers to realize just how corrupt and cynical the political system really was that replaced Communist rule in Russia. At least for some, this understanding also entailed an awareness that this corrupt and cynical system had the potential to one day infect the United States.

In September 1999, James A. Leach, chairman of the House Committee on Banking and Financial Services that had held the hearings on Russian money laundering, was struck by the notion that some of the laundered money could have seeped into the American political process. He remarked:

> When we look at Russia today and we see the infiltration of former KGB into the financial system, into the economy, and we wonder what is unique about Russia, because there

are other kleptocracies in the world, but one of the unique aspects of Russia today is: A, that it is so large and extraordinary; and B, it is a backward economy in many ways, but it is immensely sophisticated in many other ways, for example, intelligence. The combination of kleptocratic greed, coupled with centralized controls and bureaucratic expertise and coercion of a historical nature is something that the world has never seen before.[18]

Back in 1999, the American congressman couldn't know how prescient he was. In the years to come, Russian money would flood into the United States by the billions. Russian oligarchs became investors in America. They sought out, made, and cultivated important political connections. For many years they acted on their own behalf, not the Kremlin's.

But Russian foreign intelligence was never far behind. And the collapse of the Soviet Union hadn't changed them much.

CHAPTER 18

SOME HABITS DIE HARD

In the wake of the fall of the Soviet Union, a weighty question hung in the air: What would become of the KGB? The Communist Party no longer existed. It made perfect sense that the KGB—the Communist Party's most trusted instrument for protecting the regime, both inside and outside the country—would also dissolve or at least change beyond recognition. Thus in the 1990s, under Yeltsin's democratic government, the KGB's foreign intelligence apparatus was doomed.

Or was it?

Early on a sunny October morning in 1990, a year before the collapse of the Soviet regime, the head of the KGB's foreign intelligence, a middle-aged man with neatly combed dark hair and thin, tightly pressed lips, stepped out of his dacha. One of twenty wooden houses in the Yasenevo Forest (*Yasenevo* means "plenty of ash trees") just a few miles southwest of Moscow, Leonid Shebarshin's house was part of a dacha colony situated on the edge of a large compound occupied by the KGB's foreign intelligence service headquarters.[1] These houses were well looked after and furnished with servants to clean the rooms, do laundry, cook meals, and tend the garden.[2]

This morning Shebarshin took his time as he strolled through the woods on his way to work. Fifty-five years old, sardonic, aloof, and highly ambitious, he had been at his current post—head of the entire Soviet foreign intelligence operation—for just under two years.

It was a lonely, twenty-five-minute walk to his job—a daily routine that gave him a chance to think.[3] The living compound was quiet, and the manicured path through the woods felt completely deserted. The security fence encircled such a large area that, here in the woods, it was nowhere to be seen.

Shebarshin spotted an early morning runner on a side path. The man, who was wearing a blue sports suit topped by a motley knitted hat, was waving his arms, doing some kind of gymnastic exercise. Shebarshin recognized him immediately as Vladimir Kryuchkov. Once a protégé of Andropov, Kryuchkov was now the chairman of the entire KGB and Shebarshin's boss. Kryuchkov's office was in Lubyanka, in downtown Moscow, but he still held on to his beloved dacha in quiet Yasenevo. Shebarshin bowed and kept a respectful distance; he admired his boss.

Shebarshin also felt that he owed Kryuchkov for the meteoric rise of his own career. When Gorbachev had made Kryuchkov head of the KGB two years earlier, Kryuchkov had in turn tapped Shebarshin to run the KGB's foreign intelligence.

Shebarshin was a surprising choice. He had spent most of his spy career in the East—India, Pakistan, and Iran—rather than dealing with the Main Adversary, as the United States was known in Lubyanka.

But Kryuchkov felt that Shebarshin's experience dealing with Afghanistan in the 1980s justified his promotion to the post. As head of the foreign intelligence agency, Shebarshin oversaw roughly twelve thousand people.

After a twenty-minute walk in the woods, Shebarshin approached a checkpoint. The sign by the gate read Science Research Center—the cover name adopted by the KGB's foreign intelligence service for its forest headquarters when it relocated from Lubyanka in 1972. The guard recognized him, and the iron gates opened noiselessly. Beyond the checkpoint, Shebarshin took a path that led through a grove of maples to a stumpy seven-story concrete building.

It was probably no accident that this compound in the woods reached that particular height. The old CIA headquarters at Langley were also exactly seven stories high, and the KGB's spies always seemed to have their American counterparts on their minds. Who knows? Maybe this relationship was more emotional than commonly thought. The resemblance was strong enough that within Moscow's CIA station, people referred to the Yasenevo compound as "the Russian Langley."[4]

The seven-story building was only one part of the forest headquarters. Behind it, toward the west, rose a twenty-two-story office high-rise; to the east was a shorter structure with two wings, like the tail of a dove. This swooping building housed shops with discounted prices, a department store, and a clinic; there were two saunas, a swimming pool, several gymnasiums, and multiple tennis courts. All in all, it had the feeling of an exclusive American country club—and if an officer was short on time, a masseuse could be summoned to his office.[5]

This morning, like every morning on entering the giant lobby, Shebarshin passed beneath the inevitable, stern-faced, granite bust of Vladimir Lenin. It was relatively early—9:00 a.m.—and the corridors were still empty. A private bank of elevators whisked him to the third floor. A duty officer opened the door to the waiting room of Shebarshin's office, which was inhabited by two very noisy parrots in a birdcage—a gift from colleagues at the Cuban secret services. Their cries drowned out the ticking of a loud electronic clock—also a gift from colleagues, this time from Vietnam.

Everything looked normal and proceeded according to the usual routine. But the second-most powerful man in the KGB was anxious. He entered his office and glanced at the huge table with eight phones on it. Four portraits—Lenin, Dzerzhinsky, Andropov, and Gorbachev—stared down at him from the wall. All four men played crucial roles in the fate of the Soviet secret police; Lenin and Dzerzhinsky created it, and Andropov enlarged its role. But Gorbachev's new policy of *glasnost* ("openness") was undermining the KGB by revealing the truth about Lubyanka's crimes.

Shebarshin scanned the first reports of the day. One from Berlin contained the depressing news of what he termed the "reprisals" being carried out against former employees of the Stasi—the once powerful and feared East German secret police. In January, angry citizens had stormed the Stasi headquarters in Berlin, and Stasi leaders were jailed. Today's report said that the newly reunited Germany had just created a new government agency to deal with the Stasi files—a first step toward making the top-secret documents available to the public. Shebarshin shook his head. He didn't like it at all. His pack of cigarettes was almost empty, but he lit another one. Thinking of his beleaguered German colleagues, he made a mental note to remind the Kremlin of its obligations to old friends.

At the regular afternoon conference that day, Shebarshin looked around. What he saw, sitting before him, were men in their fifties and sixties with tired, nervous faces. These KGB generals were clearly on edge. They described what they saw as failing discipline within Yasenevo—officers had started drinking in their rooms, leaving empty bottles everywhere. There were tensions between senior staff and personnel; a deluge of anonymous letters from agents were full of complaints about their superiors.

Shebarshin knew that the political climate in the country was changing, and he understood that the KGB was under attack. All the people in his office that day were saying the same thing in one way or another: they were not sure the Kremlin still needed them or that it would continue to protect them. That's why people were quitting. Now he had more bad news for them: Gorbachev was supportive of the KGB but would not act for its support. "We need to lobby hard in parliament and the journalistic corps, and with civic organizations," he told his subordinates.[6] In other words, the KGB could not count on the Kremlin anymore. It would have to find a way to protect itself.

That idea was groundbreaking. The KGB had always been a party instrument, its role to serve as the Communist Party's advance regiment. And it had always been completely under party control: the party presided over every KGB section, department, and division. But that spring, in March of 1990, the Congress of People's Deputies of the Soviet Union had changed the Soviet Constitution, removing the article pronouncing the Communist Party the leading political force in the country. The KGB was suddenly and simultaneously left without a boss, protector, and supervisor.

Shebarshin was working on a solution. He shared his idea about what his people in Yasenevo should do in new circumstances. "The Plan of Action should be prepared,"[7] he explained. To save itself, foreign intelligence should act on its own, independently from the KGB in Lubyanka. To implement this plan of action, Shebarshin chose the department called Service A.

Service A usually dealt with disinformation. One of its main tasks was to conduct "active measures"—that is to say, to spread fake news made up by the KGB around the world. As Shebarshin described it, "Service A generates and formulates specific ideas, produces false papers, publishes literature and media reports authored by dummy authors."

Shebarshin had come to think that Yasenevo could be saved only by deceiving the public—in other words, by applying at home the methods that the KGB's Service A had been using abroad for decades.

Shebarshin knew and trusted Service A: "several dozen experienced and intelligent people" as he put it. Service A was also led by an old friend, a man he had shared a room with while at the KGB spy school and who he trusted to this day.[8] Furthermore, Service A was one of the most competent and industrious units in Yasenevo.

"The ideology of our active measures during the Cold War was simple—to inflict maximum political and moral damage on our opponents," Shebarshin later wrote in his memoirs.[9] If this sounds more like the description of weapons capability than of the objective of an intelligence unit, it is for good reason: Shebarshin and others saw foreign intelligence as exactly that, a weapon. And in October 1990, Shebarshin decided to redirect this weapon and aim it at the Russian people.

All of a sudden, Service A became so precious that Shebarshin felt he personally needed to safeguard its existence. To accomplish this, he chose the usual tactics: denial and deceit. "There is no Disinformation Directorate within the foreign intelligence," he assured the public that same year in an interview.[10] "We completely rule out violence, brutality, and interference in the internal affairs of other countries."[11]

Shebarshin secured the approval of his colleagues and dismissed the meeting. Now he could turn to the document that was lying on his table. It was a draft titled, "On the active measures of the foreign intelligence service of the KGB," prepared by his old friend, the head of Section A. Shebarshin read the paper very carefully. Several ideas were forming in the back of his mind.

Eight months later, in August 1991, KGB chairman Kryuchkov led a military coup d'état against Gorbachev, who was vacationing in Crimea. Three days of the standoff on the streets of Moscow followed. Then, on August 21, inspired by the charismatic Boris Yeltsin, the democratic crowds of Muscovites defeated the putschists. Shebarshin played his cards well during the putsch, distancing himself from his boss and from Lubyanka. When Shebarshin returned to Moscow, Gorbachev made him temporary chairman of the KGB. He had the job for one day: on August 23, he was replaced by a liberal outsider. But Shebarshin held on to his position as chief of foreign intelligence for another month. Then he left—after all, this new democratic Russian government was determined to reform the KGB.

Two months later, as part of the same effort, foreign intelligence was split from the KGB. In December, the Soviet Union ceased to exist.

Foreign intelligence got a new name, the SVR (*Sluzhba Vneshney Razvedki*, or Foreign Intelligence Service), and a new chief, Evgeni Primakov, an imposing, heavy-set, high-ranking Communist Party official with the looks of a respectable academician.

Primakov was an expert on the Middle East, just like Shebarshin. Cunning and cautious, Primakov was the Soviet answer to Henry Kissinger; he had spent decades shuttling between Moscow and the regimes in Lebanon, Egypt, Syria, Iraq, and Israel.

It was an uneasy time for many generals in Yasenevo. The threat of being completely disbanded still loomed large: the new democratic Russian government under Yeltsin had begun investigating the KGB's role in the failed coup d'état. Foreign intelligence, or SVR, badly needed to rebrand its public image. The goal was to do that without actually making any internal changes—which meant that Shebarshin's plan of action still looked like a valid option.

Primakov immediately invited Shebarshin back to Yasenevo to serve as his deputy. Shebarshin politely declined—he was too ambitious to accept a subordinate role. Undeterred, Primakov set off down the path that strikingly resembled the one Shebarshin had laid out just a few months earlier with his Service A team.

To implement the plan, Primakov first created several new organizations devised by the Service A specialists. He green-lighted Shebarshin's initiative to set up the Association of Veterans of Foreign Intelligence, an old-boys network of former generals of the PGU (*Pervoye Glavnoye Upravlenie*) and KGB, as a front organization. This "veterans association" formed the unofficial channel of communication for outsiders—journalists and historians—with the team at Yasenevo.

Next, a few easygoing officers were chosen to man the newly established Foreign Intelligence (SVR) press office, which occupied a blue-and-white mansion on quiet Kolpachny Lane in central Moscow. There, the press officers would welcome Russian and foreign journalists. After that, with the help of the veterans association, these press officers set off to promote a remarkable four-part narrative.

The first part of the message was that, given that intelligence methods had never varied, from biblical times to the CIA to the KGB, there was no need to reform Russia's foreign intelligence.

Second, during the Cold War, the KGB's spies spent the bulk of their time in the West. Thus, according to the message, it was only logical that they were more open-minded than the rest of the KGB. With their broader frame of reference, Foreign Intelligence officers were also much more critical of Soviet reality than their in-country KGB counterparts.

Third, as spies based abroad, they couldn't, and therefore didn't, take part in the disgusting business of prosecuting dissent in the Soviet Union.

Fourth and finally—went the narrative—Soviet intelligence ceased the practice of carrying out assassination operations abroad as early as the late 1950s. In fact, claimed the press officers with bold specificity, the very last operation was the cyanide gas poisoning of the head of the military wing of a Ukrainian émigré organization on the streets of Munich in 1959.

This narrative was, to say the least, fantastical. Nonetheless, the SVR used it successfully, skillfully cultivating an image of the agency as the natural embodiment of the old KGB's most liberal elements.

Primakov added his own touch as well: in January 1993, he made a public presentation of the first-ever "SVR Analytical Report." The report, reflecting on the global threat of the dissemination of weapons of mass destruction after the end of the Cold War,[12] constituted an effort to make the SVR look like a sort of foreign policy think tank. That, of course, was the reason Primakov made the report nonclassified. He also renamed officers at Yasenevo: instead of "operatives," they were "referents"—consultants. The SVR even ceased, officially, to treat the United States as the Main Adversary; Primakov merged the first, North American section, which dealt with the United States, with the section that covered Latin and South America, signifying that now things were no longer political—it was just about geography.

The rebranding operation was a success. This new image of foreign intelligence was even accepted by many of Russia's liberal journalists. The use of active measures within Russia proved effective, just as Shebarshin had imagined.

Now it was time to try to promote this progressive, new image abroad, namely, in the United States.

CHAPTER 19

COOPERATION AND REBRANDING

The CIA director rose from his chair, glass in hand. Robert Gates was just forty-nine years old in September 1992 as he looked at his audience—ten Americans facing ten Russians across a long table in the SVR's villa on Kolpachny Lane in Moscow. He had spent twenty-six years of his life serving at the CIA and on the National Security Council, most of it dealing with the Soviet threat. "I would like to propose a toast," he said.[1]

Among themselves, the Americans called the blue-and-white villa the Beria House—a reference to Stalin's dreaded secret police chief. (In fact, that was not quite right; the villa had belonged to another minister of state security under Stalin.[2]) Now, it was used by the SVR for dealing with outsiders—the press and the Americans.

Gates had traveled to Moscow to establish a liaison relationship between US and Russian intelligence. In response, the SVR and the Russian counterintelligence agency that would soon be known as the FSB hosted a dinner on Kolpachny Lane in his honor. Gates continued his toast: "I am here today," he intoned, "because the relationship between our two countries demands that our intelligence agencies work together in areas of mutual interest. It is time to turn a page in our history, without forgetting our past and present differences, in order to eliminate the threats we face in this new era."

The Russian generals were obviously pleased. "Cooperation" was exactly the message the generals of the SVR wanted to promote.

The following year, Primakov made a visit to the United States. It was the first official visit of a head of Russian foreign intelligence since Kryuchkov had gone to the United States in 1972. That visit was different, though, in that Kryuchkov had traveled in the guise of an ordinary diplomat. This time the trip was official. Primakov had a meeting with James Woolsey, the Clinton administration's head of the CIA.[3] The following month, Primakov hosted Woolsey in Moscow.

At one of the meetings between the CIA and the SVR, Russian intelligence agreed to cease the practice of active measures. "It was a gentlemen's agreement between the American and Russian intelligence agencies," a former SVR employee told us. Service A was officially gone.

"There was never a written agreement between us," said Rolf Mowatt-Larssen, who headed Moscow's CIA station in the early 1990s and who was present at the dinner on Kolpachny Lane. "But in the late 1980s there was a mutual understanding that it was better to be cautious so as not to undermine the talks between Gorbachev and Reagan."[4]

Now the SVR began making every effort to win the trust of the Americans. For that to happen, the public image of the agency was to be improved.

They had a plan at the ready. The operatives at Yasenevo started working on it before the collapse of the Soviet Union, but it came to fruition four years later in 1993.

This delay almost ruined the whole thing.

By 1993, the former Soviet Union had changed beyond recognition. It was a market economy, wild and brutal. Social guarantees for people employed by the state—including in foreign intelligence—had ceased to exist. The compound at Yasenevo, with its heavily guarded shops and masseuses, began looking shabby. Smart, cunning opportunists were leaving the SVR by the hundreds.

Among those who wanted to sell their skills elsewhere was an easygoing young officer named Alexander Vassiliev. Once captain of the North American section in the First Chief Directorate, he landed a prestigious job at the popular newspaper *Komsomolskaya Pravda*.

In summer 1993, thirty-one-year-old Vassiliev, a moon-faced man with long blond hair and a ready laugh, published a big story. It was about the KGB's most successful active measure ever: an article the KGB had planted in the mid-1980s in the Indian newspaper *Patriot*. According to this active-measure article, the Pentagon had developed the AIDS virus as part of a set of "experiments to design new and dangerous biological weapons." The story went viral, and millions of people in Africa believed in the US military conspiracy.

Vassiliev's story was not the first to expose this particular KGB measure. The West had known about the Soviet disinformation campaign for several years. Yet Vassiliev was the first to get the head of foreign intelligence, Evgeny Primakov, to confirm the story. And Vassiliev's piece did something else, something far subtler. In it, he claimed that the AIDS scandal story had been planted by the KGB in response to the CIA spreading a false rumor that the KGB had masterminded an attempt to assassinate Pope John Paul II. Vassiliev's story thus made the two adversaries look alike—that they had simply exchanged strikes, and the KGB's active measure was a perfectly reasonable response to the CIA attack that had preceded it. Foreign intelligence must have been pleased. This fit in perfectly with the master narrative they were pedaling.

The day after the publication, Vassiliev got a phone call from Yuri Kobaladze, an SVR spokesman. Kobaladze invited the colleague-turned-journalist to the blue-and-white mansion on Kolpachny Lane for a talk. Vassiliev went to the meeting. "I thought they would scold me for my story on active measures," Vassiliev said. Instead, Kobaladze had an offer for him.[5] Explaining that the foreign intelligence agency was supervising a very ambitious publishing project, he invited Vassiliev to join the team. The project was high profile: the Association of Veterans of Foreign Intelligence had just signed an agreement with Alberto Vitale, then chairman and CEO of Random House, for the publication of a series of five books that looked at the KGB's Cold War operations.[6]

The KGB had initiated the publishing project before the collapse of the Soviet Union. It began with a contract for a book about Alexander Orlov, the most famous intelligence defector during Stalin's regime, to be written by two authors—a KGB officer and the British historian John Castello.[7] (Among other things, Orlov had supervised Nahum Eitingon in Spain.) After the book was successfully published, the SVR came up with an idea for five new books: The first would tell the history of Soviet spy operations in the United States in the 1930s and 1940s. The second would cover the standoff between the KGB and the CIA in Cold War–era Berlin. The third would discuss operations in Britain before and during World War II. The fourth would be about the Cuban Missile Crisis (or, as the Russians call it, the Caribbean Crisis). The fifth and final book would tell the story of Leon Trotsky's assassination.[8] Each book was to be written by two authors, one Russian and one Western. The principal agreement with Random House had been reached in June 1992, and Kobaladze had been looking ever since for a suitable candidate from the SVR side for the first and most sensitive book about KGB operations in the United States. This was the book Vassiliev was invited to work on.

The SVR had a clear idea of what it wanted when it agreed to the publication deal. Namely, the agency wished to produce a sanitized version of its own bloody history geared specifically toward a Western audience. The project's respectful American and British historians, they believed, would lend legitimacy to the Russian agency's authorized histories. Western scholars would not get direct access to the KGB files—that was reserved for the Russian researchers, some of them former or active Foreign Intelligence officers. In other words, Russian Foreign Intelligence planned to control the narrative tightly. The project was supervised from the very top. "Primakov was running things out at Yasenevo during the final, protracted stages of negotiations," remembered James O'Shea Wade, who was vice president of the Crown imprint at Random House at the time and supervised the project from the Western side.[9]

Not everyone was thrilled by the Random House publication plan. The British journalist and intelligence expert Philip Knightley, who was the first to expose Kim Philby in the 1960s, turned down Random House's offer to write the book about the Cambridge Five. He feared, rightly, that the books would be propagandistic. When the book about Orlov was published in 1993, Knightley went further, denouncing it as "disinformation."[10]

Sitting in Kobaladze's office, Vassiliev considered the offer. He knew close to nothing about the KGB's history in the United States. "Of course I knew about the Rosenbergs' trial, but that was all. In my time in Yasenevo, you had to obtain special permission from your superior to get to the archives, which were all top secret, and given all the scandals about defectors and traitors in the late 1980s, nobody wanted to raise suspicions by asking for access to information above one's pay grade." But Vassiliev had a gut feeling: "I had a full impression it was another active measure; they just wanted to fool the Americans." He didn't want to be a pawn in an SVR operation. When he reminded Kobaladze he was not an officer anymore, Kobaladze assured him he would be given access to the real KGB files, not just spoon-fed whatever the officers now in charge decided to show him.

In that light, Vassiliev saw the offer as a chance to do something both important and well paid. He also believed Stalin's operations in the United States had been a good thing and that the story deserved to be told. "There was nothing to be ashamed of. It was a glorious past. They stole the bomb and changed world history, and they didn't participate in repressions," Vassiliev said.[11]

That official version of the agency's history was, of course, exactly the view the Foreign Intelligence Service now wanted to project to the public. And having been brought up through the ranks of the Foreign Intelligence Service, this narrative was what Vassiliev had been taught and expected the files to confirm. From Kobaladze's point of view, the assignment was a perfect fit.

Vassiliev and Kobaladze shook hands.

For the next two years, Vassiliev worked from 9:00 a.m. to 5:00 p.m. every day at the blue-and-white SVR mansion on Kolpachny Lane. He shared a table with another "historian," who was also an SVR officer, and worked on the book about the operations in Britain. Each day, they read through file after file brought in from Yasenevo.

Vassiliev knew what to ask for; he was familiar with the KGB's internal procedures from his days in Yasenevo. He began hunting for pale green or brown folders with aged yellow sheets inside— the files of agents' correspondence, or DOPs (*Dela Operativnoy Perepisky*). Indeed, these files proved to be jewels. They consisted of decades of cypher telegram exchanges between Moscow's Center on Lubyanka and Soviet spies in the United States—crucial, heretofore unknown parts of the story of Soviet atomic espionage. (The reports of Vasily Zarubin and Liza Gorskaya were among them, and it's thanks to Vassiliev that we now know the details of the attempts made by Zarubin to bring Jacob Golos to heel.)

Vassiliev made notes in his notebook. Once he had filled a notebook to the end, he was allowed to take it home for safekeeping. He eventually stored eight notebooks full of information.

Kobaladze, trusting his former brother-in-arms, didn't bother to have Vassiliev sign a nondisclosure agreement. That was the first mistake. The SVR had overlooked the fact that in the 1990s, they could no longer exert the kind of control over Vassiliev that the KGB had enjoyed for decades. This was not the Soviet Union anymore, and they couldn't rely on intimidation and fear the way they used to. The SVR compounded this mistake by failing to offer Vassiliev any money for his work; the American publisher alone was supposed to pay him.

This left Vassiliev a free agent. In January 1996, the former spy realized he was in possession of a treasure trove—and that it was probably time for him to move. Vassiliev later claimed he could feel things heating up and referred to a cloak-and-dagger-type operation: "There was a hidden Communist Party cell in the SVR, and they became threatening to me."[12] The timing question might well be simpler than that, though. That same month, the SVR head Primakov was made foreign minister, so Vassiliev may have merely worried that, with his chief patron out of the agency, the SVR would cancel the project and want their files back.

Vassiliev scanned his notebooks and left the digital copies with his friends. He quickly secured British visas for his wife and himself through his contacts at the UK embassy and flew to London. In his hand luggage Vassiliev had a laptop—completely empty, as he suspected he would be searched at Moscow's Sheremetyevo airport—and several floppy disks containing the digital copies of his precious notebooks.

Vassiliev then enlisted the help of American scholars. Together they turned his notebooks into two books about Soviet operations in the United States in the 1930s and 1940s that would become the most damning exposés of their kind ever written: *The Haunted Wood: Soviet Espionage in America—The Stalin Era* (1998) and *The Spies: The Rise and Fall of the KGB in America* (2009).[13]

Vassiliev was neither a hero nor a whistleblower. He was just a smart opportunist who saw an opening and took full advantage of it. But his actions shed much-needed light on one of the most secretive organizations in the world. In 2009, the notebooks, translated and digitized, were put online on the Wilson Center's website.[14] Finally, the United States had proof from inside Yasenevo about the crucial role that the Communist Party of the United States played in Soviet espionage—something the SVR had always denied. Some American nuclear physicists' reputations were cleared as well—most notably that of Robert Oppenheimer, the leader of the Manhattan Project, who had never been a Russian agent.

What had started as a cunning Russian intelligence disinformation operation ended up a cataclysmic disaster for the SVR. Vassiliev didn't even have to defect; he just left the country. The Foreign Intelligence Service had been too slow to understand that the country's borders were now porous. Meanwhile, books still worked.

The Foreign Intelligence Service was so embarrassed that it never even tried to start an investigation of Vassiliev. "I'm not a traitor—they let me in!" Vassiliev told us, with a smile, from his home in the United Kingdom.

True, if the agency had complained, its top leadership would have been the first to blame, and nobody wanted that. So Vassiliev was left in peace. But he never returned to Moscow.

In the end, only four of the five books outlined in the Foreign Intelligence plan were published, counting Vassiliev's. The project about the assassination of Trotsky was abandoned—Yasenevo most likely decided it was not ready to open the KGB files on the killing of the Soviet Union's most prominent political émigré. Nahum Eitingon's secrets remained safely sealed, probably forever.

At the time, it looked as if the failed book operation was just a last hurrah from the old guard on its way out—a last attempt by a dying breed to influence the way history was remembered. That assessment would continue to seem correct for several years. After all, all of Yasenevo's top positions were still occupied at the time by generals who had come up through the ranks of the KGB. And you can't teach an old dog new tricks.

Soon enough it became clear that while the old dogs would retire and the KGB itself would fade away, the new Russian security and intelligence services were not ready to abandon the old tricks either.

In the late 1990s, when we started writing about Russian intelligence, we were constantly hearing from our more experienced colleagues that the secret services were conducting disinformation operations, although the details were vague. There were rumors that the Russian spies had just changed the names for their long-standing disinformation operations—that "active measures" had become "assistance programs" or "assistance operations," in the sense that operations that succeeded in changing a foreign government's policy or position would "assist" the Russian government.

In 1999 we received confirmation of this particular rumor. It came, somewhat surprisingly, from the FSB—Russia's domestic security agency—when an FSB spokesperson proudly presented himself to journalists as head of the new "department for assistance programs," a department that included the FSB's press office. Many FSB case officers were embarrassed to hear he had revealed what was presumably a confidential term.[15]

In 2010, disenchanted FSB officers leaked documents that showed the FSB was behind a disinformation operation in Ukraine, the goal of which was to prevent Kiev from purchasing gas from Turkmenistan rather than Russia. (The FSB planted a false story in the Ukrainian media that the Ukrainian secret services funded the Turkmenistani opposition.[16]) Nearly two decades after the collapse of the Soviet Union, the FSB was clearly sticking with the KGB's tool kit.

Was Russian Foreign Intelligence also using the old KGB tricks abroad? The SVR kept its cards closer to its chest than did the FSB. The SVR didn't say anything about whether or not it was bold enough to continue conducting disinformation operations in the West. But in spring 2013, more than twenty years after Robert Gates toasted the dawn of a new era of cooperation between US and Russian intelligence services, we learned the answer.

*　*　*

The ugly concrete high-rise on Sixty-Seventh Street between Third and Lexington in New York City, the premises of the SVR's rezidentura in New York, was referred to informally as the submarine by the agents who worked there.

The twelve-story building housed the Russian mission to the United Nations, and it was a fortress, pure and simple. Built in the early 1960s, it was heavily guarded and protected by a fence, supplemented by CCTV cameras surveilling every angle. Across the street, near the entryway festooned with the tricolor flag of Russia, was a New York City Police Department precinct and several police cars constantly parked there.

In May 2013, on the eighth floor, two officers were deep in discussion. The eighth floor was a fortress within a fortress. There were no windows here, and no phone lines connected the submarine to the outside world. The interior ceilings on the eighth floor were a foot shorter than on other floors because of the extra-thick walls. The electricity and ventilation systems were self-contained to prevent outsiders from planting listening devices.[17]

The two officers were in shirtsleeves. A decades-old rule was to leave all suit coats and jackets in the eighth-floor cloakroom in case a listening device had been discreetly placed in an officer's jacket by the insidious Americans.

"Zhenya drafted, what do you call it, a proposal," said the first officer.

"Aha," said the second.

"I will have to process it now," pressured the first.

"What's the subject matter?" asked his interlocutor.

"He drafted, as I told you before, the proposal about Bombardier planes."

The first officer was referring to the Canadian company Bombardier, which was in talks at the time with the Russian government about a possible joint project manufacturing airplanes.

"So what's his idea?" asked his colleague.

The first officer elaborated: the idea was to set up the midsize airplane assembly plant in Russia.

"That's an important point," the second officer agreed.

Knowing they were in a highly secured area, the two officers didn't think twice about speaking openly with one another. But they hadn't accounted for human error.

Stuck somewhere among the papers in the room was a file binder, brought into the submarine by the first officer. He believed he had recruited a promising asset, an American, and had accepted a delivery from him—a file binder containing an analytical report of interest to Russian intelligence. Unfortunately for Russian intelligence, the SVR officer's asset was, in fact, an undercover FBI agent who had a planted a listening device in the binder. Now the device was recording the entire conversation about Bombardier.

The first officer kept pushing. He believed the deal would bring modern technologies to Moscow and could open up production and export possibilities for Russia. He also deeply respected Zhenya and his proposal. "Zhenya" was, in fact, Evgeny Buryakov, deputy head of the Manhattan office of Russia's state-run bank. The bank's head, Buryakov's boss, was a KGB foreign intelligence veteran, and Buryakov himself was, in fact, a Foreign Intelligence officer who operated under nonofficial cover, meaning he did not have diplomatic immunity.

The first officer said that there was a problem with the deal and explained that the Canadian workers unions were resisting it. However, he had a solution: put pressure on the Canadian unions.

"Therefore," he told his colleague, "the proposal for MS is geared toward pressuring the unions and securing from the company a solution that is beneficial to us."

The FBI agents listening in might well have asked themselves who or what the mysterious MS was.

Sergei Tretyakov, a high-ranking KGB/SVR officer who served as the deputy head of the Russian Foreign Intelligence Service's submarine headquarters in New York before his defection in 2000, provided a clue. Tretyakov explained that the gentlemen's agreement the Russians had made with American intelligence back in the early 1990s to put a stop to active measures had been a ruse from the beginning. "We said, 'OK, now we are friends. We'll stop doing this' and the SVR shut down Service A," Tretyakov told us. "But Service A simply underwent a name change. It became Department M." The old KGB active measures were renamed MS (*Meropriyatia Sodeystvia*; Assistance Measures or Operations).[18] "The same people who had run it under the KGB were still doing it for the Foreign Intelligence," Tretyakov told us.[19]

So the MS proposal under discussion in the submarine in May 2013 was just this—active measures, slightly rebranded.

In January 2015, Zhenya was arrested by the FBI and charged with conspiracy to act in the United States as an agent of a foreign government. Two other Russian intelligence officers, identified as such by the FBI, left the United States. Zhenya pleaded guilty and received thirty months in jail. In April 2017 he was released and put on an Aeroflot plane bound for Moscow.[20]

Two decades after the collapse of the Soviet Union, a new generation had taken over Russian intelligence. Many had no experience serving in the KGB (e.g., Buryakov had been only sixteen years old when the Soviet Union collapsed), yet they ran the same kinds of operations. The post-Soviet intelligence officers followed tradition and stuck with the old KGB methods, primarily the use of disinformation. Russian intelligence proved to be a self-reproducing circuit.

Disinformation and deceit was a foundation stone for Russian intelligence, the essential tool in its tool kit. Foreign intelligence had refused to give up active measures tactics in the 1990s, essentially as a matter of survival. After the collapse of the Soviet

Union, the Russian spies kept using active measures with just a slight rebranding to repel criticism at home. And they used active measures beyond their own borders—first, and largely successfully, to improve their own image abroad and, second, to do what they had done all through the Cold War: help the Kremlin to achieve its ends in the West.

PART III

PUTIN'S PROJECT

CHAPTER 20

A FRESH START

On October 12, 2001, men in the dark suits of the President Protection Service blocked every conceivable entrance to the Hall of Columns in the House of the Unions in Moscow.

The blue-and-white classical building, just a stone's throw from the Bolshoi Theater, had once been a ballroom venue for the Assembly of Nobility. After the revolution, the hall hosted important state events, including party congresses and funeral services. It was in this hall that Lenin, Stalin, and Brezhnev lay in state before being taken to their final resting places in the Kremlin necropolis (Lenin's body was displayed here for five days before being brought to the wooden mausoleum on the Red Square, where a frozen Zarubin would guard it). This evening, however, the Hall of Columns was hosting the First World Congress of Compatriots—an updated version of the previous congresses organized by Tolstoy in the early 1990s. This time, however, Vladimir Putin was in charge. The new Russian president had not approved of Tolstoy's congresses of 1991–1993, and now, as the title of the event indicated, he wanted to start fresh. Mikhail Tolstoy was not even invited.

The massive chandeliers sparkled brightly, illuminating the twenty-eight gilded columns that gave the hall its name as well as numerous red-velvet curtains and chairs. It was a far cry from Tchaikovsky Hall, a plain space nearby that had long served as a haven for the impoverished Moscow intelligentsia and fans of classical music, where Tolstoy's congress had been held.

As the ceremonies commenced, Putin took his seat onstage at a long table under the new emblem of the congress. The emblem for Yeltsin's congress had been made up of three curved lines—the white, blue, and red of the Russian tricolor—with a curve to symbolize the Soviet era's distortion of the smooth course of Russian history. Putin's congress adopted a new image. The emblem was a globe with the map of Russia marked in black—a symbol of the president's international ambitions.

Putin took the pulpit. In the audience, delegates from forty-seven countries hushed. From his very first words, it was clear that Putin saw the huge Russian diaspora as something the Russian state could use to advance its interests. "A strong diaspora can only exist if there is a strong state," he proclaimed, noting that the Russian-speaking community, including Russian citizens, was the fifth largest in the world.[1] His message contrasted sharply with that of Yeltsin and Tolstoy. Yeltsin had wanted to correct the historical injustice that had forced millions of Russians out of the country with no hope of ever returning. Putin, on the other hand, saw this diaspora as a valuable asset for the Russian state. This speech also marked the first time Putin invoked the term *Russky Mir* (Russian world)—the worldwide community of Russian-speaking people with an identity firmly connected to Russia's history, culture, and language—which would, in time, become a Russian foreign policy concept.

Unlike Yeltsin, Putin was not interested in asking Russians abroad for help building a democratic Russia. Rather, he wanted to send a message to the Russians abroad that Russia had once again become a strong state—and that it was high time for her compatriots to advance Russia's positions beyond its borders. It was no accident that Putin, a former state security officer, chose the word "compatriot" for his address. The term directly evoked KGB terminology. Tolstoy had used the term just a decade earlier in an attempt to bypass KGB interference, but Putin's use of it represented a 180-degree change from Tolstoy's approach.

Putin also talked about the need to create a coordinating body to oversee the diaspora. Soon after, the Kremlin launched not one but several government-funded organizations to do just that. These organizations ranged from civic engagement groups to dozens of media outlets, including journals and websites.

Putin didn't stop there. Within a few years, the Kremlin launched a federal agency under the Foreign Ministry to monitor the diaspora, commonly called the *Rossotrudnichestvo*.[2] This agency in turn became an umbrella body for a collection of foundations that supported compatriots abroad and provided funding for Russian-speaking media. These generously funded groups joined the Russian culture centers—traditionally, a disguise for intelligence operations—in operating all over the world.

Using culture as a guise for intelligence was a time-honored tradition. The KGB's 1968 manual, "The Use of the Soviet Culture Committee for Cultural Ties with Compatriots Abroad in Intelligence Activity," put it this way: "The main operational task for our intelligence to conduct through the Soviet Committee is to use the official work, propaganda and other means of influencing compatriots to prepare the grounds for the deployment of recruitment and other intelligence and counterintelligence measures using emigration as an operational base."[3]

In October 2001, Putin's message resonated at the congress, and the majority of the delegates were fully supportive of the Russian president.[4] But that was not enough for Putin. He expected something different from the congress in the Hall of Columns—a big idea that could help engage the emigrants in the Kremlin's project of expanding its influence abroad. He also needed someone to implement and execute the idea, somebody from the other side— an émigré, not a Russian government official. Putin didn't see such a person among the participants of the congress. When the congress was over, he fired the minister who had been in charge of putting the event together.[5]

In Putin's eyes, what was at stake was nothing less than the security of his regime. Only ten years had passed since the collapse of the Soviet Union, which had come as a complete surprise to the KGB. Only three years had passed since the major—and equally unforeseen—economic crisis that had shuttered Yeltsin's government. The KGB always looked on emigrants with suspicion, as a hotbed of subversives ready to challenge the authority of the Kremlin if something ever went wrong. Putin wanted to "prepare the grounds for the deployment of recruitment," as the KGB's textbook put it.

In the Hall of Columns, an elderly, gray-haired man was watching Putin closely through his old-fashioned, horn-rimmed glasses. Alexei Jordan was the leader of the United Russian Cadet Corps in the United States. Jordan hailed from a prominent, religious family of White émigrés of German ancestry that was proud to have ancestors among Crusaders—thus his non-Russian-sounding name.

Despite his advanced age—Alexei Jordan was now in his late seventies—he was still full of energy. Ever since 1991, he had spent several months each year in Russia promoting the cadets movement, a network of all-boys military schools that the White army established abroad after its members fled the revolution. In the generations since, the cadets movement had become a tool to keep the Russian military's largely aristocratic traditions alive for the next generations of emigrants.[6] Jordan's efforts were met with great enthusiasm in Russian military schools; the disoriented post-Soviet army saw the cadets movement as a lifeline tying the uncertain present to a glorious imperial past.[7]

Alexei Jordan's activities were funded by his son, Boris, an American financier who made a fortune in Russia in the 1990s. Alexei had always been close to his son. He knew that Boris had recently tied his fate to the political regime in the Kremlin; in fact, Boris had recently helped Putin bring a rebellious TV channel to heel. Now, as Alexei Jordan listened to Putin, he was deep in thought.

Meanwhile, the organizer of the original congress, Mikhail Tolstoy, had married a participant of that first congress—a descendant of the first wave of emigration whose family had made its way from Russia to China and then to the United States. Now Tolstoy left Russia, as had many Tolstoys before him. He moved to the United States, settled in Menlo Park, California, and thus became a compatriot.

CHAPTER 21

THE SIEGE

In Russia, the dawn of the twenty-first century brought with it a new idea: the rules, it was clear, should be tightened. The country had barely survived a devastating economic crisis that was preceded by a government default on debt that had knocked out the middle class. Yeltsin had let the country run dangerously wild—that was the opinion shared by both elites and angry businessmen. Russians wanted more order.

To sort out the mess, they talked about the need to bring in some sort of Pinochet, the infamous Chilean dictator. But Russia was not Latin or South America. Historically, order in Russia originated not in the military but in state security. In 2000, Russia got the order it had been missing in the 1990s in the form of a new president. Tough and energetic, Vladimir Putin also happened to be a former officer of the KGB.

The job of state security is to police society. One of the first steps is the establishment of government control of the media—and Putin embarked on that task immediately.

During the previous decade, Russian Americans had helped open the door to Western financial markets. In the new circumstances of the early 2000s, some found new roles to play. One of that special group was Boris Jordan, the energetic thirty-five-year-old investment banker.

Boris started with television.

The TV channel NTV had drawn the ire of the new Russian president when the channel began to report critically on the Second Chechen War. Putin perceived the critique as a conspiracy to undermine his war effort and his prestige. Therefore, the channel needed to be crushed—and, gradually, so did the media empire of which NTV was the flagship.

NTV had been built by Russian tycoon Vladimir Gusinsky. A bespectacled, corpulent man with a defiant smile, a stage director by training, Gusinsky made his fortune in the 1990s by building up his bank empire, as had many other oligarchs of the first generation. But then he made a dramatic turn: he aspired to become a media magnate. In just five years, he built his media empire—a newspaper and a magazine, radio and television—and he built it from scratch, unlike other tycoons who had gotten slices of national property from the government at bargain prices. Emotional and highly ambitious, Gusinsky thought of himself as the Russian Ted Turner; he even sent his best journalists to CNN for training. He was also a political player, and he had supported Putin's competitors—the side that lost—in their bid for the Kremlin.

Now the Kremlin was landing punch after punch. Special forces in balaclavas raided Gusinsky's offices, and Gusinsky himself was jailed in an effort to make him sell the channel. The attacks finally forced him out of the country, and the Kremlin placed NTV in the hands of the state-owned corporation Gazprom.[1]

But the NTV journalists, led by the channel's CEO and chief editor, Evgeny Kiselev, refused to accept the change. They kept working, and they kept speaking up on air despite and against the Kremlin's pressure.

They effectively turned the most popular NTV talk shows into permanent protest rallies, inviting political opposition leaders, human rights activists, experts, and journalists to talk about the channel's precarious situation. The highest-ranking official to accept the invitation was probably Boris Nemtsov, a tall man with curly hair and a ready smile, who was leader of the liberal caucus in the Russian parliament and a former deputy prime minister. His position was to try to find a compromise between NTV journalists and Gazprom.

But the stalemate continued, for days and then weeks.

One day, Evgeny Kiselev got a call from Nemtsov: "Evgeny, I have great news for you! They want Boris Jordan to be the new CEO of NTV. He is a Russian American, so he would not choke your journalists."[2] Kiselev responded, quietly, that he knew who Jordan was but didn't share Nemtsov's enthusiasm about his appointment.

Boris Jordan was not a government official or a TV professional but a financier. Cherubic, blue-eyed, and just thirty-five years old, Jordan had already earned a prominent place in recent Russian history.

Every door opens on both sides, and the door between the Russian and American financial markets was no exception. Vladimir Galitzine and Natasha Gurfinkel at the Bank of New York had flung it wide open on the American side, letting the Russian dollars stream into the United States. But there were also American dollars eager to come to Russia, particularly when the privatization of large chunks of Soviet state property began. Someone had to open the door on the Russian side, and another pair of Russian émigrés with American passports—one of them Boris Jordan—was more than happy to oblige.

The path of this second émigré pair mirrored that of Galitzine and Gurfinkel in many ways.

Boris Jordan, a New Yorker, was a descendant of the first wave of White Russian emigration, an aristocrat connected to the best prerevolution Russian families and a devoted member of the Orthodox Church.

In 1992, he went to Moscow along with his best buddy, who had been born to a Jewish family in Leningrad and moved to the States when he was a teenager.[3] The two were twenty-six years old, and they were in Russia seeking opportunities to make a quick buck. In three years the pair launched the Renaissance Capital investment bank. Within a few years it was the largest bank attracting Western money into Russia. Jordan even briefly contemplated getting Russian citizenship but abandoned the idea—the American passport was still much more convenient.[4]

Boris Jordan was crafty and ambitious. He had succeeded financially in the 1990s, when everything in Russia was about money. Now he wanted to keep on succeeding.

Among other things, this meant finding a way to cooperate with people from the security services. They came back to prominence after Yeltsin consecutively appointed three prime ministers whose main qualifications seemed to be that they had been tied to the security and intelligence services. Finally, Yeltsin made his bet on the KGB man Putin.

Jordan's Renaissance Capital brought two Foreign Intelligence generals on board. The first was Yuri Kobaladze, the very same SVR spokesman who had so disastrously invited Vassiliev to join the SVR's active measures book project. The other, Yuri Sagaidak, was a colleague of Kobaladze's who was known mostly for having been expelled from London, where he had served in the guise of a journalist, in the late 1980s after he had tried unsuccessfully to recruit a British member of Parliament.[5] When Kiselev got the call from Nemtsov, he remembered that, together, these two generals had already tried to organize a back channel of communication with the besieged NTV station in very traditional secret-service style.

Even before Nemtsov's call, Kiselev had gotten a call from Kobaladze inviting him to the Renaissance Capital office to talk.

Kiselev understood that Kobaladze wanted to talk about NTV, so he agreed to come. At that meeting, Kobaladze and his colleague had a message to deliver. The message, it turned out, was from the counterintelligence agency now known as FSB. "Some big shots at the FSB want to talk to you about NTV," Kiselev was told. Kiselev refused to come to Lubyanka—he feared the FSB could record him entering their offices and then use the video to try to compromise him. After all, Lubyanka was the same building that had once housed Stalin's secret police, and the new Russian president had arisen from that building to rule the Kremlin. Hearing that Kiselev didn't want to meet inside Lubyanka, the FSB canceled its invitation.[6] That first attempt by the Russian secret services to impact the fate of NTV, using the traditional KGB tool kit and the Renaissance Capital connections, had failed. The second attempt failed when Kiselev was not swayed by Nemtsov to step down as CEO and accept Jordan.

On April 3, 2001, Gazprom convened a meeting of the channel's board. At that meeting, the board elected a new chief executive—Boris Jordan—along with a new editor in chief. Most of the channel's journalists rejected the new leadership, and the stalemate continued.

It was a classic seize-and-capture operation, the kind typically practiced by Russian special forces. The thirteen-story rectangular Ostankino TV center in northeast Moscow was the nerve center of Russian television, housing nearly all of the country's TV channels. But in the early hours of April 14, 2001, it was very quiet—after all, it was Holy Saturday, the day after Good Friday. The building was barely lit when a group of heavily built, short-haired men in dark suits made their way beneath the entrance's concrete canopy and in through the glass doors.

One of the men spoke briefly with a sleepy policeman, who promptly let the men into the large lobby. There they divided into two groups: the first went to the elevators, and the second took the stairs. They met on the eighth floor, which was marked NTV in huge green letters. This floor had its own security guarding the NTV channel. One of the men in dark suits produced a letter signed by the channel's new CEO, Boris Jordan. According to the letter, from this moment on, these men were in charge. They burst into a long corridor, and the man heading the group quickly directed a dark suit to stand at every door. He placed two people by the door of Evgeny Kiselev's office, just in case.

The news team's night shift was taken completely by surprise. The men in dark suits told them, very politely, that they could either comply with the new bosses or vacate the premises. Most decided to comply, but one journalist made an outside call. In a few minutes, Moscow's largest radio station, Echo Moskvy, broke the news: NTV had been seized. It was just before 5:00 a.m.

One NTV news program editor was home but not asleep—her new baby was very active. She was a news junkie and kept her radio on and tuned to Echo Moskvy at all times. When she heard of the takeover, she immediately picked up the phone and called her boss, Vladimir Kara-Murza. He was at home too; it was the only day of the week when he had no program to run.

Kara-Murza, then forty-two years old, was an anchorman on NTV's nightly news program, easily recognizable thanks to his trademark black turtleneck, gray jacket, and ducktail beard. His unmistakable intonation and intelligence made him one of the most respected voices in Russian television. When he heard what had happened, Kara-Murza immediately got dressed. He threw on his gray-and-black outfit and went out into the street.

A descendant of a distinguished Moscow family, whose scions—among them, historians, scholars, and lawyers—had long belonged to the intelligentsia, Kara-Murza had a soft voice and good manners. But he was also a man of action outraged at pressure from the Kremlin—an attitude naturally inherited from his father, a journalist who had spent several years in Stalin's labor camps.

When Kara-Murza had studied at Moscow University in the late 1970s—the fourth generation of his family to study there—he had almost been thrown out. A group of students in the dormitory had had a party during which they accidentally set fire to the political notices board on the wall. Unfortunately, when the board went up in flames, so did the photo of Soviet leader Leonid Brezhnev that was on it. One of the students, most likely Kara-Murza, threw the burning stand out of a seventeenth-floor window. Of course, the heretics burning the Soviet leader's portrait were denounced at once. All of them faced expulsion from the university. Luckily, the decision fell to a Komsomol leader, a grandson of Stalin's foreign minister, who had been a friend of Kara-Murza's family. He downplayed the case, and Kara-Murza graduated with distinction. Nevertheless, he determined never to work a single day at a Soviet institution. Instead, he made his living by tutoring, and at night he worked in a boiler room.

When the Soviet Union collapsed, a former classmate, Oleg Dobrodeev, was a heavyweight working in television. He invited Kara-Murza to come work with him in the burgeoning Russian TV scene. By April 2001, Kara-Murza had spent almost a decade at NTV. His career on television made sense to him as part of the Kara-Murza family mission; it was the kind of role Moscow liberal intelligentsia should play in Russian society. He was proud that his nineteen-year-old son already shared his sense of public mission. Vladimir Kara-Murza Jr. was already a part-time journalist and was helping Boris Nemtsov at the parliament.

The news of the takeover shook Kara-Murza to his core. It was about a fifteen-minute drive to the Ostankino TV center from his apartment. He took a cab and tried to collect his thoughts.

What was happening inside Ostankino looked like the final stage of a government-sanctioned hostile takeover, something NTV journalists had been dreading for almost a year.

Kara-Murza believed that with Boris Jordan as CEO, the new leadership could have already blacklisted the dissenting journalists.

If Kara-Murza was on such a list, they would not let him up to the eighth floor. He needed to think fast. He asked his cab driver if he could buy the driver's sunglasses and then asked to be dropped off at the Ostankino back entrance. Using his still-valid ID, he took an elevator to the eleventh floor, walked along a maze of corridors to the other end of the building, and descended to the eighth floor and NTV's offices.[7]

There he bumped into a cameraman named Zhenya. He and Zhenya had worked together in many hotspots, including Chechnya. Taking his sunglasses off, Kara-Murza spoke in a commanding tone. He ordered Zhenya to turn on his Betacam camera. He then approached a new security guard at the entrance to the floor and said in a loud, firm voice, "I'm Vladimir Kara-Murza, NTV TV company. Who are you? Your name and surname!" Faced with a TV celebrity who was instantly recognizable in his black turtleneck and gray jacket, the astonished guard let him in.[8]

Taking the cameraman with him, Kara-Murza slid into the corridor of the hijacked station. Almost immediately he saw two people approaching. One was the new chief editor, a man appointed with the full approval of the Kremlin. That was anticipated. But the second was truly a surprise: Oleg Dobrodeev, a bulky, solid man in old-fashioned glasses, had been CEO of NTV just a year earlier. When NTV started scrapping with Putin, Dobrodeev deserted the battle. Rather than incur Putin's displeasure, he moved to head up the state-owned media mammoth known as Russian state television. Ever since, he had been busy buying up journalists leaving the beleaguered NTV. When Dobrodeev saw Kara-Murza, he turned away, but Kara-Murza blocked him with his hand.

"Turn on your camera, Zhenya! A question for our viewers. Why has the chairman of the state-owned TV corporation, at"—Kara-Murza looked at his wristwatch—"5:30 in the morning on a Saturday, found himself on the premises of the TV channel NTV?"[9]

"Because I'm no longer a representative of Russian state television," Dobrodeev said and turned away. He was pretending to have resigned from state television to fool people into thinking that he had come to NTV as a friend.

Kara-Murza wasn't buying it. He followed Dobrodeev.

"OK, so why didn't we see you here yesterday or a year ago?" he asked.

"Well, we all needed to think about what's going on. And you too," Dobrodeev replied.

"To think about what?" Kara-Murza exclaimed. "Zhenya, keep rolling! . . . Please confirm that the program scheduled for tonight, the one about a takeover of NTV, will be aired as planned. The program that also looks at Beria and Yagoda." Kara-Murza was referring to Stalin's chiefs of state security, directly implying that the takeover of NTV amounted to government repression. He continued to address Dobrodeev, not the new editor in chief. His gut feeling was correct: he didn't know then that Dobrodeev had been driven to Ostankino after his meeting with Putin in the Kremlin.[10]

Dobrodeev kept walking away. Then he suddenly stopped and turned to Kara-Murza. He started in a surprisingly thin voice: "You want to talk about freedom of speech? Freedom of speech, Volodya [diminutive for Vladimir], is not only you, alas. And you understand this perfectly." He hinted that Kara-Murza, too, was not completely free in his actions. For months, state propaganda had been attacking NTV journalists. In these attacks, they claimed that NTV journalists were extremely well paid by Gusinsky, implying that the journalists had traded their integrity for big salaries and low-interest loans on apartments. But if Dobrodeev was accusing him of having sold out to the oligarch, Kara-Murza wanted him to say it explicitly, on camera.

"Please, look into my pockets!" Kara-Murza exclaimed. Offended, he opened his jacket wide. He asked where the evidence was of his being paid. "I do not understand your hint . . . I do not understand your hint," he repeated, slowly enunciating each word.

But Dobrodeev kept walking away.

It was the end of NTV as its Russian audience knew it. Most of the station's prominent journalists left in protest of its hostile takeover.

It was also the end of a twenty-five-year friendship. Oleg Dobrodeev had been Kara-Murza's friend since the days they were both studying history at Moscow University. Their families were friendly, too. Kara-Murza was godfather to Dobrodeev's son. It was Dobrodeev who had invited the unemployed Kara-Murza to work in television in the first place, at the channel Dobrodeev himself had founded. He had also kept giving Kara-Murza wristwatches, which Kara-Murza kept losing. One day Dobrodeev took off the wristwatch he was wearing, which had been specially made for NTV's top executives. It was an expensive, classic-looking piece engraved with "NTV Channel," but he gave it to his friend. That had been just seven years ago.

That precious gift Kara-Murza never lost. It was this wristwatch, in fact, that he consulted when he asked Dobrodeev what he was doing on the premises of the occupied NTV at such an early hour.

Always a professional, Kara-Murza made several copies of the recording of his walk-in and encounter with Dobrodeev and sent the tapes to his Russian and foreign colleagues. The tape aired the same day. But that, of course, didn't have any effect on the fate of NTV.

A few hours later, the glass doors under the entrance's concrete canopy opened. A tall, chubby-cheeked man in an impeccable suit appeared outside. He approached the crowd of journalists and TV cameras that had gathered there. He began speaking with a slight American accent.

"Today I'm so busy with the affairs of the TV company because of the very difficult situation the company found itself in after the departure of some of the employees that I had no time to look into personnel issues. But I think first thing we need is that people take a rest from all this, all of them," he ended cheerfully.[11]

Boris Jordan had every reason to smile. He was quite pleased with himself and the way the operation had been implemented, especially since, at the end of the day, it was his special project.

With Vladimir Putin in the Kremlin, the quest for success became focused on politics and control over society. Boris Jordan, offspring of an aristocratic Russian émigré family in the United States, had been called upon to help the Kremlin take over the rebellious TV channel. He had played his family history card and used his American citizenship. The day Jordan was appointed, Nemtsov said of him, "It was a very smart decision by the government to appoint Boris Jordan. Why? He is an American citizen; his ancestor was a minister of education under Tsar Alexander I. His father studied at the Cadets Corps in Belgrade; he himself has a very good noble pedigree. And I cannot imagine how the US State Department would criticize Russia for suppressing press freedom with an American citizen, formally or informally, heading this company."[12]

Now Jordan was standing proudly at the steps of Ostankino before the flashbulbs of dozens of cameras. He had gotten rid of troublemakers by using the methods practiced by Russian oligarchs in their wars for plants and factories. The security guards in dark suits who had taken over the premises of NTV in the early hours were employees of his investment company. This phase of the operation had gone well.

It was time for the second phase: to prove his usefulness in running the television channel. It was, essentially, his first day at his new job. Very soon that job was to include fighting for the hearts and minds of Russian Americans, as NTV happened to be the most popular Russian-speaking channel beyond Russian borders.

CHAPTER 22

GETTING OUT THE MESSAGE

Vladimir Gusinsky, once the most powerful media tycoon in Russia, was now forced out and in exile and didn't want to give up so easily. He wanted to stay in the game. The only option he saw open to him was to launch a television channel for Russians abroad, primarily those in America. So he did, investing his money and energy into a new project. But Boris Jordan's NTV would follow him, and the fight for the hearts and minds of the emigrant compatriots began.

The night of September 27, 2001, Russians in Europe, Israel, and the United States watching the Russian-speaking TV channel NTV International saw their TV sets suddenly go dark. This was no technical error. The channel's broadcasting system in the technical center in Ostankino had been shut down.[1]

After taking over the station in April, Jordan had spent the summer seizing control of Gusinsky's numerous other companies. Those he couldn't lay his hands on, he tried to kill. By September, NTV International was the last remnant of NTV still under Gusinsky's control. The oligarch had launched the channel, an extension of the

NTV brand, five years earlier to reach out to the Russian diaspora. NTV news and shows launched first in Israel and Europe and then, in 1999, in the United States. By the fall of 2001, NTV International was the most popular Russian-speaking TV channel in the world.

As a company registered overseas, NTV International was out of reach of both the Russian authorities and Boris Jordan. But because it was broadcast from Ostankino, the station was vulnerable.

In the end, the September 27 blackout lasted only a few hours. Jordan's argument that Gusinsky's company was switched off because of outstanding debts was easily dismissed by Gusinsky's lawyers, and broadcasting resumed. It was a failure for Jordan and a first, modest victory for Gusinsky. Stripped of all his media assets and having fled Russia, the oligarch was nonetheless still resourceful. NTV International, he believed, could serve as a launching pad to start a counteroffensive against Putin.

But there was a problem. NTV International didn't create any original content. Gusinsky had to fill his airtime with old shows, series, and movies. He had a way to reach out to Russians abroad but almost nothing to broadcast. Boris Jordan, on the other hand, had content generated by NTV but no way of reaching international audiences. Gusinsky understood that the blackout was a preemptive attack and that Jordan was already building a direct competitor to his international channel.

Jordan had registered a US branch of his NTV. Gusinsky, motivated by profit, had launched his first oversees broadcasting in Israel because that country had the biggest Russian-speaking audience outside Russia. Jordan made a different choice: his first move was to rent luxury offices in North Bergen, New Jersey, just across the river from upper Manhattan, for NTV's American branch. It was absolutely clear that Jordan wanted to reach out first to the Russian audience in the United States. He claimed it was all business. But was it really?

* * *

Two months later, in November 2001, Vladimir Putin visited the United States. From Moscow, he flew to Washington, DC, where the Bush administration ensured that he was hosted in grand style. Among other events, Putin met with the US Congress and received a confidential White House briefing from the head of the CIA. It was a time of the thaw between Russia and the United States, and Putin exploited to the full the fact that he had turned out to be the first foreign leader to express condolences when he called Bush on September 11 after the al-Qaeda attack on the World Trade Center.

From Washington, Putin flew to Houston, where he gave a speech at Rice University. From there, it was just a short trip to the Bushes' ranch outside Waco. Putin was the first foreign leader ever to visit the sixteen-hundred-acre Prairie Chapel Ranch. "I want to show him some of my favorite spots," Bush said. When he did meet Putin, he called him "a leader of a new kind, a reformer."[2] After enjoying a few days with the Bushes, Putin flew to New York. He visited Ground Zero, gave an interview on NPR, and attended a sermon at the Russian Orthodox Church mourning the Russian victims of 9/11.

During the US trip, Putin was accompanied, unsurprisingly, by high-level Russian officials. More surprising was another of his companions. As the *Washington Post* noted, "Shadowing Putin across the country was Boris Jordan, a Russian American financier given control of NTV when the country's only major independent television network was taken over by a state-controlled company."[3]

Indeed, Jordan's presence was highly unusual. Normally, a Russian American who didn't hold any official position would not mix with the Russian foreign minister, the head of Putin's personal security service, and the secretary of the Russian Security Council at all, let alone on a diplomatic trip abroad. But there he was. In fact, Boris Jordan was following along right behind Putin when Rudy Giuliani showed the Russian president around the ruins of the World Trade Center.

Did Jordan accompany Putin to help him sell the takeover of NTV? His bright American smile and constant talk about future Western investment that would ensure both the channel's integrity and financial sustainability made him well suited to the job. And selling the takeover was surely one of his main tasks.

In early December 2001, the *New York Times* published a letter to the editor written in response to a story exposing the Kremlin's efforts to place Russian TV under government control.

"There will not be 'virtual government control over national television' in Russia," the letter asserted. "An objective review of news reporting in the eight months since Gazprom took control of NTV after prior management defaulted on its loans would show the network provides Russia's most thorough and hard-hitting news coverage." The letter was signed by Boris Jordan, chief executive, NTV.[4]

Jordan kept proving his usefulness to the Kremlin, but he also worked on his image in the United States. A month after he had taken control over NTV, Jordan hired another Russian emigrant. Savik Shuster had the reputation of a true cold warrior but from the American side. Born in the Soviet Baltics, he had emigrated along with his parents to Canada in the early 1970s. He had initially considered a career as a physician, but then the war in Afghanistan started, and soon he found himself in Afghanistan helping local mujahedeen. He was twenty-eight years old. He started freelancing for international media and that kicked off a journalistic career, but he also was involved in propaganda operations organized by Bukovsky's Resistance International—he helped smuggle the mock-up *Red Star* issue into Kabul in January 1984.[5] Since 1988 he had worked for Radio Liberty in Munich. He had helped build the Moscow office from scratch and been head of the office from 1996 to 2001. Jordan made Shuster NTV's leading anchorman and gave him the flagship show, *Svoboda Slova* (Freedom of Speech), obviously intending to show his critics abroad that such freedom did exist on his channel.

* * *

Gusinsky knew that if he wanted to fight back, he needed to be running exclusively original content on NTV International. For that, he needed a new TV channel. In early 2002 he started a project he called RTVI (Russian TV International), a Russian-speaking channel geared toward the Russian diaspora. Although based in Russia and the United States, the channel would not reach the Russian audience at home. The Kremlin made it crystal clear that there was no way for Gusinsky's channel to get a license to broadcast in Russia.

Gusinsky, like Jordan, chose New York for RTVI's headquarters. He rented a ground-floor studio at 304 Hudson Street in Lower Manhattan and equipped it with the best TV technology he could buy. He was involved in the smallest details of his new project, weighing questions like the design of the news anchorman's table for days.

Gusinsky invited journalists he had worked with in the 1990s at NTV to join RTVI. Not all of them agreed to take part in his overseas enterprise. In March 2002, a group of oligarchs loyal to the Kremlin launched a new TV channel. This channel, TVS, appealed to journalists for several reasons. For one thing, it was based in Moscow, not far-away New York. For another, the new channel seemed to offer journalists a chance to keep working for the Russian audience. It also held out the promise that in Putin's Russia, there was space for an independent-minded TV channel. Unlike Jordan's NTV, which was under full control of a state-owned corporation, TVS was not owned by the government. The oligarchs provided at least some distance from the Kremlin.

Many of the journalists who had been expelled from NTV went to work at TVS, including Vladimir Kara-Murza. He was given three programs: a nightly news show, a daily review along the lines of *Meet the Press* but with no guests invited, and a satirical show.

Meanwhile, in April 2002, RTVI went on the air, televising five newscasts daily. Gusinsky promoted it as a Russian CNN, but in truth, RTVI lacked the people and resources needed to make good television. Because RTVI couldn't broadcast in Russia, Russian newsmakers and experts were often reluctant to be interviewed; to them, it seemed like a waste of time. Despite these handicaps, RTVI was a Russian TV channel that was totally independent from the Kremlin, and this made it interesting to Russian-speaking viewers abroad. In less than a year, RTVI was seen in two hundred thousand homes in the New York metropolitan area. It counted an additional thirty thousand subscribers on Dish Network in the United States.[6]

Competition between Jordan and Gusinsky was fierce for the rest of that year. In September, Jordan also signed a contract with Dish Network, and his brainchild—NTV America, backed by the might of the NTV in Russia—finally appeared in American homes. But NTV America had fewer than thirty thousand subscribers.

Still, it was a start. As usual, Boris Jordan had a plan for how to proceed. What he did not know was that, just a month later, a devastating terrorist attack in Moscow would finish off Jordan's career in Russian TV.

CHAPTER 23

THE CRISIS

The crisis began on Wednesday, October 23, 2002. That day, the theater on Dubrovka Street—a large concrete building built in the 1970s as a cultural center to give the local factory youth something to do—was performing Russia's first Broadway-style musical, a show called *Nord-Ost*. The first act was coming to a close when three minivans approached the main entrance. In a few seconds, a large group of Chechens armed with Kalashnikovs and pistols rushed into the theater, shooting into the air. The entire audience—almost a thousand people, sixty-seven foreigners among them—was taken hostage. The terrorists ordered the captives to call their relatives and tell them to organize a demonstration against the Chechen war.

The hostage crisis lasted for three days before special forces troops stormed the theater and put an end to it. The price was high: 130 hostages died, most of them poisoned by a gas that these same special forces pumped into the theater. That fact didn't prevent Putin from calling the operation a victory.[1]

Both NTV America and RTVI drew the attention of mainstream US media, as their coverage of the tense standoff during the crisis was picked up by CNN and CBS. In New Jersey, NTV

America managers quickly made use of this, pointing to their coverage of the terrorist attack as a sign that the station was not censored by the Russian government.

NTV's coverage was good indeed, much better than anything else done by Moscow-based TV channels, and the channel's managers would have been correct if their coverage had no repercussions. But it did. The furious Kremlin went on the offensive against the journalists who had covered the attack. Authorities accused the media of having sabotaged the rescue operation, justified terror, disclosed crucial details to the enemy, and so forth. (We reported the siege and experienced the pressure firsthand—the FSB raided our newspaper editorial office, seized our computers, and interrogated us, along with our colleagues, for hours in the FSB's Lefortovo prison.)

Jordan's Russia-based NTV came under huge government pressure. Before long, Jordan was told by the Kremlin's officials to fire several journalists, including Savik Shuster, who had angered the Kremlin by interviewing hostages' relatives.[2] If Jordan failed to comply, the Kremlin advised, it could find another manager.

Jordan rushed to Washington, DC; he needed help. He wasn't ready to give up Shuster. It would affect his reputation in the United States badly. Besides, NTV was a precious asset, and he had personally invested a lot into it. He didn't want to destroy it.

Jordan arranged a talk at the National Press Club regarding the situation. At the club, he praised the NTV coverage of the crisis. He also defended his journalists' work and said the Kremlin had most harshly condemned the channel's decision during the crisis to bring relatives of the hostages on air, where they pleaded with the special forces not to storm the theater.[3] The Kremlin had wanted to downplay the terror attack, but Russian journalists hadn't let them. As part of his defense strategy, Jordan brought Shuster with him to Washington. Jordan had Shuster interview President George W. Bush, who was about to visit Russia. The anchorman was well received, and the American president declared himself a supporter of the freedom of speech. "The more freedom of speech, the better the world would be. Don't you think?" said Bush at the beginning of the interview.[4]

But it was November 2002, not November 2001. Enlisting Bush's support didn't count anymore in Moscow.

A week after Jordan's trip to Washington and a month after the *Nord-Ost* tragedy, Vladimir Putin gathered the editors of Russia's major media outlets at the Kremlin. The editors tried to calm Putin down and presented him with a conciliatory joint letter. "Some actions of journalists and the media during the last terrorist act in Moscow were wrong," the editors admitted, but "these were just mistakes."

Putin said sharply that he didn't agree. The broadcasting of special forces actions by "a national TV channel" was, he said, "a deliberate act of neglect of the agreements signed with the Press Ministry."[5] He was singling out NTV. An able manipulator, Putin accused the channel of airing information about the movements of the special forces just minutes before they stormed the theater, which had not been the case. This showed, Putin concluded, that the TV channel had acted in the interest of higher TV ratings and, ultimately, a desire to make more money. He stressed that it was unacceptable to "make money with the blood of our citizens, if, of course, those who do it identify themselves with our citizens."[6]

With this statement, it was clear: Putin was talking about Boris Jordan personally. The moment had come for Jordan to pay the price for his American passport.

Jordan was hardly in a position to complain. He had fallen into a trap of his own making. Two years earlier, when interviewed by PBS, Jordan had said of Putin and the concept of economic fair play, "I do believe that he will, from time to time, probably violate international codes of operation because he has to roll back a little bit the chaos created by Yeltsin. That's not to criticize Yeltsin. I think he had to do it. But Putin has to rein that in a little bit."[7]

Now Putin had violated the rules regarding Jordan's channel. And he had made it personal.

In January 2003, Jordan resigned and left television for good. Two years later, Shuster left NTV, and Russia, for Ukraine and relaunched his *Freedom of Speech* on a Ukrainian TV channel.

Late on the night of June 21, 2003, a young man with high cheekbones framed by a beard and mustache finally opened the door to his room in a cozy, five-story Holiday Inn set in the woods just outside Moscow. He shut the door behind him and sighed with relief. The hotel was filled with members, like him, of the Union of Right Forces, a liberal opposition party led by Boris Nemtsov. They had spent the day planning their campaign for the upcoming elections for the Russian parliament, and the young bearded man was one of the candidates.

Vladimir Kara-Murza Jr., as he preferred to be called, to distinguish himself from his famous father, was twenty-one years old. He looked a lot like his father, but he was OK with that; he was eager to take up the mantle of his family's mission. He was understandably anxious. This was his first political campaign.[8]

He had spent the entire day in a suit because he thought he looked too young and talked too fast, and he wanted to come across as serious. He briefly reminded himself that he was not entirely green when it came to politics. After all, he worked not just for some ordinary member of parliament but for Boris Nemtsov, a former vice prime minister and protégé of Yeltsin. Plus he had spent years in journalism—he had been writing since he was sixteen years old. On the downside—there was always a downside—he had lived abroad for the past seven years; he'd been taken to London by his mother. Now he had a British passport along with the Russian one—not a good thing in the eyes of the Russian authorities, but the lawyers who the party had consulted said it was fine, at least for now. Vladimir had always wanted to make a political career at home in Russia.

It had been a long, tiring day, and his mind was still racing. He reminded himself that he was graduating from Cambridge in three days, and he needed to make it back to the United Kingdom on time. He needed and deserved some rest. To unwind, he turned on the hotel's TV set and switched to the channel TVS, his father's channel, a years-long habit.

He watched until midnight, and then the broadcasting suddenly stopped. An enlarged white TVS logo appeared and above it the line, "Farewell! We were disconnected from the broadcast." Soon after, the sign was replaced with the logo of a sports channel. Later on, the Press Ministry would say the channel had been terminated "in the interest of viewers."

Kara-Murza Jr. was shocked, but at least now he knew one thing for certain. In three days, when the time would come to get his Cambridge diploma (a "double first") and to kneel at the throne in the Senate Hall in a hood of black-corded silk lined with white silk, both of his parents would be there. His father, who was always busy with the three shows he hosted on TVS and had been reluctant to promise he could attend the ceremony, now could definitely come to Cambridge.

On that lovely, sunny day in dreamy medieval Cambridge, the Kara-Murzas, senior and junior, both knew that the time had come to face some cold facts. Kara-Murza Sr. would never work in Russian mainstream media again. That period of Russian history—and of his life—was over.

When Boris Jordan had first taken command of NTV, he had canceled the station's top satirical show, which featured *kukly* (puppets), one of which was a caricature of Putin. The last program TVS aired before being shut down was another show focused on political satire and hosted by Vladimir Kara-Murza Sr. It marked the very last time the Russians would see political satire on their TV screens. Such programming was clearly not acceptable anymore.

A short time later, Gusinsky offered Kara-Murza Sr. a job at the Moscow bureau of his RTVI channel. Kara-Murza understood that he would no longer be reaching a Russian audience, but he took it. And in December, Kara-Murza Jr. lost his election, and his party didn't make it into the parliament. Apparently there was no room left in the country for either his ambitions or for his father's.

In February 2004, Kara-Murza Jr. followed in his father's footsteps and joined RTVI. On his first day on the job, a bomb exploded at the front door of the apartment occupied by well-known Russian journalist Elena Tregubova. She had just published a revelatory book about the Kremlin. Among many juicy stories was one about her rendezvous with Putin in a Japanese restaurant that seemed more like a date than a meeting. The book immediately became a bestseller. It also angered Putin. An interview with Tregubova recorded on NTV was taken off the air. And now her apartment had been bombed.

The police cordoned off the building and effectively locked Tregubova inside it. An RTVI editor told Kara-Murza Jr. it was his story to cover. He was given a TV crew and sent to Tregubova's. He found her home phone number and called her. He called many times, each time speaking in his fast, exaggeratedly polite manner. Finally, he talked her into slipping behind the policemen's backs to come out to the street and give him an interview. She did, and he got his story.

A few days later, Kara-Murza Jr. got a call from Gusinsky's top lieutenant. He was offered a new job: launch and then head a new RTVI bureau in Washington, DC. Kara-Murza Jr. readily accepted. In two months he moved to a country he had never lived in before.

Gusinsky's RTVI became the most popular television broadcasting network for the Russian audience abroad—much more popular than the radio stations the US government had launched at George Kennan's instigation—and it emerged at the very moment when the number of Russian-speaking people outside Russia dramatically increased. People kept leaving Russia, but they also were now leaving the former Soviet republics, including the Baltics, where everybody still spoke and understood Russian. There was also a substantial audience of Russian speakers in Eastern Europe and the huge community in Israel.

But Gusinsky's channel lacked funding to become truly international television. It was, essentially, a startup funded mostly from Gusinsky's pockets. And despite Gusinsky's energy and determination, it could not survive long with that level of funding. The big opportunity to create a major media outlet for the Russian emigrants (and, with the advent of internet, for the audience inside the country, too) was missed.

Boris Jordan had played a disruptive role for Russian television. The NTV takeover operation had so split the community of journalists that when Putin turned on Jordan, nobody came to his or the channel's defense. Jordan fell victim to the game in which he had been an eager player, but there were other, much more important victims as well.

Boris Jordan lost the game on one of his chessboards; Vladimir Putin, personally, had turned the board upside down. The Russian president's intense suspicion, instilled in him during his career as a KGB officer, that an uncontrolled media undermined his authority was simply too strong to beat. As a good investor, Jordan knew the rules: one needs to be on good terms with Putin to stay successful in Russia. Jordan needed to repair their relationship and quickly.

Jordan had another game going. It was a big game and a tricky one; although riskier than NTV, it could help him win back Putin's trust. That game included exploiting his connections in the United States, in the Russian émigré circles where his family was widely respected. If he were successful, he would deliver a precious gift to the Russian leader, something no one in the Kremlin had even dreamed of being able to attain.

CHAPTER 24

COURTING THE WHITE CHURCH

Before the revolution, the church in Russia had always been closely connected to the Russian state. Its borders matched the borders of the Russian empire, and the Russian tsar was the head of the Orthodox Church. The revolution changed this relationship dramatically. Two churches emerged—one in Moscow, under control of the Communists, known as the Red Church, and one launched in Europe and then in the United States, called the White Church. The latter was officially known as the Russian Orthodox Church Abroad and became the church of the Russian emigration. The White Church was the first truly globalized Russian institution with parishes extending from France, Germany, and England to the United States. The White Church also embodied the idea of the "other Russia," that of the intellectuals, artists, industrialists, writers, and officers; of an elite uncompromised by cooperation with the Communists. The other Russia was an imaginary, inchoate, ultimately unrealizable vision of the country but a very appealing idea, even for many who lived in the realm of the Red Church.

Putin wanted one united Russia. He didn't like alternative versions.

* * *

When Putin had visited the United States in November 2001, things had started out swimmingly. He had met with Bush at the White House, been welcomed warmly by the US Congress, and anticipated enjoying himself at the Bushes' Texas ranch. But before he left Washington for Texas, something occurred that he found profoundly frustrating—something the Kremlin had not foreseen.

On November 14, the Russian embassy had thrown a large reception, inviting more than 250 people, to honor the new Russian president. The crème de la crème of American business came to the white-marble Russian embassy to hear Putin, along with prominent Russian émigrés—including artists, writers, and athletes. In the marble and glass Golden Hall of the embassy, framed by gold curtains and two walls of dreadful panels—one set depicted the capitals of fifteen Soviet republics and the second fifteen Russian cities, all on gold backgrounds and all drawn in the primitive, overoptimistic style common to children and Soviet official art of the 1970s—a long line formed to talk to Putin. The first to reach him were the leaders of the Jewish community.

They seemed to like Putin a lot. "The eyes of the American Jewish leaders have opened. They shine! They did not believe that in Russia now there is such a man—Vladimir Putin," exclaimed chief Russian rabbi Berel Lazar, who was ordained at the Central Lubavitch Yeshiva in New York and who had lived in Moscow since 1990.[1] Indeed, Rabbi Lazar was so excited that he promised to lobby for the cancellation of the Jackson-Vanik Amendment. That piece of legislation sanctioned the countries that did not allow the free emigration of Jews and was still law, although not in use anymore. Russia had been determined to be in full compliance with Jackson-Vanik every year since 1994.[2]

"I liked him," said Ernst Neizvestny, a sculptor who had left the Soviet Union in 1976 and lived in New York.

"What a speech! How many thoughts! Especially that part that everyone should unite," added Slava Fetisov, a former legendary defenseman of Soviet ice hockey. His brave and public fight for the right to emigrate to play for the National Hockey League in the United States made world headlines in the late 1980s. He succeeded and won the Stanley Cup playing for the Detroit Red Wings and was now an assistant coach with the New Jersey Devils.

Putin enjoyed this gathering much more than he had the World Congress of Compatriots, held just a month earlier in Moscow's Hall of Columns. The people who came to greet him now, at the Golden Hall of the Russian embassy, really mattered.

But Putin had expected another important guest to come. The Kremlin had asked the Russian embassy to pass on an invitation to His Eminence the Most Reverend Metropolitan Laurus, the head of the White Church. Putin wanted to meet Laurus to invite him to come visit Russia.

Whereas the first Russian president, Yeltsin, hadn't known much about the religion, Putin made it known from the beginning that he was deeply religious. He also didn't hesitate to use his religion as a tool to win the trust of world leaders. At his very first meeting with Bush in June 2001, Putin told the American president a story about how he'd saved the Orthodox cross his mother gave him from a fire in his dacha. The story so resonated with Bush that he famously told the press after that meeting, referring to Putin, "I was able to get a sense of his soul, a man deeply committed to his country and the best interests of his country."[3]

Still, this was a personal matter for Putin. Officially, the church in Russia has been separated from the state since the Bolshevik Revolution, and the collapse of the Soviet Union hadn't changed things. Strictly speaking, it was not Putin's call to invite a church leader to the country.

The Orthodox Church in Moscow was very sensitive about visits to Russia by the heads of other churches. The Russian Orthodox Church treats Russia as its territory—70 to 80 percent of Russians profess to be Orthodox—and jealously guards it from competitors.[4] Pope John Paul II spent years trying to get invited to Russia but failed. The relationship between the Orthodox Church in Russia and the White Church was even more strained. The two churches were like close relatives who not only did not trust one another but who each suspected the other of downright treachery.

There was a lot of bad blood between the two churches. The White Church was founded in May 1919 by a motley group of hierarchs of the Orthodox Church who, horrified by the Bolsheviks' advance, had fled Moscow for territory controlled by the White army. When the Bolsheviks' Red army besieged and stormed Crimea, the last holdouts of the White army evacuated the priests along with the troops to Constantinople. The last commander in chief of the White army, baron Pyotr Wrangel, decided not to disband the troops but rather to maintain the army in exile. The priests made a similar decision. They formed the Russian Church Abroad, the White Church, to serve the army in exile. As it happened, the officer corps, which still had a strong aristocratic element, would always have a decisive say in the church's affairs.

In 1921, the White Church established its headquarters in Serbia along with many of the Russian émigrés. When World War II broke out, those Russians stayed in Serbia under German occupation. Toward the end of the war, in the face of approaching Soviet troops, the church heads, along with masses of émigrés, fled to Germany and reached the American occupation zone. In 1951, the church leaders moved to the United States. They put down roots in New York and stayed there.

The descendants of the first wave of emigration and the White Church stayed close. That proved true for many prominent families, including Boris Jordan's.

The Jordans, a Russian aristocratic family, went through a lot after the revolution. Just like the church's leadership, they settled in Serbia. While Boris Jordan's grandfather became a leader of a local Russian community there, his position was a mere shadow of the status he'd enjoyed in Russia, where his wife had served as a maid of honor under the empress and could go every day to the Winter Palace in St. Petersburg.

Sticking to traditions, Boris's father, Alexei, went to the Whites' Cadet Corps. He joined the Russian Protection Corps, a Wehrmacht unit, when the Germans invaded Serbia. By the end of the war, the Jordans fled to Germany and eventually moved to the United States. There, Alexei went to banking. He remained close to the church; for decades, he had helped the White Church handle its finances.

When Boris, Alexei's son, went away in the early 1990s to make big money in the new capitalist Russia, he remained close to his father, and his affiliation with the White Church remained important to him.

The White Church, although never very large or wealthy, could always count on the support of the Russian aristocracy in exile, including the Galitzines and the Jordans. Many Russian émigrés shared mistrust and contempt for the Red Church.

After the revolution, the atheist Communists had attacked the priests who had remained and destroyed most of the churches in the country. Humiliated and devastated, the church was forced to recognize and adapt to Soviet rule. Later on, the Kremlin eased the repression but still kept the church under firm control. For seven decades, the White Church considered the church in Moscow to have been largely corrupted by its cooperation with the Soviet authorities. It believed, rightly, that the KGB had penetrated the Moscow organization at every level.

The Orthodox priests in Moscow, in turn, looked at the White Church with a mix of suspicion and envy. After all, the White Church was the single ideological institution that united the millions of Russians living abroad, from Australia to Canada to the United States to Europe. And it was completely out of reach of the priests in Moscow.

It didn't help that the two churches were very close to one another spiritually and, at times, geographically. In New York, the Red Church was (and is) headquartered in St. Nicholas Cathedral, a Russian-style church with seven domes above a dark redbrick facade trimmed with limestone, squeezed between two four-story apartment buildings on East Ninety-Seventh Street. The White Church's headquarters were (and are) located a mere seven-minute walk away, at the corner of Park Avenue and East Ninety-Third Street, in a redbrick and limestone mansion.

Vladimir Putin, an ex-KGB officer visiting Washington, took an unprecedented step: he invited the head of the White Church to the Russian embassy—his territory. It was not just a polite gesture. Putin wanted to meet Laurus to bring him over to his side. More than that, he wanted to take over the "other Russia."

Laurus chose not to come to Putin's reception in Washington, nor did he accept Putin's invitation to visit Russia.[5] It became clear to Putin that he needed a subtler approach to this sensitive matter. Perhaps a gentle push by someone inside to urge the church to come to terms with Moscow. But who was in position to act as go-between and push the church?

He found this person in Boris Jordan. Jordan had proved himself useful with the NTV just half a year earlier—even if things hadn't gone so well in the end—and he wanted to stick around. The president met with him at a one-on-one meeting in Moscow. They had a long conversation about many topics—Putin was very interested in Jordan's family story.[6] Then the topic of reunification was raised.[7]

"I understand that you're involved with the church, that you're a religious person," the president—a former officer of the Soviet secret police—said to the Russian American financier, a descendant of an officer of the White army who had fled with his family from the Soviet secret police. Putin continued: "I believe that the reunion of the churches is a very, very important thing. One of the most important things you can do, much more important than anything you're doing in television or business, is to help in the reunification of the churches."[8]

Jordan was excited. Personally, he didn't have any problem with Putin's origins in the Soviet secret police. "He was a chekist, yes, but that doesn't mean he is bad. He is a religious person, close to the church. I support him because I saw what happened while he has been president—he got more people out of poverty than any Russian leader before him. And look, these days, you can see the icons in the offices of the heads of secret services," he told us.

Jordan was ready to invest his personal prestige in the reunification of the churches.

Now he needed a proper battle plan.

CHAPTER 25

REUNION

The small resort town of Sea Cliff, twenty-five miles east of Manhattan on the North Shore of Long Island, became home to many White Russian emigrants, including the Jordans. The first Russian families arrived in the 1930s, and the community of Russians continued to grow steadily. The Russians built several tiny churches topped with onion domes where their children learned the language and religion on Fridays and Saturdays, and Russian was often spoken on the streets. In the 1970s, when Boris Jordan grew up, there were still people alive in Sea Cliff who remembered how they had been thrown out of their homes by Bolsheviks.[1]

Now Boris Jordan needed to convince his neighbors, who had never forgotten where they came from, that they could pray alongside the Russian president from the KGB.

Jordan obviously needed some help.

In the 1990s, while Boris was busy making his fortune in Russia, his father had traveled across the United States giving lectures about Russian army traditions before the revolution. That was why Alexei Jordan had been invited to Putin's World Congress of Compatriots. He thoroughly enjoyed the attention of the Russian military. All of a sudden, his family had once again become important in the motherland.

When Boris Jordan set off to promote the idea of the union of the churches, his father, although seriously ill by then, stepped in to help. In August 2002 he wrote a letter to Laurus asking him to consider the union with Moscow. Half an hour after he had finished the letter, he died.

Alexei Jordan's letter had no immediate effect. So Boris Jordan flew to New York, visited Metropolitan Laurus in his monastery, and during a long conversation tried to convince him to meet both Moscow's Patriarch Alexy II and Putin.[2]

But months passed, and the progress was slow.

What was needed was someone from the White Church who was ready to push from inside. As it happened, there was such a person in Laurus's entourage—one Peter Holodny, a priest and treasurer of the White Church.

Everybody in the Russian community knew that Holodny was pro-reunification. In fact, his grandfather, a prominent priest, had been expelled from the White Church for cultivating a close personal friendship with Moscow's patriarch and, in the 1990s, moved to Russia, where he died. Holodny chose the career of financier, working in the late 1980s and early 1990s at JP Morgan, First Boston, and Lehman Brothers. In 1993 he was picked by the White Church to be treasurer for his financial talents. Quite conveniently, he was also ordained as a priest.

Like Boris Jordan, Holodny had spent years in Russia and was privy to the Russian financial world. And since 2000, he had combined his priesthood with work for the Russian oligarch Mikhail Prokhorov, who, as it happened, was also on friendly terms with Boris Jordan. Here was a new opportunity for achieving Putin's goal.

In September 2003 Putin returned to New York. This time his goal was not to win George W. Bush's trust but to advocate for Russian companies by discussing the American president's most controversial project: the war in Iraq.

Putin stayed at the Waldorf Astoria, where he played world leader, meeting five heads of foreign governments in a row.[3] He also delivered a speech at the UN General Assembly. That didn't go very well—no journalists other than the Russians brought from Moscow came to listen to him.[4]

Putin also tried once again to arrange a meeting with Metropolitan Laurus. Once again, Laurus was invited to talk on Putin's territory—at the Russian consulate in midtown Manhattan. This time, Laurus did meet the Russian leader.

Laurus walked into the consulate accompanied by five priests. One of them, the youngest, dressed in bright blue among the rest in black, was thirty-nine-year-old Peter Holodny, treasurer of the White Church and Laurus's chief negotiator.[5] The priests were ushered into a large hall trimmed with white and gold panels, lit by massive chandeliers. A grand piano was in the corner, and next to it, an oval table was set for a meal so as to make the meeting look less formal.

Holodny had been entrusted with carrying a gift to the Russian president—a massive icon of the last Russian empress Alexandra, killed by chekists. If the gift was intended to send a message to Putin, Putin knew how the game was played. "I want to assure all of you that this godless regime is no longer there," he said at the meeting, although after he returned to Moscow, he ordered the erection of a monument to Yuri Andropov, the longest-serving chairman of the KGB and a celebrated chekist.[6] "You are sitting with a president who is himself a believer," Putin pressed.[7] The priests listened intently.

The meeting lasted more than three and a half hours and ended on a high note: Laurus accepted Putin's invitation to come to Russia. Laurus also made it clear that he was ready to talk to the Red Church. The ground was prepared.

Now it was time for the two churches to talk business. In two months, five priests—including four who had attended the meeting with Putin in New York, Holodny among them—flew to Moscow. On arrival, they were brought to Sretensky Monastery, in the Lubyanka District, a stone's throw from the KGB headquarters. They were greeted by Tikhon Shevkunov, Putin's designated negotiator, known for his anti-Western views.

Shevkunov's standing within the Red Church was officially modest; he had nothing to do with the department of the church that handled diplomacy. But he happened to be the abbot of the monastery—a church and collection of chaotically spread three-story buildings behind a low wall—strategically located in the corner of Bolshaya Lubyanka Street and Rozhdestvensky Boulevard.

In the mid-1990s, many FSB officers became religious, and they ended up going to Shevkunov's monastery. They were met by a young, easygoing, well-versed priest who talked about religion using modern language—Shevkunov was a screenwriter by training. Soon Shevkunov was on friendly terms with many generals, including Putin, whom he had known since 1996.

The relationship between the church and the security services improved dramatically in the early 2000s and proved mutually beneficial.[8] Just the year before, the FSB had expelled five prominent Catholic priests from Russia, helping the Orthodox Church to protect its territory against what it saw as Catholic expansion.

Shevkunov showed the five priests from New York around the monastery. He walked them to the monastery's church, where the liturgy included a prayer for the health of the heads of the two churches. Finally, he invited the visitors to breakfast at his office in the abbot's modest building.[9]

The five priests brought with them a list of talking points addressing property issues, the legal status of the White Church, and personnel policy—for example, who would get positions in strategically located parishes and who would have a say in these appointments. It was a long and successful conversation. Later there would be a meeting with the Moscow patriarch, followed by a series of meetings with church hierarchs. But in that spacious room on the second floor of the abbot's mansion, its windows overlooking the quiet Moscow courtyard, the six priests in black came to terms regarding how best to lead the two Russian Orthodox churches to reunification.

The next item on Putin's agenda was to get Metropolitan Laurus to come to Russia. In spring 2004, accompanied by Peter Holodny, Laurus made the first official trip. He was given a reception fit for a head of state. The visit was reported by the biggest Russian state media. Putin received him, along with Moscow's patriarch, in his residence at Novo-Ogarevo. All went well—and then something completely unexpected happened.

On July 9, Evgeny Kiselev was sitting with his friends at a restaurant in the Barvikha Luxury Village, a luxury brands shopping mall in Rublyovka, known as Russia's Beverly Hills, when Boris Jordan rushed to his table. It was their second encounter after Jordan's security guards had thrown Kiselev's team out of their NTV offices. The first time they'd run into one another after the ouster, the ever-jovial Jordan had pretended they were good friends. Now he was uncharacteristically serious. "Evgeny!" Jordan exclaimed. "Paul Klebnikov has been killed. Do you know who killed him?"[10]

Paul Klebnikov, an American journalist and a founding editor of *Forbes Russia*, had been gunned down on the street when he left the *Forbes* offices in the east of Moscow. Like Jordan, Klebnikov had been born into an aristocratic Russian family in the United States, and the two men, who were roughly the same age, had known each other for twenty years.

It was a high-profile assassination. Klebnikov was a well-known and widely respected investigative journalist both in the United States and in Russia, where he had spent years investigating and exposing criminal connections of Russian oligarchs.

Although Putin had downplayed the assassinations of Russian journalists more than once, he didn't downplay this one. He made a point of personally condemning the crime.[11]

Jordan was in deep shock. "We all felt, including Paul, that they're no longer hiring assassins in Russia, they're hiring lawyers to settle their disputes," he said to the *Washington Post*. "The fact is, that doesn't seem to be the case."[12]

The Klebnikovs had been very religious, and a question arose about where to have a memorial service for Paul. The Klebnikovs were parishioners of the White Church in New York, but they had also occasionally gone to St. Nicholas Cathedral, the seat of the Red Church, on East Ninety-Seventh Street. They were on friendly terms with all main drivers of the reunification from both churches. Everything about Paul's death suddenly became political and high profile.

Tikhon Shevkunov, always energetic and a quick thinker, wasted no time. First, he brought Klebnikov's body to his monastery and organized an overnight vigil for him. Second, he arranged a memorial service for him at the Christ the Savior Cathedral.[13] The Soviet authorities had destroyed the original cathedral, built to celebrate the Russian military victory over Napoleon, and put a huge swimming pool in its place. In the 1990s, Christ the Savior was built anew to signify that Russia was reclaiming its religious identity. The resurrected cathedral started to play the same spiritually symbolic role for the Red Church that St. Peter's Basilica in Rome did for Catholics.

Klebnikov's coffin was put on display in the grand hall of Christ the Savior. Tikhon Shevkunov held the service, with Holodny in attendance. Then Klebnikov's body was transferred to New York, and a second memorial service was held at St. Nicholas Cathedral—that is, in the Red Church.[14] It was a very powerful message for the Russian émigré community in the United States.

At this point, the reunification project still lacked the White Church congregation's official approval. For that, the Kremlin and the White Church had to wait for two more years.

In May 2006, the White Church gathered for conference in San Francisco.[15] Boris Jordan personally helped fund the conference and was given a chance to speak. He urged the conference to approve the reunification. "It was my personal thing. I was personally interested in making it happen," he told us. After four days of debate, the conference voted for reunification.

On May 17, 2007, the two churches signed the accord, known as an Act of Canonical Communion, in an elaborate ceremony at Christ the Savior Cathedral in Moscow—where Shevkunov held a service for Klebnikov three years earlier. Jordan was present at the ceremony.

Prominent figures of the Russian first wave of emigration, including Vladimir Galitzine, the retired vice president of the Bank of New York and now leader in Russian American aristocratic circles, voiced approval of this news. They had similarly voiced approval two years before, when the remains of a renowned commander in chief of the White army and of Ivan Ilyin, a chief philosopher of the White movement, were transferred to Moscow.[16] This operation was also funded by Boris Jordan.[17]

The entire reunification project, from beginning to end, took Putin six years. During this same period, Putin was also busy crushing his opposition inside Russia, attacking media freedom, and promoting former and current KGB members to important positions—effectively making them the new nobility of the country.[18]

The Russian president's successful absorption of the White Church essentially nullified the "other Russia."

Why was this move of Putin's so readily accepted by the descendants of the first wave of the émigré community? We have asked ourselves this question dozens of times. They should have detested his KGB past and been suspicious of his use of Soviet symbols—a practice that included the reintroduction of Stalin's hymn, with the words just slightly changed.

The only theory we have come up with is that the descendants of the White Russian émigrés shared something with Putin. In the course of his career, the Russian president repeatedly demonstrated his excellent tactical skills—in particular, his understanding of what made particular Western politicians tick—but strategically, he lived in the nineteenth century. The bon mot coined by Tsar Alexander III in the late nineteenth century, that "Russia has just two allies, the armed forces and the navy," resonated deeply with Putin. (Indeed, Putin was present at the 2017 opening ceremony of a monument to this tsar in Crimea that had these very words inscribed on it.[19])

The descendants of the first wave of Russian emigration remained, institutionally and personally, stuck in the memories of the glorious imperial past. They were naturally given to this nineteenth-century thinking. And seven years after the Act of Canonical Communion, Putin's imperial message after his annexation of Crimea would be enthusiastically received by many Russians abroad.

This commonality provided a deep emotional bond—one that Putin exploited to the full.

In November 2018 in an Italian restaurant on Bolshaya Ordynka, in the historical center of Moscow, priest and financier Peter Holodny was sipping his tea. He was a tall, thin man with a bony face and gray hair cut short, wearing a white shirt under a dark sweater. He made it crystal clear: he didn't want to talk for the book we were writing. He brought his grown son with him to the meeting, probably as a witness.

"Forgive me for not being as naive as I used to be. You have an ambiguous reputation, and you have powerful enemies," he said. He was referring to the FSB, the Russian security service. "Now you want to write about the reunion. I'm telling you—there was no money, no one bribed anyone, there was no coercion."

Nobody had asked him about money or coercion.

Then Holodny started talking about Putin. "Vladimir Vladimirovich, with him there is so much freedom for a Russian man, more than ever before!"

He became emotional and waved his hands. As he did, one could see his cufflinks—they were in the colors of the Russian flag. Twenty minutes passed. It was clear that the meeting was over, then all of a sudden Holodny asked, "So, what do you think about the Skripal case?" He was referring to the poisoning earlier that year of a Russian former spy living in England.

It was clear that the story of a Russian poisoned in the West worried him greatly.

PART IV

MEANS OF OUTREACH

CHAPTER 26

POLITICAL EMIGRATION: RESTART

The 1990s were the first decade in Russian history in which there was no political emigration.

The long tradition of Russian political exiles being forced to live out the remainder of their lives in the West was broken for the first time in 1991, when Mikhail Tolstoy forced the KGB to let émigrés who had been thrown out of the Soviet Union return to Russia. With that, Russian political emigration of the Soviet era effectively ended. In Yeltsin's Russia, people might leave the country because of the problems with the Kremlin, but they always returned. Yeltsin didn't banish his enemies from the country.

Putin, however, did.

In May 1999 Yeltsin's chief of staff summoned media magnate Vladimir Gusinsky to the Russian White House on Krasnopresnenskaya Embankment for a little talk. The Kremlin official explained clearly that Yeltsin wanted a safe, predictable presidential election come March 2000. Gusinsky's freewheeling NTV could jeopardize that. The Kremlin wanted Gusinsky to leave the country and to stay out of Russia for roughly ten months. The government would compensate him for his trouble. "We can help you with all your debt problems," Gusinsky was told. Then the official added, "We are even prepared to give you 100 million US dollars if you will just leave the country until the presidential election."[1]

In May 1999 Yeltsin was still the president—the game was not over. So Gusinsky refused.

Things stayed as they were. The Kremlin team prepared the country for the forthcoming election, and Gusinsky's media companies continued to operate as they had been doing, independently from the Kremlin.

That summer Yeltsin named the new Russian prime minister: Vladimir Putin, promoted as a Russian strongman dealing with separatists and terrorists. Meanwhile, NTV remained to provide critical coverage of the hottest political topic of the day—the Russian war effort in Chechnya.

Putin won the presidential elections in March 2000 and took the oath of office on May 7. Two months later, in the course of the Kremlin's NTV takeover, Gusinsky was imprisoned and "encouraged" to sell his media assets in return for his freedom. After three days in jail, Gusinsky was released and allowed to leave the country. He fled to London and exile.

The period of absence of political emigrants proved to be a very short one in Russian history. It lasted nine years, just a split second by historical standards. Now it was over.

Vladimir Putin had been running the country for less than a year when two more prominent people fled to the West. Former FSB officer Alexander Litvinenko, a blond, fit man in his late thirties with strangely light eyes bearing no expression, flew to London with his wife and a son, in fear for his life. He was soon joined in London by the Russian oligarch Boris Berezovsky.

Berezovsky, a middle-aged, round-shouldered man with receding hair and lively brown eyes, was a powerful oligarch and a familiar face to everybody in Russia. He was on the front pages of the newspapers, on the covers of magazines, and on TV screens. Berezovsky might meet with top Kremlin officials on Monday, warlords in rebellious Chechnya on Tuesday, and finish his week at a party with fellow oligarchs, and all of it would be covered by media.

A mathematician by training, Berezovsky was a born go-between. He made his first fortune in the early 1990s by becoming a middleman between the Soviet-era automobile manufacturing giant Avtovaz, organized crime that controlled the car dealer networks, and ordinary Russians trying to buy a car. He achieved political prominence when he placed himself as a middleman between the Russian oligarchs and Yeltsin. But he learned well that to be an effective go-between, there need to be two groups with two well-defined positions to navigate in between.

The Kremlin was such a group, but the oligarchs were not. Each rich and powerful man in the "new Russia" had different interests, priorities, and ambitions. So Berezovsky put a lot of effort into shaping the oligarchs into a unified group with a shared political agenda. He turned his club/office—a fancy one-story late nineteenth-century mansion in the historical center of Moscow on Novokuznetskaya Street—into a meeting place where Russia's wealthiest people could discuss issues and forge consensus positions that Berezovsky could later represent to the Kremlin. To make the oligarchs look more cohesive to the public, he told the *Financial Times* in 1996 that a group of seven people made most of the decisions in Russia. He provided the list of names of the people who would become known as the Big Seven Bankers,[2] claiming that together they controlled more than 50 percent of the Russian economy.

In the late 1990s, he readily stepped in as a middleman in disputes between many parties, including the Kremlin and the Chechen separatists (Yeltsin made him deputy head of the Russian Security Council for that). When the time came to secure a transfer of power from Yeltsin to Putin, Berezovsky tirelessly toured the country to help Yeltsin's entourage obtain support from regional elites and oligarchs. As a result, many, including Berezovsky himself, believed that it was he who had given Putin his victory.

But soon after the election, Putin broke up with the oligarch. He didn't want to be dependent or perceived as dependent on anyone, especially on such an energetic and media-friendly character as Berezovsky.

Berezovsky was forced to leave Russia and chose London as his permanent address, joining Gusinsky and Litvinenko in the first post-Soviet wave of emigration. This wave would be joined by various other oligarchs who fell out with Putin and their clientele. But Berezovsky, still a very wealthy man in his early fifties, was not ready to go into a comfortable retirement.

A go-between by nature, he believed that he could play another game with the Kremlin. In London, he had no well-defined group with a shared agenda on whose behalf he could talk to the Kremlin, but this kind of obstacle never stopped Berezovsky. He immediately set off to create a group that would represent and define the political opposition to Putin abroad. Just as he had done in 1990s Moscow, he turned his office in a redbrick four-story mansion on Down Street, adjoining Piccadilly, into a meeting place for everybody who fell out of favor with Russia's president. He joined forces with Gusinsky in funding the TV channel RTVI aimed at the Russian-speaking audience abroad. He launched several news websites and published op-eds and stories critical of the Kremlin. By naming his own publication *Kolokol*, he consciously invoked the memory of Alexander Herzen, the most prominent Russian liberal in exile in the second part of the nineteenth century, and the censorship-free Russian periodical *Kolokol* (The Bell) that Herzen published in London.[3]

The Kremlin's propaganda quickly made Berezovsky an archenemy of Putin. Berezovsky was accused of plotting horrendous terrorist attacks in cooperation with the CIA and al-Qaeda and of committing high-profile murders, including the murder of journalist Paul Klebnikov. Documentaries were made and books published describing his crimes.

Apparently, this was not quite enough.

In December 2004, the blockbuster movie *Lichnyy Nomer* (meaning "dog tag" in Russian but titled *Countdown* in its English-language release) hit Russian cinemas. The movie provided a fictionalized account of two actual terrorist attacks: the 1999 Moscow apartment building bombings and the 2002 Dubrovka Theater siege. The portrayal of the events themselves was left largely unaltered except that the theater was replaced with a circus. But in the movie, an oligarch living in exile in the West is shown to have been colluding with the terrorists on a hostage-taking plan targeting the circus. The depiction of the treacherous oligarch bears a striking resemblance to Berezovsky.

Despite its $7 million budget, the movie was not a commercial project; it was an active measure by the Russian security services. The film was shot with the security services' support, and a deputy director of the FSB advised the film crew.[4] The main producer and author of the script was Yuri Sagaidak, a former KGB agent, journalist, and colleague of General Kobaladze, who headed the infamous SVR book project. Sagaidak was also the second man in Kobaladze's conversation with Evgeny Kiselev trying to lure him to Lubyanka during the hostile takeover of the NTV. The Kremlin, apparently, had a pretty short bench for sensitive operations. The film was a relative success and aired scores of times on Russian TV.

It was not Berezovsky but rather his friend Litvinenko who was hated the most at FSB headquarters in Lubyanka.

Litvinenko had made his mark serving in the Russian secret services' most corrupt department, which was in charge of taking down organized crime. The department often used brutal methods but was also tasked to interfere if the mafia attacked wealthy businessmen. That was how Litvinenko met Berezovsky. In the mid-1990s, before Putin's ascension, Litvinenko openly switched allegiance from his masters in the FSB to Berezovsky—a very unorthodox thing to do. Litvinenko became Berezovsky's best foot soldier in the FSB, with wide connections within the secret services. He also became the first Russian whistleblower from the post-Soviet secret services.

When Berezovsky got into trouble with the FSB, Litvinenko helped organize an incendiary press conference. At this press conference, he and several colleagues announced that FSB leadership had ordered them kill Berezovsky. The director of the FSB lost his job and was replaced by Vladimir Putin, who didn't like this kind of political game. Litvinenko was thrown into jail. Released at the end of 1999, he fled to the UK a few months later.

In London, Litvinenko remained close to his patron. His affection for Berezovsky was genuine. The former operative had humble family origins in a far-away region in the North Caucasus, had spent his life first in the barracks and then in Moscow dealing with gangsters, and had done time in the hotspots. He told us in London that the oligarch had opened his eyes to a new world of breaking the established rules. "He told me, there is always a line. To become truly free, you need to cross it; you need to step over the line."[5]

We met Litvinenko in 2003 on a rainy evening at Piccadilly Circus. When we arrived, Litvinenko was waiting for us at the corner in an oversized blue jacket, a dark shirt, and black slacks. He didn't have an umbrella, and it didn't bother him. "I'm a warrior. I can sleep on bare ground!" he exclaimed.

Although three years had passed since Litvinenko's escape from Russia and resettlement in London, he was still struggling to learn English and adjust to British ways. Berezovsky had continued helping Litvinenko financially, but the former FSB officer was trying to establish his own way of making a living by helping recent Russian émigrés get their money out of Russia. (Much later it was made public that he was also helping the British and Spanish secret services fight Russian organized crime.) He also kept publicly exposing the FSB, providing verifiable details and real names.

At the time, Berezovsky was seeking a flag, a theme to organize people around, to build up the Russian exile community. The apartment bombings in September 1999 in Moscow, which killed more than three hundred people and terrified the country, provided one. It was true that after the bombings, many Russians became more supportive of the Russian war effort in Chechnya, and it was Vladimir Putin who promised to find and kill terrorists. After the bombings Putin's popularity skyrocketed. But many others felt that the apartment bombings had not been properly investigated and suspected that they were, in fact, the work of the Russian secret services.[6] To Berezovsky, it was a story of Putin securing the presidency via a mass killing of fellow citizens, pure and simple.

In his office on Down Street, he welcomed anybody who could offer any information about the tragedy.

Berezovsky had a special assignment for Litvinenko. The former FSB officer had coauthored a book with a historian, a Soviet emigrant in the United States who worked for Berezovsky. The book, called *Blowing Up Russia*,[7] elaborated on the assertion that the apartment bombings had been organized by the FSB to propel Putin to power.

On November 1, 2006, Litvinenko was poisoned at the bar of the Millennium Hotel in central London. He died a few weeks later. The British determined that Litvinenko was poisoned with highly radioactive polonium-210 that had been put in his teapot by two Russian agents, one of them a former KGB officer, under the orders of the Kremlin. The assassination was straight out of the early days of the Soviet Union when the operatives of Stalin's secret service had fled to the West, published revelatory books, and ended up hunted down and killed by Stalin's agents.[8] It was textbook Nahum Eitingon.

*   *   *

Another presidential election came and went, and Putin stayed in power. Another election would be held in 2008. In April 2007, a now desperate Berezovsky announced his big plan to the *Guardian*: "There is no chance of regime change through democratic elections. If one part of the political elite disagrees with another part of the political elite—that is the only way in Russia to change the regime. I try to move that."[9] He added, "There are also practical steps which I am taking now, and mostly they are financial."

The FSB took him seriously. Lubyanka charged Berezovsky with conspiring to seize power and opened a large-scale criminal investigation. The secret service also harassed Luke Harding, a Moscow correspondent for the *Guardian* whose name was one of the three in the byline of Berezovsky's interview.[10]

Berezovsky had spent millions by then plotting in London, but it was Litvinenko who made the biggest impact on public opinion in Russia and the West. The English-language edition of his book was published posthumously that same month by Encounter Books, a politically conservative American publisher based in New York. Though criticized as a conspiracy theory, Litvinenko's allegations became part of the widely accepted narrative of Putin's rise to power. His poisoning and death gave his story in *Blowing Up Russia* all the more traction. Emigrant books worked once again.

Berezovsky's call for regime change had no impact on Russian society. The number of people unhappy with Putin's policies remained relatively small throughout most of the 2000s. In fact, they were being marginalized as an emerging middle class grew more and more comfortable under Putin. That middle class, and Russian businessmen, thought they understood the game—until Putin changed it.

CHAPTER 27

ILLUSIONS CRUSHED

Why did so many smart, Westernized, financially successful people feel so comfortable under Vladimir Putin in the first decade of the twenty-first century? The KGB had a horrifying reputation, and Putin never condemned the organization that defined him. On attaining the presidency, he immediately moved to suppress the media freedoms Russians had come to savor under Yeltsin. He put KGB people into top positions in government, and soon a number of businessmen started to be sent to jail.

And yet, many people remained supportive of his policies. They continued to like him. Why? That question tortured many Russian liberals in the 2000s.

The popular radio station Echo Moskvy, essentially a talk-radio outlet, had been a haven for liberals since the early 1990s. But over the next decade, Echo's hosts and their guests felt increasingly isolated from the rest of the country. Every year Putin tightened his grip on the political system, but few in the country seemed to care. The middle class in big cities enjoyed ever-growing prosperity secured by high oil prices. The economy was booming. Comfortable compounds popped up in suburbs, while new shops featuring trendy clothes opened in Moscow every month. Echo's editorial office was on the fourteenth floor of a high-rise with old elevators and Soviet-era wood-paneled walls, but below the Novy Arbat Highway was filled with brand-new cars. A mile to the west, a bunch of skyscrapers were rising in Moscow City, a new international business center for the Russian capital. Journalists felt they were losing touch with their audience.

To bridge the gap, Echo created an ongoing show called *One Family in the Times of Vladimir Putin*. The concept was to invite an ordinary family on air to talk about everyday life to try to understand what made them tick under Putin. In May 2007, the featured guests on the show were Ilya Zaslavskiy, a twenty-eight-year-old manager of the oil company TNK-BP—a highly profitable joint Russian-British venture—and his girlfriend, Veronika.

Soft-spoken, smiling Ilya was very sure of himself. Oxford-educated, he also held an American passport. His family was Jewish and had moved to the States in 2000, first to Connecticut, then to New York. Just a few years later, Ilya and his older brother Alexander returned to Russia when they saw opportunities to make money opening in Moscow. The best options, they thought, were in the area of gas and oil, so the brothers went into that business. Now Ilya enjoyed a good position at TNK-BP; he cleared the equivalent of more than $7,000 a month after taxes and rented a spacious apartment on Mayakovskaya, in the heart of Moscow. He had spent $12,000 producing an independent movie—about an oil trader—and was thinking of a career in the film business. Indeed, Ilya sounded like a poster child for Putin's economic boom.

A program host asked Zaslavskiy what he thought about the past seven years under Putin.

"Honestly, it's basically nonsense, the idea that your well-being depends on Putin or Yeltsin," said Zaslavskiy. He added, cheerfully, "Your well-being depends, if you don't live in an authoritarian country, more on you than on Putin."[1] He seemed to be under the impression that he was not living in an authoritarian country.

Less than a year later, in March 2008, Ilya Zaslavskiy was in his second-floor office in the posh brand-new TNK-BP building on Arbat when he got a call from his father. "Your brother has been arrested!" his father told him. "You need to get home now and deal with your computers and flash drives, just in case."

Ilya rushed out. But when he reached the street, three plainclothes operatives snatched him and threw him into a car—a Russian Lada with tinted windows.[2] They brought him to Lefortovo prison. They forgot to search him and failed to take his phone away, so he made a brief call to his father and warned him that he, too, was detained. Zaslavskiy was then brought to the small room on the second floor of Lefortovo where he was interrogated by an FSB officer. After hours of interrogation, he was taken to his apartment to see it thoroughly searched by FSB operatives.

He had learned that he and his brother were to be charged with industrial espionage.[3] Allegedly, they had tried to access some confidential information about a Russian state-controlled gas company, but Ilya already knew the case against them was just a pretext. The brothers Zaslavskiy found themselves at the center of a monumental battle over control of the highly profitable Russian-British joint venture, with the Russian secret service helping the Russian side by applying additional pressure on the British to squeeze them out. (This goal was ultimately achieved.)

The Zaslavskiys were just two small fish living in still, warm waters in a corporate aquarium. Then the moment came when the aquarium was smashed to pieces. Nobody cared about the brothers—the FSB didn't even bother to throw them in jail. It just used them as an excuse to raid the BP offices and harass top managers. After a while, Ilya and his brother were sentenced to one year of probation.

Ilya suddenly understood that his career and reputation had been destroyed by powerful forces—just like that—and his personal tragedy went completely unnoticed. Ilya's corporate bosses didn't stand by him.

It was time for him to say goodbye to illusions. But he didn't accept that he had been treated as a small fish by both the Russian state and the Russian oligarchs. He was not that kind of person.

Moscow 2005. The warm August day was perfect for a wedding. A bride in a beautiful white gown was standing by her tall groom, who looked solid and wealthy in a dark blue suit. They were a power couple—famous TV anchor Olga Romanova, thirty-nine years old, had a son and a daughter from a previous marriage, and financier Alexei Kozlov, age thirty-one, had a son—and they knew very well what they wanted from their marriage.

Olga, an attractive, sharp-tongued blonde, had grown up in a family of doctors in a working-class Moscow suburb. Her parents had sent her to a music school, obligatory at that time for girls from a good family, where she made headway playing piano. She also loved singing but not the classical music repertoire. Rather, she loved singing "gypsy" (Roma) folk songs she had learned from her neighbors in a nearby Roma district. Her parents did not encourage her friendship with the Roma, but they couldn't stop Romanova from having relationships with whoever she wanted.

In the early 1980s, she enrolled at the prestigious Financial University. Each day she traveled to Moscow by commuter train to attend classes. Often she rode home on the last train of the day, which was usually deserted, inviting trouble with hooligans wandering the cars. Romanova was not afraid of them. Many of her classmates had joined criminal gangs, and when a suspicious person approached her, she called out the names and nicknames of the most dangerous, implying she knew them. It usually worked well.

But she really wanted to have a car. Finally, her parents gave her one—a Soviet-made blue Lada sedan, which was quite a luxury gift for a girl in the Soviet Union. Her father, who didn't own a car or drive himself, started taking driving lessons along with her. He wanted to be able to lend her a hand with driving when she needed it. One day he was driving with an instructor and the car crashed, killing them both.

Her father's death made a lasting impact on Romanova. She blamed herself for having had the stupid idea to get a car and for letting her father learn to drive. It was in her nature to be accountable and to always accept responsibility for the part she played in things.

In 1989 Romanova was a young professional with a son from a short-lived student marriage. Her career developed fast; she worked as a financier at the Ministry of Trade and tried her hand at economic journalism, but she didn't know what to do next with her life.

Romanova was very sociable and made many friends at the ministry. One of them, a young lawyer, approached her with a surprising idea. He had just been offered a great job in New York. He was not married, and in 1989 that meant he was not allowed to work abroad. He offered Romanova a deal: marry him and move to New York, with no obligations. Romanova said yes. She still blamed herself for what had happened to her father. She decided to start from scratch.

In New York, a small apartment on the ground floor of a three-story building on Lexington Avenue was awaiting her. She did not even have to pay for it—her husband, who immediately left her on arrival, as they had agreed, took care of it—but she still had to make a living. She went to Brighton Beach and landed a job in a Russian-emigrant nightclub. Her job was to entertain guests before the star singer appeared on the stage. Her gypsy songs turned out to be very useful. But after more than a year of singing and waiting tables, Romanova felt she was going nowhere.

In August 1991 she learned there had been a KGB-orchestrated coup d'état in Moscow. She felt she had to get home, to be there at this uncertain time in the life of her country, so she boarded the next plane she could.

In Moscow, Romanova soon joined the liberal newspaper *Segod-nya* as chief economic observer. That kicked off her media career and, in a few years, landed her a job as a TV anchor. In the mid-2000s, it made her famous although still not financially secure. Alexei Kozlov was a man who would stand by her side. And for Kozlov, Romanova was a prestigious prize—one he had grabbed right from the TV screens of millions of Russians.

The wedding guests were from two different worlds. Kozlov was personable, serious, and very rich. His friends were rich too. Their wristwatches cost more than a month's salary for the journalists invited by Romanova. Under Putin, journalists had gradually been losing their social standing and were paid less and less.

Two older men circulating among the guests didn't belong to either group. They were bossy and frequently stood to offer loud toasts to the newlyweds. Kozlov had invited them because they had been crucial to his business career. Both were from the murky world of the secret services, but so had been his beloved grandmother Zoya Zarubina. In fact, Zoya Zarubina—daughter of Soviet spy Vasily Zarubin, stepdaughter of the brutally efficient operative Nahum Eitingon—had introduced Kozlov to the two bossy men in the first place.

Zarubina had taken care of Alexei since his childhood. His parents had separated when he was small, and he had struggled in relationships with both of them. His grandmother had stepped in gladly to fill their shoes, and she invited the boy to move into her spacious flat on Arbat in the center of Moscow. There he started meeting people like US ambassador Matlock and his wife, Rebecca, who were frequent visitors. When he would go out to buy bread in a shop around the corner, he often met members of Gorbachev's inner circle. Alexei grew up as a true golden boy who learned from childhood that he belonged to the elite, thanks to his grandmother's connections.[4]

He kept his room in his grandmother's apartment until he got married. It was an apartment with a distinguished history—Trotsky's assassin Ramon Mercader was a family friend and had dropped by regularly when Eitingon was alive.

. While the Soviet regime was falling apart, Zoya encouraged Kozlov to go to university rather than join the KGB. Always ambitious, Zoya was determined to help her beloved Alexei establish a career. In the 1990s, all ambitions in the city were centered on money and the West. Zoya got Alexei a part-time job as an interpreter with one of the first American banking delegations to come to Moscow. He became interested in banking, and she helped him go to the United States to study. She located a suitable USAID (US Agency for International Development) program, and off he went, to George Washington University, to study finance.

In 1996, Alexei returned. He wanted to have a career in banking in Russia, and now he had a specific dream: he wanted to make $1 billion by his fortieth birthday. He knew he had an advantage. The presence of KGB foreign intelligence officers was palpable in the Russian banking business.[5] And his grandmother happened to know just the right people.

Zoya introduced Alexei to a former KGB general who in 1991 had helped KGB chairman Kryuchkov draft his plans for the doomed coup d'état. In the 1990s, the general had a top-ranking position in a big Russian bank. Zarubina thought he could help with advice and cover her grandson's back. In Putin's Russia, it seemed, Soviet-era KGB family connections were just as relevant as they had been in Zarubin's time.

The general, son of a prominent Soviet spy himself, had admired Vasily Zarubin and was happy to help his family. The retired general-turned-banker became Kozlov's godfather in business and got Kozlov his first job at the bank. The unusually tall general proposed most of the toasts at Kozlov and Romanova's wedding.

The second guest, also an acquaintance of Kozlov's grandmother, was head of the SVR Foreign Intelligence training academy. For seven years, Alexei paid a stipend named after Zarubin to the most accomplished student at the Russian spy school. It was a smart investment. The head of the academy put Kozlov in touch with big shots in the economic department of the SVR. Kozlov speculated on Russia's foreign debts from time to time, and this game was always under the close watch of the SVR.

At age thirty-one, Kozlov already possessed a brilliant résumé: he had experience as a deputy CEO of a large Russian company and as the vice president of a well-known bank. He also had the backing of former and active generals in Russian foreign intelligence. What could possibly go wrong for a guy like Kozlov in Putin's Russia?

After the wedding, the couple set off for Kozlov's country house in Rublyovka. It was a big, brand-new, three-story mansion. Its garage was packed with an Audi A8, a Mercedes sports convertible, and a Lexus. It also had a swimming pool on the second floor, next to the hosts' bedroom, just as Kozlov had insisted. In the billiards room, Kozlov had two portraits on the wall. They were of his two great-grandfathers—Vasily Zarubin and Nahum Eitingon. The one of Eitingon irritated Romanova from the start. Her family, peasants in the Tambov region, had unhappy experiences with the Bolshevik repressions.[6]

But the portrait didn't darken Romanova and Kozlov's relationship. In a way, theirs was a perfect match: a famous and smart TV news anchor who happened to be on a first-name basis with plenty of Russian oligarchs and government officials and an ambitious young financier with the right connections to foreign intelligence. It seemed like a win-win combination for the kind of economic system Putin was building.

Romanova and Kozlov spent three years in the mansion at Rublyovka. Then things started falling apart. Kozlov was eyeing his dream of $1 billion, but he was getting reckless. Romanova suspected that he took a lover on the side.[7] He also fell out with his godfather, a retired KGB general.

By then, Kozlov worked at a large investment group run by a well-connected tycoon, a job his godfather-general had helped him land. The tycoon had just gotten himself a senate seat and left Kozlov to run his business.

The senator was twenty years older, much richer, and much more influential than Kozlov. A conflict broke out about a tannery in Moscow. The factory was not an issue, but the huge piece of land it occupied was worth tens of millions of dollars. The senator decided that Kozlov had tried to help his competitors take over the factory, and he had police investigating the case. Kozlov hadn't expected such a development.

On a sunny summer day in 2008, his career as a successful financier ended. The police came to the corporation's office. They arrested Kozlov and took away his phone. He kept a second burner phone, and in a crowded elevator, he found a way to make a brief call to Romanova. Kozlov was incarcerated in Butyrka, an old, dirty, crowded redbrick prison in the center of Moscow.

At that point, Romanova and Kozlov were on their way to divorce, but she still lived in Rublyovka. It was the mansion where she got Alexei's call. She went into the billiards room, looked at the portrait of Eitingon, and tore it off the wall.

Next she went to Butyrka to see Kozlov. He seemed to have lost weight, although only days had passed since his arrest. She made up her mind: She was his wife. She didn't want to fail another man in her life. As she had done many times before, she took responsibility.

It was a new, tough job for Romanova—coming to prison to see Kozlov. The prison authorities were reluctant to let her in, and she tried many pretexts. She soon found the most effective was to come disguised as a member of a Butyrka church choir. Kozlov declared his deep religious feelings that required him to make frequent visits to the prison's church.

She paid money for a better cell for Kozlov, for normal food for him, for a hot shower. She paid the expensive lawyers. But months passed, and nothing worked out. Kozlov stayed in prison.

Every time Romanova went to Butyrka, she met a long line of women—wives and girlfriends of inmates. One day she invited some women to her apartment to talk and to think about what could be done to help their men. They decided to fight for the rights of the imprisoned and formed a group. Romanova dubbed it Russia Behind Bars.[8]

She started with a small action. She taught women terrified and humiliated by the Russian prison system to put on a bright red dress when they went to court. The stunt worked in two ways: women lost their fear, and judges (usually women) began paying attention to the wives of prisoners.

She also convinced Kozlov to start writing a blog—named after Butyrka—detailing the harsh conditions of everyday life in Russian prisons. She asked her friends in the media to publicize it, and the blog soon became so popular that the prison's administration took notice.

Russian society took notice too. Romanova and Kozlov had successfully removed the stigma from public debate about prisons. All of a sudden it became clear that not only criminal outcasts but regular people fell victim to a prison system that was very little reformed since the days of Stalin's gulag. For Romanova and Kozlov, that was the first step.

By the end of the 2000s, the businessmen and the middle class—the very people who had prospered under Putin—started to emerge from a dangerous delusion and realized that just knowing and playing by the rules guaranteed nothing. Their jobs, their houses, even their freedom could be taken away swiftly. Their fate depended not on them, as Zaslavskiy put it at Echo Moskvy, but rather was at the mercy of the new, repressive regime.

In 2010 Ilya Zaslavskiy and his brother left Russia for the United States for good.

But he couldn't forget what happened to him. He had some plans forming in his mind. He was thinking about what could be done from abroad.

Meanwhile, some prominent opposition politicians were also thinking hard along the same lines.

CHAPTER 28

"WE NEED SOME TARGETED HITS"

By September 2011, Boris Nemtsov, Yeltsin's first deputy prime minister, was clashing openly with Putin. He published several reports, like "Putin: 10 Years" and "Putin: Corruption," that exposed Putin's corruption, and he went to anti-Putin protest rallies. If he had once been protected in any way by his status as a former high-ranking official, that was no longer the case. Earlier that year, he had spent fifteen days in jail for taking part in a rally against restrictions on public protests.

Nemtsov, a big, tall, powerfully built man, was always cheerful, with a ready joke and laugh. But he had come to think not much could be done about Putin's regime from inside. After the troubled 1990s, the more time that went by, the more the Russian people seemed to hate liberals. The Kremlin blamed them for all kinds of troubles the country had gone through after the collapse of the Soviet Union—from the upsurge of violent crime to economic downturns—and ordinary Russians seemed to accept that narrative.

The Kremlin also made sure that all attempts to launch a popular liberal political party or form any kind of liberal coalition failed. Nemtsov's party had lost its presence in the Russian parliament back in 2003, and the Kremlin was determined to further marginalize the opposition.

But the country was not isolated like the Soviet Union had been. Its borders were porous and Russia was globalized, as was the Russian elite—the oligarchs but also the highly placed officials, who had kids in British public schools, nice mansions abroad, and foreign bank accounts. Presumably they would not like to lose all that. And in theory, that made Putin's system vulnerable.

By 2011, Nemtsov had been working to prove this theory for four years.

His efforts began in December 2007 in a nineteenth-floor office in east Moscow. The occupant, former prime minister Mikhail Kasyanov, had also fallen out with Putin and was trying to find his place in opposition politics. In the room with Nemtsov and Kasyanov were Vladimir Bukovsky, a Soviet dissident and one-time head of the 1980s anticommunist organization Resistance International, and Vladimir Kara-Murza Jr., who had come from Washington for the meeting. They had been talking for hours about opposition strategy for the upcoming election when Nemtsov suddenly had an idea. "We should work on getting sanctions on the personal visas of important figures in Putin's political regime," he exclaimed. "These guys are in charge of repressions and falsifying elections, yet they want to enjoy Western ways, keeping their money in Western banks and their kids in Western schools." He paused, then quietly added, "We need some targeted hits."

The group thought about who might be targeted first in such an effort. Nemtsov suggested starting with Vladislav Surkov, Putin's gray cardinal. Surkov was the deputy head of Putin's administration in charge of dealing with political opposition. Surkov was believed to be behind most of the attempts to transform Russia into what he called a "sovereign democracy," a term coined by Surkov, meaning that democracy in Russia should have different rules from that of the world outside. These projects included creating pro-Kremlin youth organizations who could take to the streets to counter popular demonstrations. Some pro-Kremlin youth movements were devoted to activities like public burnings of books by liberal writers and displayed portraits of prominent human rights activists and opposition politicians defaced with swastikas in their summer training camps. One of those portraits was of Nemtsov.[1]

The idea was approved. It was the right moment to start in on Surkov. His pro-Kremlin activists were even now harassing the British ambassador for attending an opposition conference. Everywhere the ambassador went, he was met with posters of his face with the inscription "loser" drawn on his forehead and with screams and shouting.

British officials were receptive when Nemtsov and Kara-Murza Jr. approached them asking whether they should be letting Surkov come and go to London as he pleased to quietly enjoy his time there. As a result, Surkov was summoned to the British embassy in Moscow and told, very politely, to stop harassing the ambassador. Diplomatic staff hinted that if he persisted, he would not be allowed back into his beloved London. Surprisingly, despite Surkov's usual "don't give a damn" attitude, the tactic worked.[2]

The next year, Nemtsov's idea of visa sanctions got a surprising backer: American investor Bill Browder, a grandson of the one-time US Communist Party leader Earl Browder, who had been an agent of the Soviets and a comrade of Jacob Golos in the 1930s and 1940s. Bill Browder had been making good money in Russia since the 1990s as the head of an investment fund, but in 2005 he and the Kremlin had had a falling out. As a result, the Russian authorities started prosecuting his businesses. One of his employees, lawyer Sergei Magnitsky, was jailed and tortured to death in Butyrka prison. Browder had drafted and started to lobby the US Congress for passage of legislation to punish the Russian officials involved in Magnitsky's prosecution by banning them from traveling to or having assets in the United States.

At the end of 2010, Nemtsov went to Washington to talk to US senator John McCain. He brought Kara-Murza Jr. along with him to the meeting in the W Hotel, near the White House. Nemtsov had known McCain for years and trusted him as a fierce and determined critic of Putin.

Nemtsov and Kara-Murza explained to the senator that they wanted to expand Browder's legislative initiative to make it open. This meant including an option to add to the list of sanctioned people not only those who had played a role specifically in Magnitsky's tragedy but also any officials who violated the rights of Russian citizens. McCain was sympathetic, and Nemtsov returned to Moscow, leaving Kara-Murza Jr.—then head of the RTVI bureau in Washington—to continue lobbying in DC.

Kara-Murza sensed that getting involved in political lobbying could be perceived as undermining his journalistic integrity, but he believed that he was still ethically aboveboard. He didn't cover Russian politics as a journalist and reported only US news.

Kara-Murza got down to business in early 2011, at the start of the new congressional session. "From January to May, I went to the Congress almost every day. For four months I met people, explained why it was important," Kara-Murza told us. The Obama White House was not very supportive. The State Department didn't feel the need for special sanctions. It argued that the US government had already put a dozen Russian officials on the visa-ban list for human rights violations in the wake of Magnitsky's death, without having to enact new legislation.[3] But the names of these officials were not made public, and their assets were not frozen.

Another issue was sensitive when it came to formal legislation. Bill Browder, although he had renounced his American citizenship to obtain a British passport some time ago, had been born in the United States. But Nemtsov and Kara-Murza Jr. were Russian citizens, and now they were lobbying in the US Congress to change American policy toward Russia. They were not, as had been the case during the Cold War, Russian émigrés carefully selected by some

George Kennan initiative. They were activists and politicians from the country itself. For the very first time in history, the Russians had come to Washington, DC, to lobby for legislation that would, as Putin's officials made crystal clear in their conversations with their American counterparts, inevitably harm the US relationship with the Russian government. It made several US officials uncomfortable. Nevertheless, in May 2011, the new, expanded draft was introduced to Congress.

This initiative turned Nemtsov and Kara-Murza Jr. into major enemies of the Kremlin. The Russian authorities made no secret of the fact that they loathed Browder; he was portrayed on Russian TV as a thief and scoundrel and gradually replaced Berezovsky as archenemy number one, but still, he was a foreigner. Nemtsov and Kara-Murza were different—they were Russians.

Nemtsov understood the danger, but he raised the stakes even further when he made it personal. The day he was released from jail in late January 2011, Nemtsov told journalists that the West should cancel any sanctions against Russia as a whole but introduce sanctions against specific people: "This new list should begin with the name of Putin! Because this person, having a legal education, trampled and tore up the Russian Constitution and justice using his feet, hands, teeth, with particular cruelty and contempt."[4]

Throughout 2011, Nemtsov kept pushing for the sanctions, and in early September, he flew to Washington to help Kara-Murza Jr. on the spot. President Obama had just signed a proclamation that strengthened the State Department's authority to impose visa bans on people who participated in human rights violations. The State Department used it as a way to fight against the Magnitsky legislation.[5]

When Nemtsov returned home, he learned that a video had just been posted on YouTube showing a meeting that Nemtsov had held in a Washington, DC, coffee shop with an American rights activist and a Russian environmentalist. It was titled, "Nemtsov is getting instructions in Washington."[6]

It was not a popular video, and it was not widely used as propaganda by the Kremlin. Its intention was slightly different. It was addressed not to the public but to the opposition, and its message was, "You might be out of the country, but we are still watching you."

CHAPTER 29

DESPERATE TIMES

n late 2011, mass protests hit Moscow. People were angered by
Putin's decision to reclaim the presidency. He had already served
two full terms—supposedly the constitutional maximum. He had
then ostensibly "stepped aside" and supported his former campaign
chairman and supporter Dmitry Medvedev for the presidency, but
the new president immediately appointed him premier, in which
position he remained just as powerful as before. Now he was taking
the unprecedented step of "running" again, and "running" inevitably
meant winning. The public protests against his candidacy became
the first internal political crisis Putin faced as leader of the country.

Unlike his predecessor, Yeltsin, Putin never engaged in public
political competition and, even during election campaigns, never
took part in debates. Now the urban middle class, once so supportive of him, was chanting slogans demanding him to step down and
waving placards mocking him. In the face of such public spectacle,
Putin's charm seemed to dissipate overnight.

He didn't manage the crisis well. Month after month, people
kept taking to the streets. This scared him.

* * *

December is always a bad time to be in Moscow. Muddy snow covers the town, and the sun disappears for weeks.

On December 24, 2011, over a hundred thousand angry protesters gathered on the Sakharova Prospect, an eight-lane urban thoroughfare in the center of Moscow named after the famous Soviet dissident. Olga Romanova was onstage announcing the protest speakers—liberal journalists, opposition politicians, TV presenters, and a writer of popular thrillers.

Now people knew Romanova not as a TV anchor and journalist but rather as a public campaigner for her imprisoned husband and for the rights of other Russian inmates. She still appeared on TV frequently, but now she talked only about the terrible conditions in Russian prisons and violations in the penal colonies. Romanova had spent three years fearlessly fighting for her husband and, ultimately, was successful. Three months earlier, the Supreme Court decided to revisit Kozlov's case, and he was freed from prison during deliberations.

Right from the beginning of the protests, Romanova had a tricky role: to collect money. A proper protest needed a good sound system and big screens, not to mention a stage. Romanova was in charge of collecting money through Yandex.Money, the Russian version of PayPal.

She knew nothing about the technology of online fundraising. After his release, Kozlov stepped in to figure out the best way to raise money online. He didn't hesitate to become political—inspired not only by his prison stay but also by Putin's decision to return to the Kremlin. The Yandex account he and Olga registered became known as Romanova's purse. The system worked fairly well: to stage this protest rally on Sakharov Prospect, the organizers needed three million rubles, or about $100,000. In just four days, they had what they needed.

The hundred-thousand-strong protest rally on Sakharova Prospect was enough to scare Putin. He didn't understand why people had turned against him and strongly suspected an American conspiracy. He sent his personal friend, a former finance minister, to the stage to speak to the protesters and suggest that they were being duped. From where we stood in the crowd, he didn't sound convincing.

Putin was watching carefully. Many people who came onstage to address the crowd were completely unknown to him. The Kremlin had made a deliberate effort to marginalize the liberals and had been successful to a large extent. But a new generation had emerged with its own charismatic leaders and new ways of communicating.[1]

Two people onstage stood out to him. The first was Nemtsov, Yeltsin's deputy prime minister, tall, smiling, and handsome. The second was a short, energetic man in a peaked cap who spoke in a fast, agitated manner familiar to millions of Russians—Garry Kasparov, legendary world chess champion turned opposition activist. Kasparov had been involved in politics since 1990, and in the late 2000s, he and Nemtsov ran the opposition movement *Solidarnost* (Solidarity). Kasparov's speech that day was optimistic. "There are only a few of them [Putin's cronies], and they are huddling behind the police," he said. "They are scared because we have lost fear."

To the crowds on Sakharova Prospect, Kasparov was not the most popular speaker, but that hardly mattered to Putin. Back in November 1985, Kasparov, then a young chess genius, challenged the reigning Soviet champion, Anatoly Karpov, in a monumental battle broadcast live on Soviet television. Everybody knew that Karpov, who had the bland and unimpressive look of a government bureaucrat, was supported by the Communist Party and, by extension, the KGB. Putin's colleagues at the Soviet intelligence post in Dresden, Germany, viewed Kasparov as "an extremely impudent upstart."[2] But Putin, then a thirty-three-year-old Soviet intelligence officer, made it no secret that he favored the upstart. Kasparov won the championship and was a superstar while Putin was his modest fan. Twenty-five years later, when Putin became important, it looked like the idol from his youth was attacking him.

In March 2012 Putin won the election. No opposing candidate had effectively united the opposition. On May 7, Putin was inaugurated in a grand ceremony at the Kremlin, to which he was driven in a black Mercedes through empty Moscow streets cleansed of passersby.

Now safely in the Kremlin, he began his counteroffensive using the time-honored tactics of selective repression combined with squeezing troublemakers out of the country. The authorities commissioned more than two hundred investigators to prosecute protesters. The protesters tried to fight back and elected an opposition coordination council to represent all the anti-Putin political groups from liberals to nationalists, but it was a lost cause. With every rally, fewer and fewer people dared to come into the streets. The Kremlin kept sending protesters to jail, and dozens of political activists fled the country. Of thirty people elected to the opposition coordination council by direct vote, nine left the country and several found themselves in prison.

In March 2012 the court tried Kozlov a second time. He was found guilty again and thrown back into jail, where he would spend another year and a half. Romanova lost her temper and cursed the judge in the courtroom.

Vladimir Kara-Murza Jr. was a member of the opposition coordination council, although, as head of RTVI's Washington bureau, he was in the United States for most of the protests. But Putin believed the protests were backed by and even organized in Washington. And Kara-Murza was—not coincidentally, in Putin's mind—walking the corridors of the most powerful government institutions of the United States, lobbying for the imposition of sanctions against Putin's friends and associates. From time to time,

Nemtsov would fly to Washington to add more political weight to Kara-Murza's lobbying.

One sunny day, Kara-Murza Jr. and Nemtsov left the US Congress after another series of exhausting meetings about the sanctions. They decided to walk and enjoy the beautiful weather. As they walked along, a car abruptly stopped alongside them. A tinted window rolled down and a hand appeared, holding a camera pointed straight at them. They were openly under surveillance.

On July 12, 2012, the National Day of Russia marking Russia's official sovereignty from the Soviet Union, Kara-Murza Jr. drove to the Russian embassy on Wisconsin Avenue for a press briefing. As usual, he gave his name through the intercom and waited for a security guard to open the gate. A brief pause followed. Then a voice said, "You are banned from entering the territory of the embassy of the Russian Federation." Kara-Murza was puzzled. "Why? Could you give the reason?" he asked. But he was told that those were the orders.

Kara-Murza Jr. called a spokesperson. "Zhenya, what's going on?"

"Sorry, but this is straight from the ambassador. I can't do anything about it."

He called a journalist friend and asked her to call the embassy for an official explanation. The spokesperson explained that Kara-Murza Jr. had no right to enter the embassy because he was no longer a journalist at RTVI and therefore had lost his accreditation.[3] That was how Kara-Murza learned he had been fired—not from his bosses at the TV station but from the Russian ambassador Sergei Kislyak.

Only four months had passed since RTVI's founder, Vladimir Gusinsky, disenchanted and desperate, had sold the channel to a little-known individual whose previous experience in media was running a TV station for the Russian Ministry of Defense.[4] Now the TV channel Gusinsky had personally invested in so much to make it the global Russian voice, independent from Moscow, was firing a journalist in the United States, and the Russian embassy was the first to learn the news.

The next day, Kara-Murza was trying to wrap his mind around how he would now support his three young children, all of whom had been born in the United States. Nemtsov called from Moscow and told him that, according to his contacts, the Kremlin had had Kara-Murza blacklisted. No Russian media would hire him.

It was, effectively, a total professional ban.

If 2012 was a bad year for the Russian opposition, 2013 was going to be even worse. People didn't see the point of taking to the streets anymore, and the opposition coordination council dissolved itself. Protest leaders felt crushed and confused. Putin was in the Kremlin and supported by the majority of the country.

In February, Garry Kasparov decided that he would not return to Russia. The law enforcement agencies had started poking around, and he feared imprisonment. Kasparov settled in New York.[5]

The next month Boris Berezovsky died mysteriously at his multimillion-pound mansion, Titness Park, near Ascot in Berkshire, England. A bodyguard found the Russian oligarch's lifeless body lying on the floor of a locked bathroom with a ligature around his neck. It remains an open question whether Berezovsky took his own life or if somebody helped him.[6]

His death effectively marked the symbolic end of the first wave of political emigration under Putin. Concentrated in London, Berezovsky had spent years leveraging the public's perception that he had made Putin president and thus could probably crush him. That era was over.

Another oligarch was withstanding treatment similar to that of Gusinsky and Berezovsky. A bespectacled man with a habit of speaking in soft, measured tones, Mikhail Khodorkovsky, once the wealthiest Russian oil tycoon, had fallen out with Putin in the early 2000s. They had clashed over the country's oil resources. At one point, an overconfident Khodorkovsky publicly challenged Putin in a meeting at the Kremlin.[7] Putin promptly had him imprisoned, and by 2013, Khodorkovsky had spent ten years in jail and been stripped of most of his assets.[8]

Nevertheless, to Putin, Khodorkovsky remained a problem. The Kremlin suspected that the money he still had was being used to recruit liberal intelligentsia to raise their voices on his behalf. The years-long campaign to release the oligarch became a self-organizing force. The force was not a political party, and Khodorkovsky himself was not a politician, just an oligarch. Nevertheless, the patently unfair trials that had landed him in prison also had served to cement opposition to Putin's regime. Khodorkovsky, in a penal colony first in Siberia and then in Karelia—the northern region bordering Finland—kept writing articles and sending them to Moscow's popular newspapers. The newspapers kept printing them, causing debate in Russian society. As the nonpolitician Khodorkovsky became more and more a political figure, the Kremlin liked him less and less. After the protests in Moscow, Putin lost patience. He didn't want Khodorkovsky in his country. Besides, there was little to fear by sending him abroad, given what had happened to Gusinsky's and Berezovsky's once ambitious plans.

On December 20, 2013, Khodorkovsky was summoned from his cell by prison guards and taken under guard to the St. Petersburg airport. He was put on a plane bound for Germany.

Putin had agreed to free Khodorkovsky and throw him out of the country; in exchange, Khodorkovsky made a promise not to engage in any political activity. To make sure Khodorkovsky kept this promise, Putin held a hostage: a personal friend of Khodorkovsky's was also released from prison but banned from leaving the country.

* * *

Kasparov and Khodorkovsky were abroad, along with dozens of other activists who had fled persecution. They were spread all over the world, from the Baltics to Ukraine to the United States. The new Russian opposition in exile now emerged.

Garry Kasparov worked frantically to change Western public opinion about Putin. He published a book and articles in the United States damning Putin. But his main project was to get Russian activists and opposition politicians together to talk and coordinate their efforts.

Mikhail Khodorkovsky set up shop first in Switzerland and later moved to London. He also provided the Russian activists—those who lived in Russia and those in exile—the room to gather and talk, organizing conferences in Eastern and Central Europe. His idea was to take advantage of porous borders to work with the people who stayed politically active in Russia. He kept his word to Putin and didn't organize a political party. But from his luxurious headquarters at 16 Hanover Square, he launched a civil society activists' organization called Open Russia. Although funded from outside, it was based in Russia with branches in many Russian regions.

Khodorkovsky believed he could do one other thing. "There are people who are trying to do risky things in Russia—activists, journalists—so we can help them by taking the responsibility and heat on us. We all well understand the risk—it's Novichok." Khodorkovsky was referring to the nerve agent used in the poisoning of the Russian former spy Sergei Skripal in the United Kingdom. "But we are doing this consciously to help those in Russia."[9]

Khodorkovsky hired Kara-Murza Jr. as deputy head of Open Russia. Kara-Murza, who had been kicking around Washington, DC, with no luck finding a new job, was thrilled to have a chance to go back to Russia and do some meaningful work there. The two had a meeting in New York, and Khodorkovsky very calmly said to Kara-Murza, "I strongly advise you not to take your family with you."

Kara-Murza thought that Khodorkovsky might have become a bit paranoid in jail but followed his advice nonetheless. He moved to Moscow but left his wife and three children in Washington, DC, and flew back twice a month to see them.

Both Kasparov and Khodorkovsky toured the United States and Europe giving talks and lectures about Russia's political situation. Kasparov joined Nemtsov and Kara-Murza Jr. in lobbying for the Magnitsky legislation in Washington. However, neither Kasparov nor Khodorkovsky were optimistic.

"The new wave of emigration from Putin's Russia is younger, more educated. But many of these young people are not eager to fight Putin's regime. They think it's senseless. Right now, to be honest, Putin's achievements at using emigration look better," Kasparov admitted to us in a midtown café in New York just a day after PutinCon, a conference he'd organized at the New World Stages theater near Times Square. The one-day event was intended to serve as a wake-up call to Americans. Dozens of speakers exposed Putin's reign in detail. It was an interesting gathering but hardly a game changer.[10] "The only potential I see in this emigration is that after Putin's gone, maybe 10 percent of them would be ready to get back and fill government positions," Kasparov said.

Meanwhile, politically active citizens—civic activists, environmentalists, artists, politicians, most in their twenties and early thirties—kept leaving the country. Abroad, they connected with experienced liberals—experts, pundits, journalists, economists—who had been clashing with Putin for many years.

The number of Russian applications for political asylum in the United States reached 2,664 people in 2017, a twenty-four-year record, exceeding the high of 2,117 in 1994.[11] The 2017 figure more than doubled the number of applications by Russians since 2012, when Putin had been elected to a third presidential term.

Putin's strategy of squeezing troublemakers out of the country seemed to work pretty well.

"This tactic is smart, and it is efficient," Mikhail Khodor-kovsky said.[12] We were sitting with the former prisoner in his large, semiempty wood-paneled office in London. He looked calm, as always, but during our conversation, he was constantly crumpling an empty can of Coca-Cola. "It lets off steam. When a person is fed up, he faces a choice: either he leaves the country, and loses his social status, or he stays, and he gets all kinds of problems, and he can find himself in prison. When you look at it, the loss of a social status is considered a minor evil."

He laughed sadly, holding the crumpled Coca-Cola can in his hand. "There will never be a critical mass built outside the country. Because there is no tool from outside which would work better than something inside the country. We are a mainland country. We provide 80 percent of our needs ourselves. This country is invulnerable."

CHAPTER 30

WHEN THE PARTY'S OVER

I t was a great success. The large two-story Manhattan penthouse on the fourteenth floor in a brand-new Sky Garage building in Chelsea was overcrowded that night in October 2010. Artists, executives, and journalists filled the penthouse apartment that was rumored to belong to Nicole Kidman. There was plenty of champagne, absinthe, and high-cheekboned models. Most of the guests spoke Russian. In the crowd, the billionaire Mikhail Prokhorov, at six feet eight inches tall, stood a head above everyone else.

He was pleased with himself in New York. "It's perhaps the only city in the world where the energy reminds me of Moscow," he said to Rebecca Mead of the *New Yorker*. "In all other major cities, I generally fall asleep."[1]

The crowd had gathered to celebrate the launch of the American edition of *Snob* magazine, which Prokhorov funded both in Moscow and now in New York. Masha Gessen, the magazine's deputy editor, had the mic. "In Russia a lot of the process of securing one's place in society involves building fences, both literal and figurative, to create a private space and live as you want to," said Gessen. "What the project aims to do is allow them to kick over the fence and enable people to talk to others outside their professional and social circles and engage with a larger group."[2]

Thin and angular as a teenager, Masha was dressed in a white shirt and black tuxedo for the occasion. She smiled broadly. A Russian American journalist, she had emigrated to the United States with her parents when she was fourteen years old in the early 1980s and returned to Moscow ten years later. Masha was as well known in Russia as she was in the United States, where she wrote for *Vanity Fair*. No one was better positioned than she to introduce the "Global Russians," the driving idea behind *Snob* magazine, to New York.

Beginning in the early 2000s, a new generation of smart and successful Russians had emerged—or, as the *Snob* manifesto put it, those successful, educated cosmopolites who might live in different countries and speak different tongues but who think in Russian.[3] Moving between international corporations or building their own companies, they lived in whatever country or city provided them with the best options for pursuing their careers, and when they weren't in Russia, they felt themselves to be neither exiles nor emigrants.

A group of journalists spotted them first and saw a promising market with money to spend and ambitious social aspirations. The journalists secured backing from a billionaire, Prokhorov, and launched the magazine they called, fittingly, *Snob*—born to sell elitism to people eagerly pursuing exactly that. The journalists also coined a name for the international Russian professionals they were targeting—Global Russians. It was 2008, Putin had stepped down as president, and people thought a new era was dawning.

The journalistic bet on this community turned out to be a very successful one. Two years later, the crowd in the penthouse in New York was so impressive that the party was reported in both the *New York Times* and *New Yorker*.[4]

Gessen believed that the Russian idea of emigration—of leaving the country forever—that had existed from before the revolution to the end of the Soviet Union was finally dead. "Global Russians" was a new, optimistic name for people who moved not out of fear but because they saw a good opportunity elsewhere, and neither they nor the authorities shut the door behind them.

That was how the Russian middle class also saw things in 2010. The virtual club of Global Russians identified by and with *Snob* suddenly became very prestigious. Hundreds joined in, people as different as Olga Romanova, still fighting for her husband; Peter Holodny, the financier-priest who helped reunite the two Russian Orthodox churches; and Russian American investor Boris Jordan.

For the first time in their history, Russians enjoyed total freedom to travel and to live life split between two or even more countries.

But it didn't last for long. The club members didn't know it yet, but they had only three years left.

In May 2013 approximately two and a half of those three years had expired, and the atmosphere in Moscow had changed beyond recognition.

For more than a year, Putin had been attacking Russian society with arrests and repressive legislation, introducing internet censorship along the way.[5]

Few doubted that the turning point had been the Moscow protests in 2011. Putin had watched the crowds of angry Muscovites and suspected American interference, but he also saw that some of his country's business elites had turned against him. That included Mikhail Prokhorov.

An essential Russian oligarch and towering figure in Russian high society, Prokhorov had built his enormous fortune by participating in the "loans for shares" scheme back in the nineties, in which powerful banks lent money to the Russian government in exchange for shares of some of the country's most valuable assets. Prokhorov along with his partner picked up Norilsk Nickel, the world's leading smelter of palladium and nickel, built in Stalin's time by prisoners of the gulag two hundred miles north of the Arctic Circle.

Now Prokhorov wanted more civilized rules for business, and he wanted to become acceptable in the West, which is why he funded *Snob* and cultivated the new Global Russians. In summer 2011, before the election and Putin's reascension to the presidency, Prokhorov launched his own political party, and a sizable contingent of Moscow elites was fairly supportive. But Prokhorov had not sought Putin's sanction first, and that was a mistake. He lost his own party (it expelled him under instigation by the Kremlin) a few days before Putin announced his return to the Kremlin. That was why, in December 2011, Prokhorov was standing in the crowds on Sakharova Prospect listening to Kasparov and Nemtsov. The all-powerful oligarch felt he'd been played like a gullible child.

A year later, with his fortune then estimated by *Forbes* at $13 billion, Prokhorov stepped down from his businesses and left his partners to manage his assets.[6] He hadn't given up his political ambitions, but he understood that his politics could place his companies at risk. Putin was by then firmly set on a confrontational path, and he wasn't just fighting a big sector of Russian society. Relations between Russia and the United States had slipped to their lowest point in decades. At the end of 2012, Obama signed the Magnitsky Act, lobbied for by Browder, Nemtsov, and Kara-Murza, which imposed US sanctions on Russian officials involved in human rights violations. The list of sanctioned officials started with eighteen people implicated in the jailing and death of Magnitsky and gradually expanded. Within five years it would include Alexander Bastrykin, chief of the Russian Investigative Committee—the Russian equivalent of the FBI.[7] Putin, furious, responded with an asymmetric strategy: the Russian parliament banned foreigners, namely Americans, from adopting Russian children.

On May 6, 2013, Muscovites once again gathered in the center of the city for a protest rally. This time they were not in a cheerful mood. They didn't hope for any political change. They came to the streets to protest the imprisonment of their fellow protesters, in a desperate act of self-defense.

Two weeks later, in London, the local public was invited to a debate on the subject of Vladimir Putin. The well-chosen setting was Lowther Lodge, a dark redbrick Victorian building crowned with chimneys in affluent South Kensington, overlooking Kensington Gardens. The mansion had housed the Royal Geographical Society since the early twentieth century. On that May evening, it was hosting a high-profile debate on the motion that "Putin has been good for Russia."

The debate took place in Lowther Lodge's largest conference hall, which held up to eight hundred guests, and it was full. The organizers had chosen the speakers carefully. The first to be invited was Boris Jordan. It took some effort to explain why an American investor would be qualified to talk about Putin, and the organizers decided to introduce Jordan as the author of a 2007 op-ed on Putin in the *Washington Post*, titled, "He Delivers. That's Why They Like Him."

Participating in the debate was the second step in Jordan's new public campaign. Before that, he had invited himself onto a panel on Russian-American relations at the Jordan Center for the Advanced Study of Russia at New York University. He had invited himself because he could: after all, he had funded the center and it was named after him. In New York, Jordan argued that Putin's personal expectations for Russian-American relations had not been met during his first two terms as president. He also attacked the Magnitsky Act, saying he didn't understand why the United States "interfered in Russia's internal affairs."[8] Now he was coming to London.

To oppose Jordan, the organizers approached Masha Gessen. Since 2010, Gessen had abandoned *Snob* and had worked for several publications in Russia. (She left one publication because she didn't want to send a reporter to cover Putin's flight with endangered

Siberian cranes when he led them in a motorized hang glider, supposedly showing them a new route to use to fly south in the winter—an obvious publicity stunt.[9]) She briefly headed the Moscow office of Radio Liberty.[10] Gessen had published a biography critical of Putin called *The Man without a Face: The Unlikely Rise of Vladimir Putin,* and she agreed to come to London.

The debate was supposed to be two-on-two, so the organizers added two Brits. A former British diplomat would speak for the motion alongside Jordan; in support of Gessen was the *Guardian's* Luke Harding, the first Western journalist kicked out of Moscow since the Cold War.[11]

The organizers seated Masha Gessen, dressed all in black, and Boris Jordan, now a stout man with receding silver hair and a white trimmed beard, to the right and left of the chairman at the table. The two had much in common: they were both Russian Americans and both forty-six years old. Gessen and Jordan were also two members of the Global Russians club. But now they were on opposite sides.

Masha started speaking, and she looked uneasy. She didn't feel safe in Russia anymore. The ban on adopting Russian children, a retaliation to the Magnitsky Act, affected her directly: Gessen, although living in Russia, was an American citizen and an LGBT activist with three kids, among them a boy she had adopted from a Russian orphanage. In March, a Russian ultraorthodox antigay politician and member of parliament had set about promoting the adoption ban by attacking Gessen. "The Americans want to adopt Russian children and bring them up in perverted families like Masha Gessen's," he said.[12] It was a threat worth taking seriously, and Masha consulted with a lawyer. His only advice was that she should tell her son, "if you are approached by a stranger, a government official or a policeman—run." This was not very reassuring. She was thinking seriously of leaving Russia, again.[13]

Gessen spoke softly, consistently debunking the apologists' arguments, starting with the premise that Putin was bringing prosperity to the country. "We are seeing the economy entirely dependent on oil and gas reserves. . . . Look at the social sector. If you need to get a medical test at a clinic in Moscow, you have to bring your own syringe." But she didn't think she was going to win over the audience. Putin was to host the 2014 Winter Olympics in Sochi, and the entire world was looking forward to the games.

Then Boris Jordan took the pulpit: "Masha moved to Russia in 1994, and I moved in 1992 having only learned about Russia through books, imagining myself riding through the snow in the Russian field on a troika, Russian bells ringing, and beautiful churches. And when I got off the plane it was anything but that. It was very gray, very different. I want to put you in 1998–1999—and Russia was, unlike what Masha said, a very dark place."

He repeated the Kremlin narrative: that Putin had saved the country from the criminal chaos of the 1990s. Jordan was insisting how great Putin was doing economically, bringing prosperity to the middle class of the country, but he didn't stop there. He thrashed the independent media of the 1990s, including the television channel (NTV) he used to run: "They were anything but independent! The oligarchs controlled them." Using theatrical pauses, raising his voice, gesticulating, Jordan looked like a very good salesman, selling Putin to the audience.

An angry exchange of remarks followed, and the *Guardian* journalist Luke Harding, visibly exasperated, exclaimed, "There are some people we didn't mention today." He then listed the Russian journalists and human rights activists killed in the 2000s. He looked at the audience. "The list goes on and on," he said, "and you know, brave reporters, Russian human rights workers, journalists, campaigners, often not in Moscow or Saint Petersburg, but in the provinces— these are the people who have been good for Russia, not the klepto- crats"—he pointed to his right, where Jordan was seated—"not the people who've made money from Russia, large amounts of money."[14]

* * *

Less than a year later, in spring 2014, Putin sent troops to Ukraine and, breaking all international laws, annexed Crimea. Before long, he started a guerrilla war in the east of Ukraine, sending troops, tanks, and Russian mercenaries disguised as civilians. It was clearly a new era in Russia.

Putin's illegal aggression didn't sway Boris Jordan. Three weeks after Russia's annexation of the Crimean Peninsula, Jordan, in an interview with a Russian magazine, was still waging the public relations campaign he had launched a year before in New York, talking about how to improve the world's unfair and inaccurate image of Russia. "Recently, I participated in a debate in London about what Putin has done for Russia," he said. "In the hall there were a thousand people. All criticized Putin. The only person who found anything positive in Putin's activities was me."[15]

But Jordan was not campaigning by himself. Putin's plan had worked: in his hour of need, the huge network of organizations coordinated through the Kremlin's Congresses of Compatriots came to his aid and supported the annexation. It fit their understanding of geopolitics, an understanding formed in the late nineteenth century, when Russia had last successfully expanded its empire.

Meanwhile, the community of Global Russians was dying.[16] Masha Gessen had moved her family to New York.

Putin made the death of the Global Russians' idea official in June 2014 when he signed a law requesting all Russian citizens with dual residence or a second passport to register with the Russian state. Failure to register was made a criminal offense. He wanted to keep his people on a short leash.

In late 2018, Boris Jordan was still sticking to his story. In an interview for this book, he admonished us, "You don't drag me into criticizing Putin!" He was almost shouting about how useful he was in the effort to fix Putin's image problems.

CHAPTER 31

ELIMINATING THE PROBLEM

A repressive regime has a number of options available to eliminate its critics and opponents. They can be sent to jail or expelled from the country, shot or beaten to death. All of these methods produce two desired effects: one immediate, in removing the troublemaker, and the other educational, in spreading fear in the society.

The most effective methods extend the consequences of that political choice to relatives and friends. The KGB refined this strategy to perfection. When they came after a dissident, the KGB could have the dissident's spouse lose his or her job, children expelled from university, or relatives banned from traveling abroad.

One method has been always distinctive. Poison, deadly and effective, is unique in that its victim does not die alone. Their relatives and friends share the horrific experience of the loved one's dying. In a way, this is the essence of the message.

The use of poison is even more devastating in our modern world because its effects communicate the message through global media and across porous borders, from Moscow to Washington, DC.

* * *

It was a few minutes before midnight on February 27, 2015, when Moscow lawyer Vadim Prokhorov (no relation to the oligarch) learned that his friend and client Nemtsov had been killed. A short and energetic forty-three-year-old, lawyer Prokhorov had represented Boris Nemtsov and the Russian opposition at large since the early 2000s.[1] The two had spoken just three hours earlier about an upcoming Russian television documentary that was going to depict Nemtsov as an American puppet. He knew that Nemtsov had to go to the Echo Moskvy radio station for an hour-long conversation about the protest rally scheduled for the next day and then planned to have dinner with his girlfriend. It was after that dinner, when Nemtsov was walking home with his girlfriend over the Bolshoi Moskvoretsky Bridge—a stone's throw from the Kremlin wall—that a man appeared behind them and fired six shots. Four of them hit Nemtsov in the back. He died instantly.[2]

Vadim Prokhorov was sitting at a desk in the editorial offices of the independent magazine *New Times*, checking the galleys as he usually did on Friday nights to help the magazine avoid defamation lawsuits, when someone shouted, "Nemtsov was killed! I heard the news on radio." Then his phone rang—it was a friend of Nemtsov's who was first to come to the bridge, and he confirmed the news.

Always composed, with a manner of speech reminiscent of a machine gun and a battle plan at the ready, Prokhorov was numb and speechless for several minutes. Then he stood up, ran out of the *New Times* offices, got in his Audi A4, and raced to the bridge.

He arrived at the bridge at half past midnight, and Nemtsov's body was still lying where it had fallen. In the darkness, police were rolling out white-and-red crime scene tape. Vadim Prokhorov then spotted Vladimir Kara-Murza Jr. running toward the body.[3] Prokhorov at once switched into work mode. He had spent more than fifteen years of his life fighting for Nemtsov—defending him in court against trumped-up political charges, getting him out of detention centers after protest rallies, pushing a reluctant police force to investigate the leaks of Nemtsov's private phone calls. Prokhorov took a deep breath of the icy winter air and steeled himself. He glanced at the cold stone walls of the Kremlin rising up beyond the bridge. The people in there would be glad their enemy was gone. But he could not be distracted. He knew what his job was now: he would have to fight to get law enforcement to investigate his friend's assassination.

Prokhorov stayed with the police for hours, watching them to make sure they didn't tamper with or compromise any evidence. Then he went to Kara-Murza's apartment on Ovchinnikovskaya Embankment. He got only three hours of sleep. In the early morning, he rushed back to the police station.

For three months, Prokhorov watched as Nemtsov's friends—a close circle of people, all political opponents of Putin—fell into deep depression. They were devastated. Nemtsov was a larger-than-life personality, always in an optimistic mood—someone who could always cheer up his comrades, even in the darkest times. Kara-Murza Jr. kept working for Khodorkovsky's organization, shuttling between Moscow and Washington, but he was slow to recover. He and Nemtsov had known each other for seventeen years, and Nemtsov was the godfather of one of Kara-Murza's daughters—that meant a lot to Kara-Murza.

Prokhorov saved himself by burying himself in his work. As a lawyer now representing Nemtsov's family, he was pushing the investigators to be more active. Russia in the 2000s saw a series of assassinations of high-profile journalists and human rights activists. The murders were rarely properly investigated. In most cases, the Kremlin's tactic was to attack the victim by downplaying his or her role in the society and then to claim to have uncovered the perpetrators—inevitably some small fish, hired hands—but never the motive or the masterminds. Two brutal wars in Chechnya had produced plenty of battle-hardened fighters ready to do a hit job, and they offered a priceless asset: they never spilled the beans about who hired them. This was part of their code of honor; besides, they had families to protect.

That was how the murder of the famous journalist Anna Politkovskaya, Putin's outspoken critic, was investigated. The Kremlin sent several Chechens to jail but never provided an explanation of why they had decided to kill her.

At first it looked like the investigators assigned to Nemtsov's case were doing their job. In March, three suspects were arrested, and a fourth blew himself up by grenade in his apartment in Chechnya when the police tried to arrest him. But by the end of April, the investigation had stalled. A virtual wall seemed to be preventing the investigators from getting any further on the road leading to the masterminds. On April 30, the chief of the investigation was replaced. Prokhorov had a very bad feeling about it.

On May 26, 2015, just months after Nemtsov's murder, one of Kara-Murza Jr.'s assistants called Vadim Prokhorov: "Something happened. Kara-Murza is unwell." He explained that Kara-Murza was having a meeting with him and the editor of a legal news website at the website's offices when all of a sudden Kara-Murza became sick; he vomited and then collapsed on the floor, unconscious. "Maybe it's poisoning?" Prokhorov asked. He was not particularly worried, thinking of food poisoning, mostly. "No, it looks more like a heart attack," said the associate.

Kara-Murza Jr., unconscious, was rushed to the emergency room. The next day didn't bring any improvement, and the doctors decided in favor of an operation on his heart. Kara-Murza's blood pressure levels were incredibly low: 40 over 20. The Moscow physicians thought that his heart valves must be malfunctioning and that there was an urgent need for intervention.

Kara-Murza's father had turned to radio after his expulsion from TV. He called his friend, a prominent heart surgeon. This friend hurried to the emergency room, checked the data, and put a stop to the operation: "What are you doing? He has the heart of an astronaut! Put down the scalpels; it looks like a poisoning."

The family friend saved Kara-Murza Jr.'s life. If the on-call doctors had operated, Kara-Murza likely would have died. And that would have been it—death during a heart operation, a sad thing but a thing that happens. No one would have thought twice about it.

In the hospital corridor, Vadim Prokhorov heard the news and began pacing. Was it yet another attack on the opposition, targeting Nemtsov's circle? Who else could be in danger? And why was poison chosen this time?

He tried to think about when and how the poisoning could have taken place.

He knew that two days earlier, Kara-Murza Jr. had flown to Moscow from Kazan.[4] He also knew that Kara-Murza had eaten lunch onboard—and it was common knowledge that if someone wanted to put something in your food, there was no better place than on a plane. As a rule, you eat what you are given, and you don't exchange your meal with your neighbor. Besides, there was precedent. The journalist Anna Politkovskaya had been poisoned on a plane in 2004. She barely survived, only to be shot two years later on her doorstep.

There were other options too. A day before he collapsed, Kara-Murza had had several meetings in town, including lunch at a restaurant in the city center and a dinner with his father at the usually crowded two-story Bar BQ on Pyatnitskaya Street.

For now, Vadim Prokhorov needed to stay focused on Kara-Murza Jr.'s survival. After the operation was halted, an unconscious Kara-Murza was transferred to another clinic—the First City Hospital, in a classic-looking yellow-and-white nineteenth-century building with a cupola and a portico.

Kara-Murza Sr. was of little help. The calamity had completely unnerved him, and now he was posting desperate messages on Facebook. One day he would say that his son was the victim of an intentional poisoning and then another day that he had just eaten a bad snack. The strong man who had bravely stood his ground in the face of the state seizure of his TV company, Kara-Murza Sr. was collapsing, crushed by the sight of his son in a coma.

On Friday, three days after Kara-Murza Jr. was poisoned, his wife, Zhenya, flew from Washington to Moscow while her mother flew from Moscow to Washington to look after their kids. Prokhorov met Zhenya at the airport, and they hastened to the hospital. Kara-Murza was still in the intensive care unit. "He looked like an octopus, there were so many tubes out of him," Zhenya said.

His heart had stopped, and he was given norepinephrine. His kidneys failed, and he was put on hemodialysis. Then his lungs failed, and he was given a tracheostomy and put on a ventilator. Then his liver failed, too. Now, Kara-Murza was lying there, entangled in numerous tubes with a hole in his trachea. He was still unconscious, and the medical staff looked confused. Vadim Prokhorov was trying to locate someone in the hospital who had some authority.

He learned that because it was Friday night, nobody was there— no head of the hospital, no chief of the intensive care unit. Desperate, Prokhorov phoned the *New Times*'s editor Yevgenia Albats: "Yevgenia, the man is dying, and nobody is here!"

Yevgenia Albats, a political journalist and the author of the first post-Soviet book about the KGB, *KGB: State within a State*,[5] was known as a fierce critic of the Kremlin. But in Moscow she was also a real personality with a commanding manner and a loud voice. Albats was known for her ability to get things done—she knew a lot of people in town and seldom took no for an answer. In fact, her nickname among Moscow's journalists was WMD ("weapon of mass destruction").

Forty minutes after Prokhorov had called Albats, a car pulled up in front of the hospital, and the head of the hospital stepped out. With him was Denis Protsenko, the chief of the intensive care unit. The two rushed to Denis's office. In a few minutes, they told Prokhorov and Zhenya to come in.

The head of the hospital, a corpulent man in his early forties, was obviously displeased by the interruption of his Friday night. He started by saying that he didn't believe there had actually been a poisoning. "Who would need to poison you? You're just the opposition."

Prokhorov was taken aback. "Well, Nemtsov was just killed."

"Ah, it's a different thing," the head of the hospital said.

He turned to Zhenya. "And who are you?"

"I'm the wife," she said. "I want to get his samples to check them independently."

The head of the hospital became impatient. "Look, why do you need it? It's like a train hit a man, and he is lying dying, while the train is long gone. Why care about the train when you need to think about the man?"

But Zhenya insisted.

"You don't have a right to request that," the head of the hospital snapped. "You need a signed power of attorney." It was very clear he wanted to find an excuse to get rid of them. She did not have the document.

Fortunately, as a lawyer, Prokhorov did. He presented his document. The head of the hospital checked it and shrugged. "OK, that'll do."

Now he turned to Prokhorov. "Look, why did you do that?"

"Do what?" asked the lawyer.

"Why did you phone Albats? Anything else would have been better—the prosecutor's office, the FSB, everything, but why Albats?" He was obviously unhappy to have gotten ensnared in something so politically sensitive by someone to whom he couldn't say no.

Kara-Murza Jr. was still in intensive care, and Denis, a large, bald man with a beard and smiling eyes, was fighting to save his life. Finally, hemodialysis started to have some positive effect. Kara-Murza was no longer dying, although he was still in a coma.

On Sunday, Prokhorov and Zhenya once again asked the head of the hospital for permission to take samples of Kara-Murza's hair, nails, and blood, which experts could use to try to identify the poison. That request was finally granted, although the hospital tried to downplay the situation. A theory was developed—that Kara-Murza was indeed poisoned, not by someone else but by himself. Kara-Murza had been taking a light sedative since 2014, and he also occasionally used nasal drops. These substances, combined with alcohol, could be toxic.

Essentially, the head of the hospital blamed the victim. "In general, this story is explained by the combination of some medicines with a certain type of drink that was consumed uncontrollably," he explained later to the media, hinting that Kara-Murza Jr. had been drunk.[6]

Vadim Prokhorov was in touch with people at the newspaper *Novaya Gazeta*, where two reporters had been poisoned. The editor in chief suggested three laboratories to test the samples—one in Israel, one in France, and one in the United Kingdom. Zhenya called the British embassy, asking for help in transferring the samples to the UK laboratory—Kara-Murza held a British passport. But the clerk at the embassy told her that would be impossible and offered only moral support. The embassy also made a public statement that according to the Vienna Convention, biomaterials could not be sent via diplomatic mail.[7]

Kara-Murza spent the next three weeks in a coma.

The exiled Khodorkovsky flew an Israeli toxicology expert to Moscow. The Israeli expert said that Kara-Murza had a 5 percent chance of survival, but he said nothing about the substance of the poison.[8]

Kara-Murza Jr. made it into this 5 percent, thanks to the efforts of Denis and his team. In July he regained consciousness. Very thin, with his muscles largely atrophied, he was transferred to a hospital in Washington. He flew there on a private medical jet that had been rented by Khodorkovsky.

*   *   *

Kara-Murza's full recovery took a year and a half. It was a slow and painful process. He had no memory of the past month and a half, and his muscles regained strength slowly. He was embarrassed when he tried to pour his wife some tea but was too weak to raise the teapot. He spent weeks in the hospital in Washington, DC. That was when a tall man in his early forties first approached Zhenya in the hospital corridor. He introduced himself as an FBI agent assigned to deal with the Kara-Murza case.

Kara-Murza Jr. flew back to Moscow in December 2015—six months after the poisoning—still leaning on a cane. He believed that a true Russian politician needed to be in Russia, and he wanted to make a point of coming back. He had another reason to make the trip: together, he and Prokhorov went to the police to request that law enforcement open a criminal investigation into his attempted murder.

They brought with them the results of tests done by Paskal Kintz, the head of a laboratory in the suburbs of Strasbourg, France. Dr. Kintz was known around the world as an authority on poison. His report said that four elements—heavy metals—in Kara-Murza's samples were at higher dosages than were normally found in the human body: manganese, zinc, copper, and mercury. To Vadim Prokhorov, it was crystal clear that Kara-Murza Jr. had indeed been poisoned. But the police said no. The investigation in Russia was effectively sabotaged.

Meanwhile, Kara-Murza was shuttling between Moscow and Washington, continuing his work for Khodorkovsky's Open Russia. Kara-Murza was intent on remaining active in his country, no matter what.

He spent the night of February 2, 2017, at Zhenya's parents' apartment in Moscow before an early Lufthansa flight to Washington, DC, the next morning. At 5:00 a.m. he collapsed on the floor. He managed to make a call to his wife: "Zhenya, it's a double." Zhenya got it immediately—it was happening again.

Her parents called an ambulance.

Zhenya was friends on Facebook with Denis, the chief of intensive care at the First City Hospital who had supervised Kara-Murza's recovery the first time. The previous fall, Denis had taken a new job as chief doctor of Moscow's Municipal Hospital No. 7, and Zhenya had congratulated him on Facebook. At 5:00 a.m. she messaged him on Facebook Messenger: "Denis, Kara-Murza is very sick." Denis responded at once. He agreed to take him to his clinic.[9] Kara-Murza lost consciousness soon after he was taken to Denis's hospital.

Zhenya telephoned Prokhorov, who rushed to the hospital at once. Denis remembered him and said openly, "Guys, it's the same thing." The official diagnosis this time was "acute intoxication by an unidentified substance."

The doctors put Kara-Murza on hemodialysis again, but it didn't really help. Then they replaced all his plasma. That did make a difference, and Kara-Murza started to recover. To the physicians, this was a clear sign that a poison had been used—something protein related, something strong, and something that probably consisted of more than one toxic substance.

It was clearly sophisticated, and Prokhorov believed that meant it was something only a government organization could develop.

CHAPTER 32

CHASING A POISON

Kara-Murza Jr. healed more quickly the second time, and a new struggle began: the hunt to identify the poison. With the hospital cooperating this time, samples had been taken on the second day, not the third, as had been the case in 2015. In 2017, Vadim Prokhorov was given three test tubes—blood, nails, and hair. Then he phoned Khodorkovsky's lawyer in London: "A toxicology team in Israel has agreed to look into the case. But who could take the samples to Israel?"

Khodorkovsky's lawyer called him back in a minute. "You should take them to Israel," he said. Prokhorov, surprised, expressed some hesitancy.

"Tomorrow is Saturday, so there's no court for you to attend," Khodorkovsky's lawyer insisted. So Prokhorov went home, picked up his passport, and packed a small rucksack with the insulated medical cooler the hospital had given him.[1]

He flew to Ben Gurion Airport and drove straight to the Ichilov Hospital, just ten miles from Tel Aviv. But the clinic told him that they could check Kara-Murza's samples for only three elements. That clearly would not be sufficient for identifying the poison. He called Paskal Kintz's clinic in Strasbourg—the same one that had checked Kara-Murza's samples in 2015. They promised to check the new samples for fifteen elements instead of three. Prokhorov went back to Ben Gurion Airport and boarded a plane to Frankfurt, his small rucksack with the medical kit on his back.

He was stopped at border control in the Frankfurt airport. Three German women in their late fifties told him he needed special documentation to carry biomaterials over the border. Prokhorov knew they were right, but he decided to take his chances.

"I flew from Israel, and it was fine to transfer the medical kit from Moscow to Israel yesterday," he said.

"We are not in Israel," one of the women grandly responded.

Prokhorov saw an opportunity. "Yes, exactly, and Israel exists only because of the activities of your grandfathers and grandmothers!" He went on and on, displaying a calculated rage. "My client is a political opponent of Vladimir Putin, he is dying in Moscow, and if he dies, it will be a holocaust of the twenty-first century."

They listened to him silently and then waved him in.

The Kara-Murza samples finally found their way into the hands of experts in the two-story mansion that housed Kintz's laboratory in the small French city of Oberhausbergen, seven miles from Strasbourg. But when Prokhorov got the results, they were disappointing. The report stated that there was an elevated concentration of manganese in both the blood and the hair and that "this was also observed in 2015."[2] But the report didn't answer the question of what kind of poison had been used. Once again, it only named the element levels that were higher in Kara-Murza's body than they normally were in the general population.

As a former student of history, Vadim Prokhorov was particularly interested in the history of the Soviet secret police. He knew that it had created special laboratories dedicated to developing poisons and that the poisons were intended as tools for eliminating the regime's enemies. The Soviet secret service had had a poison laboratory at its disposal since as early as 1926. From the beginning, its task was to develop poisons for use abroad.

The laboratory was known variously as "Laboratory No. 12," "Laboratory X," or just "Camera" and was headed by Professor Grigory Mairanovsky, a gaunt man with the sunken cheeks of an ascetic. In 1937 the lab was transferred from the civil Biochemical Institute to the secret service, and a year later it came under the personal control of the head of the secret service. Mairanovsky spent years testing poisons on inmates, and over two hundred people were killed.[3] After the war, when Nahum Eitingon was put in charge of the assassinations department, Mairanovsky was brought under his control. They ran several operations together, including the poisoning of Isaiah Oggins, until 1951, when Mairanovsky and Eitingon were both arrested, caught in the crossfire of internal turf wars.

Although the Soviet secret services dispensed with Mairanovsky, they did not give up on poison. The secret research never stopped. When in 1978 a Bulgarian dissident was famously killed by an umbrella shot in London, he was injected with ricin—a poison found naturally in castor beans—which the KGB had passed to their Bulgarian colleagues.

Putin's secret service also used poison.

This had become well known since the liquidation of the infamous terrorist Emir Khattab. Khattab, an Arab warlord who fought in Chechnya, made himself enemy number one for the secret service in the early 2000s. He was responsible for many terror attacks in Russia. In March 2002, he was in hiding in the mountains of the North Caucasus, surrounded by his bodyguards. He was expecting a letter from Saudi Arabia. To prevent being tracked by the Russian secret service, Khattab was communicating with the outside world using couriers—but the FSB had recruited one of them. The agency poisoned an intercepted letter with a nerve agent with the useful quality of delayed activation. The letter was delivered. Khattab opened it, read it, and threw it into a campfire. Three days later, he suddenly started foaming at the mouth.[4] In a few hours, he was dead. The FSB took credit for the operation.

Prokhorov had no doubt that the Russian secret services were somehow behind Kara-Murza's illness. And he believed he had deduced the reason why they wanted to poison his friend: the Magnitsky Act.[5]

Three people were responsible for the passing of the act: Bill Browder, who hadn't set foot in Russia for years; Boris Nemtsov, killed in early 2015; and Vladimir Kara-Murza Jr.

And Kara-Murza hadn't stopped. He traveled incessantly, lobbying other countries to adopt the Magnitsky Act or their own equivalent. Browder and Kara-Murza scored some successes. The British adopted the Magnitsky provisions that targeted gross human rights violators worldwide; Lithuania, Estonia, and Latvia barred entry to those on the Magnitsky list; and Denmark started debating similar legislation.

Since Kintz failed to identify the poison, Kara-Murza's friends and relatives kept trying to identify the substance that had nearly killed him. Kara-Murza Jr. had lived and worked in the United States for more than ten years, so he and Zhenya believed they had another option: the FBI.

When Kara-Murza had recovered well enough to travel, he and Zhenya flew back to Washington. At the airport, they were met by two FBI agents, one of them the man they had met in 2015. They had been in constant communication since Zhenya had learned of a second poisoning. Now Zhenya handed them Kara-Murza's samples to take to their laboratory.

They expected the agency to start the investigation, but months passed, and they heard nothing. Then, at the end of December 2017, Kara-Murza and the FBI agent had their meeting in the Washington coffee shop.

"We think we found an active substance you were poisoned with," the agent said. "Barium. It acts like this—it paralyzes the heart and the respiratory system." He also told Kara-Murza that the agency was preparing a detailed report that would provide details on the poison itself and include some theories about how the poisoning could have been done. He hinted that food was not the only option for delivering the poison.

He also said that given the impending meeting of the heads of the Russian secret services with the new Trump administration, they were going to hand the report over to them with the note "that there was an attempt of poisoning of a Russian citizen on Russian territory for political reasons."

Then came the January call in which the agent said, essentially, "You know, we have guidelines, that we need to run a second test, and only if the second test results match the first is the report given an official go. Unfortunately, our second test didn't match the first, so please forget everything I told you," and hung up.

Kara-Murza asked several congressmen to send a request to the FBI. They did but got a very short response: we can't give you any information on this case because it is confidential.

In February 2018, the heads of the three Russian intelligence agencies—the FSB, the SVR, and Military Intelligence—flew to Washington, DC, to have talks with their American counterparts. We spent plenty of time in the corridors of power in Washington, talking to high-level officials at the State Department and people at Congress, trying to learn anything we could about the mysterious visit. Officially, even the date of the Russian spies' arrival in DC was not disclosed, and the fact of the visit was reported by the Russian news agency, not the American press. But all our contacts just told us it was a US national security issue, so they were not in a position to disclose any details about the visit.

The talks were reportedly very productive. The secret services of the United States and Russia still needed one another. Whether or not they addressed the matter of Kara-Murza's poisoning remains a mystery.

Kara-Murza Jr. himself tried desperately to extract any information he could from the FBI regarding his poisonings. He also filed a Freedom of Information Act request. In October 2018 he went to the press, in hopes that publicizing the FBI's recalcitrance would up the pressure on them.[6]

He got silence in response.

CHAPTER 33

EVERYTHING OLD IS NEW AGAIN

I n May 2018 Columbia University brought us to New York to speak at the Political Exiles conference. The timing could not have been better; the topic of the conference perfectly matched the topic we were busy researching. We had a long list of places we needed to visit in the city, most of them in Manhattan.

One stood out from the list: Tatiana restaurant, right on the boardwalk in Brighton Beach. In this Brooklyn neighborhood, famous for its huge Russian Jewish diaspora, the restaurant was one of the brightest spots.

Tatiana, a Jew who left Odessa in 1979, had opened the big, kitschy one-hundred-table restaurant named after her in 1990. Right from the beginning, Tatiana was popular. The cuisine was Soviet-Ukrainian, and the entertainment featured dancing girls wearing bright makeup and half-dressed in transparent Russian folk costumes, along with ballerinas. The restaurant drew patrons from far beyond the immediate neighborhood. Visitors frequently included guests from Russia—artists, TV celebrities, and pop stars. Russian spies loved Tatiana, too. For years, the intelligence station in New York took every general who visited from Moscow to Tatiana for dinner.[1]

Brighton Beach was sunny and windy, just as promised. From the boardwalk we at once spotted the huge restaurant sign. Tatiana's waiters—Russian men in ill-fitting suits—ushered us inside to a small, two-person table. Large glasses of red wine, filled to the brim, promptly arrived. We looked around.

Inside, Tatiana resembled a Soviet luxury restaurant, the kind of place Irina's father, who had spent his youth in Soviet Odessa, would have recognized, shining with gold, gleaming lacquered wooden walls, and mirrors on pillars. A big family—the women in tight, glossy black-and-gold dresses and the men in open shirts with gold chains, all of them speaking Russian—was celebrating grandma's birthday at the long table next to ours.

In the hall downstairs, dozens of portraits were on the walls. The restaurant was proud to have hosted singers and actors well known in post–Soviet Union countries. But there were no photographs of another category of the visitors—the ones we were interested in— or of a particular visit eighteen years back, in the summer of 2000, that hadn't ended well.

On that sunny day in August 2000, three men walked into the Tatiana. One of them—with short hair, wearing black pants and a Hawaiian shirt—cut a particularly striking figure. Beer arrived at their table immediately. The three men were speaking Russian, and the word "Putin" was heard time and again. It was clear that the second man, in a beige suit, was playing host, entertaining the other two.

This was no casual political chitchat, however. Sergei Tretyakov, deputy head of the Russian intelligence station in New York, was having lunch with two colleagues from the secret services. Victor Zolotov, the man in the Hawaiian shirt, was the chief of Putin's bodyguards. His muscle-bound colleague was Evgeny Murov, head of the Federal Protection Service, the Russian version of the US Secret Service. These highly placed officials were meeting at Tatiana to prepare for Putin's impending visit to the United States.

Tretyakov was a shrewd Soviet and then Russian intelligence officer. He had built his career—serving abroad in Canada and then in the United States—playing skillfully by written and unwritten KGB rules. His grandmother had been head of the typists department in Stalin's secret services (quite a sensitive job). He himself had grown up in Iran in the family of a Soviet trade representative. He happily married the daughter of a Soviet diplomat. During the last Soviet years, just before being sent to Ottawa, he held a position as head of the Komsomol (the Communist Party youth organization) in the foreign intelligence department of the KGB—an incomparable position for forging useful connections in Yasenevo. Everything was in place to secure Tretyakov's successful career—an appropriate family background, a bunch of highly ranked backers at foreign intelligence headquarters. Now he faced the challenge of dealing with two new colleagues, chosen by Putin to be his right-hand men inside Russia's secret services. Both had landed their jobs just four months prior, when Putin became the Russian president.

Tretyakov knew well that the style of the Kremlin's new boss could best be detected through the people who chose to serve him. And understanding Putin's style, he thought, should be easier for people like himself. The new president was also from KGB foreign intelligence, and the gossip was that he would choose his people from the KGB flock.

But with these two men, Tretyakov felt uneasy. He thought he knew the rules, but now he was losing his confidence. These men were nothing like the kind he knew from Foreign Intelligence headquarters in Yasenevo.

At Tatiana, as the men waited for their meals, Tretyakov was struggling to entertain his guests. Putin's top security services pals had a distinctive style. Zolotov boasted about how well he had trained his men to keep Putin safe. Each was a martial arts expert, capable of killing an attacker with a single blow, he said.

Suddenly, ostensibly demonstrating his skills, Zolotov swung his hand in the air and struck Tretyakov in his temple. The blow knocked the spymaster off his chair, and he landed, unconscious, on the floor. When he regained consciousness, he heard Murov yelling at Zolotov, "You could have killed him!"

If that was the style of Putin's secret services, it was very distinctive.

Two months later, on October 11, Tretyakov left his apartment along with his wife, his daughter, and a cage containing Matilda, the beloved family cat. He locked the door behind them. They went down to the underground garage of the Russian diplomatic compound in Riverdale, in the north Bronx, where Tretyakov's car—a Ford Taurus—was parked. It was 1:00 p.m., lunchtime for the Russians working in the building, meaning it was less likely that they would run into someone they didn't want to run into.

The Riverdale compound is an ugly, twenty-story, high-rise apartment building built by Soviet engineers in the 1970s. Its roof is stuffed with antennas and transformers belonging to SVR and GRU, aimed at intercepting radio communication between FBI surveillance cars. That the Russian apartment building was the highest landmark in the area made such interception easier. The signals from the roof antennas were routed to the nineteenth floor, where technical staff engineers from the SVR and GRU worked day and night.

Tretyakov drove to the gate, pushed the intercom, and said, "Tretyakov." It was a security routine he was complying with for the last time in his life. When the gate opened, Tretyakov drove his Ford and his family straight to an FBI safe house and defected.

Did the unpleasant lunch with Putin's two friends contribute to his decision? It is possible that he saw clearly that day that his chances for a successful career among people like Zolotov were slim. Or perhaps he had seen some other sign that things were getting hot. Tretyakov had secretly worked for the Americans for several years and could be compromised. In either case, he had come to think it was the right time to leave.

By this time, Putin already had made some dramatic changes in the SVR. He shifted the agency's focus from east to west. He did it in the most effective way known in Russian bureaucracy—through personnel changes.

In the 1990s, the SVR was led by generals who had spent their careers in India, Pakistan, and the Middle East. Inside they were called the Middle Eastern mafia.

Putin picked his head of the agency from a completely different group. The new chief of Foreign Intelligence had spent his career in the West, first in Germany. Before his appointment, he was an SVR official representative to the United States. Operatives with experience spying in the United States started to fill important positions in the agency. Even the press office followed the trend. The officer chosen as the new spokesperson for the agency spent years in New York in the 1990s in the guise of a correspondent for the Russian tabloid *Komsomolskaya Pravda*.

By coincidence, for most of his time in New York, he'd been supervised by Tretyakov.

Tretyakov worked under Putin only for seven months, but he witnessed the dramatic change. Years later, he told us on the phone from his home in Florida, "Russian intelligence became even more aggressive [compared with the KGB and the early 1990s], at least if judging by the requests we started to get and what kind of appetite the center now showed. There are plenty of our former officers in the government, and we all have brains made in the same factory."[2] He meant that Putin and his friends trusted the SVR assessment much more than they did information provided by conventional diplomats.

That change didn't go unnoticed. Already in the spring of 2001, three Western countries—the United States, the United Kingdom, and Germany—reported increases in the activity of Russian intelligence abroad.[3] These allegations were to be repeated time and again as Putin's tenure in the Kremlin stretched on.

Not only did the focus change; the intelligence programs were expanded, too. According to Tretyakov, around that same time, the SVR dramatically increased spending on the "illegals program," meaning the placement of covert intelligence operatives with false identities and false names—in many cases, sending people in the guise of émigrés. The SVR believed that these sorts of spies could easily lose themselves in the West amid the huge post-Soviet wave of emigration.[4]

Ten years later it became clear that not all of them infiltrated the West as successfully as Moscow hoped.

In June 2010 the FBI arrested ten Russian illegals after having had them under surveillance for a long time, prompting the biggest spy scandal between the two countries in a decade. Eight of the ten had pretended to be not Russian; they held American, Canadian, or Peruvian passports and Western names. Two stood out in the crowd: twenty-eight-year-old Mikhail Semenko, arrested in Arlington, Virginia, and redheaded Anna Chapman, the same age, who was arrested in New York. Russian by origin, they hadn't adopted false names like the rest of the Russian spies. While Semenko had come to Washington, DC, to work for the Travel All Russia travel agency, Chapman pretended to be a new émigré.

Born in Volgograd to the family of a high-ranking KGB official, Anna had studied at university in Moscow. At a party she met a Brit, Alex Chapman, and promptly married him—getting a British passport into the bargain—and moved to London. In 2009 she came to New York and landed a job at a website selling real estate. There she was put under FBI surveillance as part of a massive counterintelligence operation, code-named Ghost Stories, against SVR spies in the United States. The federal agents discovered her contacts with known Russian spies based in the city. While sitting at a Starbucks in Manhattan using her laptop, she was caught using a private Wi-Fi network shared by a minivan driven by a Russian government official.[5]

While this marked the end of Anna Chapman's spy career, it was hardly the end of the Kremlin's intelligence scheme. In fact, the same year she was exposed, Russian intelligence openly took up the issue of the compatriots, and a high-ranking official representing Russian intelligence became a member of the Kremlin's interagency coordinating body in charge of the Russians abroad.[6]

It looked like the old KGB system, created by Andropov and Kryuchkov in the 1970s to coordinate efforts to prevent "subversive activities" by émigrés and, at the same time, to recruit them, had been restored and expanded. The age-old method of eliminating the regime's enemies was still a tool in their toolbox.

Years and decades passed, and Russian intelligence kept honoring the traditions. When Putin made KGB veteran Sergei Naryshkin chief of the SVR in late 2016, Naryshkin made it known that a portrait of Vasily Zarubin was on display in Yasenevo.[7]

Would it ever become possible to break with KGB tradition and reform Soviet intelligence to comport with a democratic system of governance and the rule of law? Yeltsin surely missed his chance, but had there ever been a chance?

On a sunny June day in London, we posed this very question to tall, smiling Richard Aldrich, professor of international security at the University of Warwick and a renowned historian and authority on British intelligence. He explained that the two systems, democratic and authoritarian, have "fundamentally different notion[s] of intelligence."

In democratic countries, he said, intelligence is about gathering information. Under authoritarian regimes, "intelligence is about protecting the regime and policing émigrés."

The KGB's intelligence branch and all its descendants belong to the latter category.

CHAPTER 34

THE FEARS OF THE SUPER-RICH

The generals on Lubyanka and Yasenevo might stick to old KGB methods, and Putin may be working hard to reinstall a Soviet style of authoritarian control. But for all that is the same, a new X factor unthinkable thirty years ago: the Russian super-rich, a new tier of influential elites with a say in the country's affairs and ways to channel their thoughts to the Kremlin privately and directly.

Thousands of them populate the most expensive neighborhoods and properties in the world, from the south of France to London to New York to Miami. Some made their fortunes in the decade before Putin came to power. Many have substantial assets in the West, out of reach of the Kremlin. Such assets could make them independent—maybe even capable of challenging Putin—if things go too far wrong.

Pretty recently, two super-rich Russians put this theory to test. Both were in more privileged positions than the rest of the oligarch crowd. They made their fortunes and reputations under Yeltsin, so they'd had time to become well established in the West. They used this time wisely—globalizing not only their money and property but also their businesses.

And both came from the KGB, so they knew better than many how to play on both the Russian and Western chess boards.

St. Paul's Church in Frankfurt was packed. Top German officials, businessmen, and foreign investors took their seats in the round, light-filled hall.

St. Paul's was no longer used for prayer. A seat of the first German parliament in 1848, its political symbolism made it a perfect venue for gatherings of the German establishment. Instead of holding Bibles, these attendees held programs detailing the schedule for the 2017 German Economic Forum.

In November 2017, the forum had invited Evgeny Kaspersky, founder of the eponymous security software company, to give a talk. He was wearing a deep-blue jacket and blue shirt, his graying hair waved Richard Branson style. Kaspersky was slightly obsessed with the British business magnate: His company sponsored Branson's Virgin Racing team. He had Sir Richard's book on his table in his office. And he bought a ticket for a journey into space from Branson's company.

Usually relaxed in public, Kaspersky looked anxious at St. Paul's. On stage, he fidgeted in his chair and joked so awkwardly that the host often failed to grasp his humor.[1]

The billionaire's anxiety was completely justified. Times were hard for both his company and for him personally. A few months earlier, at a series of public hearings held in the US Senate, six top American intelligence officials—including the heads of the FBI and the CIA—said they didn't feel comfortable having Kaspersky's antivirus software on their computers.[2] Soon the secretary of Homeland Security ordered all government agencies to remove Kaspersky software from their systems. Just a month earlier, Kaspersky antivirus was caught downloading NSA files from the poorly secured computer of an agency contractor. It caused an uproar that Kaspersky's products had been stealing confidential information from American users.[3] All of this badly harmed Kaspersky's company, which was truly global. Although headquartered in Moscow, Kaspersky had offices, and customers, everywhere.

More problems followed, this time from the Russian side. The FSB had Kaspersky's deputy, the head of the company's most sensitive department—computer crime investigations—arrested and locked up in Lefortovo prison.[4] He was accused of espionage for the United States.

Eugene Kaspersky understood perfectly well that after that arrest, his company could easily be attacked by the security service. He knew the rules—Kaspersky himself had started his career in the KGB, the FSB's predecessor.

Now Kaspersky had come to Frankfurt to fight for access to the German market, the biggest in Europe. And he wanted to make a good impression.

The host, a German journalist from the national weekly publication *Die Zeit*, was well prepared for the talk. When Kaspersky said he was "a product of a mathematical school," the journalist added, "The KGB." Kaspersky was not happy with this remark, so he countered the journalist's claim, calling it just a "cryptographic institute." Then he started talking about how great Russian engineers and hackers are. But the host was not going to let him get his way.

"Did you read Andrei's book?" the journalist asked. He meant our book, *The Red Web: The Kremlin's Wars on the Internet*.[5] Andrei had participated in the panel before Kaspersky's appearance and talked about the pressure the Kremlin was exerting on Russian IT companies after the annexation of Crimea and the Russian hacking attacks in the United States.

"No," said Kaspersky.

"Oh, you didn't?" The host in his black suit smiled. "It's interesting—you are in it. Andrei describes the situation with IT companies after the 2014 changes. The Crimea crisis changed something. Did you see it change? Did you feel it change?"

"No," said Kaspersky. This sounded firm enough, but Kaspersky decided his denial needed to be enforced and added, "Zero." And he made a zero figure with the fingers of his two hands. It looked like he wanted to show to an invisible Putin in the sky that he was firm enough not to succumb to provocation. "That's why I am not interested in this book. I think Soldatov and I, we live in different realities."

The host said his last question was about the Russian government, and Kaspersky laughed nervously. The journalist asked why Kaspersky thought his employee had been arrested.

"I have no idea," said Kaspersky. "The only thing I know is that he was arrested because of something he did before he joined our company. So it's not related to our business and his activity working in the company."[6]

The interview ended, and Kaspersky quickly descended to the hall flashing an inviting smile. He may have come to Frankfurt to win the trust of the German establishment, but as the interview played out, it looked as if he had another listener in mind. He was so eager to please this listener that he was not going to defend his man who was, at that moment, in jail but had not been convicted.

If the Russian IT industry had fooled itself into thinking being truly international made it independent from the Russian authorities, now was the time to wake up.

The wake-up call rang in other industries too, including the most sensitive one: finance.

On a sunny Sunday in July 2018, it was nice to drive a car through the manicured woods along the Rublyovka, the famous Russian road that has been, since the imperial era, a route for the elite. In Soviet times, the Kremlin granted summer homes in the villages on Rublyovka to high-ranking party members, famous artists, and prominent scientists. After the fall of the Communists, the new Russian elite took over the area.

After making a turn into the village of Razdory and into a parking lot, Andrei stopped the car. This was where Alexander Lebedev, the Russian-British media magnate, financier, and former KGB intelligence officer, had told him to come and wait.

Tall and fit, with blond hair always close-cropped, Lebedev had been born to a well-connected family that was part of Moscow's intelligentsia. His father was a professor at the Moscow Technical School, and he himself had gone to an elite school where he had become friends with many smart young men from good families.

In the late 1970s, he enrolled in the prestigious Institute of International Relations, followed by recruitment into the First Chief Directorate of the KGB in Yasenevo, the economic intelligence unit—actually just a group of a dozen operatives who thought highly of themselves because they knew something about the Western economy.

Next he was posted to London as an officer with the economic intelligence section at the KGB station. It was the late 1980s, just before the Soviet Union ceased to exist.

For the young and the enterprising, it was good to be in Moscow during the *perestroika* years. But if you were young, Russian, and really enterprising, London was an even better place to be. Many people who fell into that category were KGB officers at the Soviet embassy. A number of spectacular post-Soviet careers started there as Soviet-era go-getters found themselves in the right place at the right time.

Alexander Lebedev was one of them. Rules were changing rapidly, and soon he took to driving emerging Russian oligarchs around the city in his blue Ford.[7] They needed to open accounts in the British banks, and he was there, ready to help.

When he left the KGB's foreign intelligence department in the early 1990s, he founded a bank that started working with Russia's debts. Thanks to his time in London, he knew most of the emerging players in the Russian banking business. It also helped that this area was supervised by foreign intelligence, so his KGB connections came in handy.

That brought him a fortune. In the late 1990s, he became one of the first billionaires in Russia.

From that time on, Lebedev built his career by benefiting from both worlds—the KGB and Moscow's intelligentsia. Lebedev was smart and easygoing and took the trouble to make friends among journalists. He began supporting the liberal and respected Russian newspaper *Novaya Gazeta* and bought it outright in 2006.[8] He became friends with Mikhail Gorbachev and funded his foundation.[9] Lebedev well understood what it meant to have a good reputation in the West.

In the late 2000s, his good reputation in the West helped him achieve the unthinkable for a former officer in London's KGB station: Lebedev was allowed to acquire two influential, although financially troubled, British publications: the *Evening Standard* and the *Independent*.

There comes a point when making money crosses with politics, and Lebedev set off playing his political game. In the mid-1990s, he gave money to the Yeltsin reelection campaign and owned shares in Aeroflot, the major Russian airline run by Yeltsin's son-in-law. Lebedev was successful under Yeltsin, and he remained so under Putin.

In the 2000s, he got himself elected to the Russian parliament and ran for mayor of Moscow. He never forgot to consult with the Kremlin—Lebedev had a number of personal meetings with Vladimir Putin. As a tycoon with a background in foreign intelligence—he'd held the rank of lieutenant colonel, the same as Putin—who was better positioned to benefit from Putin's time at the helm of government?

Lebedev became one of very few Russian tycoons who became truly international—at a level much higher than any other "global Russian."

In the United Kingdom, Lebedev's media business thrived. His two publications, run by his son Evgeny, were doing surprisingly well; circulation was increasing. Evgeny, a bon vivant who sported a perfectly trimmed beard and always-extravagant outfits, was accepted by the British establishment; he was friends with Elton John, Tom Stoppard, and Boris Johnson, as well as minor members of the royal family.[10] And although Lebedev was not a Global Russian in the way of Masha Gessen and her friends, his son surely was; he had joined *Snob*'s community of Global Russians right after its launch.

In Russia, Lebedev's good luck began to run out when a small Moscow newspaper he had just launched reported on the widespread rumors that Putin had left his wife and was about to marry a twenty-four-year-old Olympic champion gymnast. The year was 2008; Putin was just prime minister at the time, not president, and it was unclear whether he would run for the presidency again. Putin was furious. "Nobody should ever interfere in others' private lives. I've always reacted negatively to those who, with their snotty noses and erotic fantasies, prowl into others' lives," he angrily commented on the ensuing scandal.[11]

Lebedev shut down the offending publication, but it was too late. It quickly became clear that he had angered Putin. And now, as in the times of the tsar, he was looking into an abyss.

Lebedev soon found most of his projects in trouble. The FSB raided his bank. He had to shut down his airline. He even sold his shares in Aeroflot to save his bank, which also got into trouble.[12] It was a downward spiral, and Lebedev was angry. In December 2011, he came to the hundred-thousand-strong protest rally on Sakharova Prospect, just like his fellow unhappy oligarch Mikhail Prokhorov, and listened to Kasparov and Nemtsov.[13]

In 2011 Lebedev was appearing on a TV talk show when the second guest, a developer known for erratic manners, announced that he had a big desire to punch Lebedev in the face. Lebedev calmly stood up and knocked the guest to the floor. The fighting was soon on air, and the general feeling was that while Lebedev had lost his temper and maybe his mind, the preemptive assault would not get him into any real trouble.

But it did. After months of interrogations, Lebedev was tried, found guilty, and convicted to 130 hours of labor. He was sent out to clean the Moscow streets and to fix up a village's kindergarten 120 miles from Moscow. State TV showed Lebedev sweeping with a broom.

It was meant to be a humiliation, and it was. It sent a clear message: you might be a former high-ranking KGB officer and an oligarch with newspapers from Moscow to London, but don't forget you are totally at the mercy of the Kremlin. Had the most globalized Russian oligarch actually gotten the message? That's what Andrei was interested to find out.

As Andrei parked his Opel Astra as he was told, a guy who looked like a former special forces officer jumped out of a black SUV idling nearby. "Andrei? Your passport. Now follow my car, but slowly."

After fifteen minutes driving along a narrow path winding among the woodland pines, the two cars arrived at a fence with a big gray mansion behind it. Andrei was told to park his car in front of the gate. Another guard in camouflage fatigues came up and asked for a passport. He took it and disappeared. While the passport was presumably being checked, Lebedev approached from the garden. In a gray T-shirt and shorts, he looked like he was about to finish his workout. He guided Andrei briskly around the house and into an adjoining veranda overlooking the garden. There was a table and two chairs. Tea was served, along with two cookies on a china plate. Lebedev excused himself and went off to a meeting inside the house. Andrei took a cup and looked around. In the well-kept garden was a trampoline, a grill, and, attached to the fence, a small bucket with a pull-rope that apparently served as an outdoor shower. A wall of glass doors divided the veranda from the house, and all of them were kept shut.

Twenty minutes passed, and Lebedev still hadn't returned. Andrei considered eating the second biscuit. Then the rain started. As the rain grew heavier, one of the glass doors opened and Lebedev appeared, motioning Andrei to come inside. Then he disappeared again.

Andrei found himself in a sitting room with two beige sofas matching the beige walls and a big fireplace. Two huge abstract paintings, both portraits of Lebedev's wife, were waiting to be hung. Bookshelves featured an odd mix of books: Ayn Rand and Sue Townsend; a history of underwear next to a John Le Carré paperback; and the memoirs of Markus Wolf, the head of the Stasi's foreign intelligence. Two copies of a recent issue of *Elle* magazine featuring Lebedev's wife and daughter on the cover were on display on the table, and a golden clutch had been left on the back of one of the sofas.

Another thirty minutes passed, and no biscuits were left. Andrei looked through an open door at what seemed like Lebedev's study—a small room with a table, a chair, and bookshelves filled with jars of nutritional supplements and the collected works of Leo Tolstoy and of Ivan Ilyin, a White émigré and philosopher beloved by Putin.

A door suddenly flung open, and a man in a chef's cap ran into Lebedev's study, calling, "Alexander Evgenevich, your lunch will be served in five minutes!" In a few minutes, Lebedev reappeared. He looked at Andrei, slowed for a moment, then changed his mind. "Do you want more tea?" he asked. Then he excused himself again and went in through the door his chef had come through. Andrei made another circle around the room. After the rain had stopped, he stepped back outside.

Almost two hours passed. In the garden a man was busy burning wood in the grill. Was he preparing for dinner? No sign was heard from inside, no movement from Lebedev's study. If the host wanted to convey the impression that he was a busy and important person, he overdid it.

Finally Lebedev showed up. Now he was ready to talk. Andrei said he was happy to catch him at home—Lebedev was always somewhere, always in the middle of a trip. He said he had come from Crimea where he was celebrating his wedding anniversary.

"I feel like a fish in water everywhere—in Italy, in France; no matter, hah! I just don't like France. It doesn't matter to me, whether I'm in Botswana or Tanzania or on the Barents Sea—there is no difference. The important thing is that it should be interesting." He thought for a second. "It was very strange behavior on the part of the Bolsheviks to close the country. Why do that? All those fences guarded with dogs? It's a big achievement now that we can travel."

He wanted to look energetic and busy, but instead he sounded a little desperate. The conversation turned to the new wave of Russian emigration, and that seemed to worry him. "The logic of our country now is to spend on defense, not to invest in human capital, and the best and brightest are leaving. We have lost hundreds of thousands of smart people, and the measure of the loss has yet to be calculated. It's done major damage. It could seem like not very many are leaving, but those who are leaving are the best. And if they succeed somewhere else—well, it doesn't look very good."

The conversation had turned to Lebedev's career when Andrei suddenly asked, "Vladimir Kara-Murza Sr. is your friend, right?"

Lebedev was instantly alert, "Yes, I know him well. His wife was my schoolmate. What happened to him? We are friends, but I have not seen him for ages."

It had not exactly been for ages. The two had stayed in contact, and when Lebedev had entered the mayoral race in Moscow, Kara-Murza Sr. had campaigned for him.[14] In December 2011, at the protest rally on Sakharova, Lebedev listened to Kasparov and Nemtsov standing in the crowd with Kara-Murza Sr. and, of course, his security detail.

Andrei said that Kara-Murza was fine but that he'd mentioned Kara-Murza's name because he wanted to ask Lebedev about his friend's son, Vladimir Kara-Murza Jr., the close associate of Boris Nemtsov who had been poisoned in Moscow twice and barely survived. The opposition suspected it was the Kremlin that had ordered the attacks. What did he think about the poisoning?

"By what, by Novichok?" Lebedev's intention in mentioning the nerve agent used to poison another Russian, Skripal in the United Kingdom, was meant to convey incredulity, that the implication the Kremlin was involved was simply absurd. But it didn't really work. It betrayed that the Skripal incident was something that jumped immediately to mind. It seemed like every Global Russian we spoke with while researching this book, from pro-Kremlin priest/financier Peter Holodny to the oligarch-turned-dissident Khodorkovsky, and now Lebedev, was thinking about Skripal's poisoning these days.

"Well, I don't know," he said. "I'm not a supporter of these conspiracy theories." He struggled to figure out a way to answer. "And, look, first, who needs to get him poisoned? There is no such practice, poisoning the opposition. There are other methods. And what do you mean, 'the opposition'? Well, as it happens, there is none. I mean real opposition. Among 145 million people, there are a few dissidents, but that's all."

It was a classic denial of a reality Lebedev didn't want to accept. There was no poisoning because such methods were not used against the opposition, because there was no real opposition. The logic was not very convincing. Surely it failed to convince Lebedev himself.

He thought for a moment and then began talking about himself and his relationship with the Kremlin.

"Look, I limited myself to a sort of reservation. I used to play on many chess squares. And later I got it, that the system had changed in such a way that you should sit in one chess square, not more. They explained to me, 'You have a billion, why don't you go buy a castle in the south of France, a yacht, and a plane?'" It was clear that Lebedev referred to Roman Abramovich, a fabulously rich Russian with a truly oligarchic way of life who always played by the Kremlin rules and, as a result, was allowed to sell his assets in Russia at a very high price and set free. "Instead you participate in elections, you print a newspaper," Lebedev continued. "'OK, so you, bitch, are suspect.' So they began 'educating' me. OK, now I know my square—small business, my family." Lebedev sighed. "And there is no way to jump from a square to a square."

And what about the British newspapers? Is the Kremlin not concerned?

"Well, I think they accepted it. And what do I write in my papers? Where it's needed they criticize Russia, and where it's needed, say, on Syria, we support the Russian position. . . . And besides, now it's calming down—maybe because they closed all my businesses. To put it bluntly—I don't have a billion dollars anymore, thus I'm harmless. They took away my airline, and all the money was removed from my bank, so they made my bank business into zero, and then I got condemned. But I was sentenced not to prison but to labor, so I understand we came to terms. Sit still and we leave you in peace. And I do."

Four years after Putin had resumed the presidency, things looked very different for men like Lebedev and Kaspersky. Once high rollers, they were brought to heel, and the hierarchy was firmly reestablished. Successful and wealthy for so many years, both had made traveling to exotic locations their passion. But it seemed that in all their travels, the two former KGB officers couldn't get rid of a tiny but insistent voice in their heads, the one telling them: wherever you are, you cannot hide from us.

CHAPTER 35

ON THE PATH TO WAR

On May 5, 2018, we were on a subway traveling to Brighton Beach, New York. At one end of the car, we spotted three tired-looking middle-aged women. Their chests were decorated in orange and black ribbons. In Russia, this decoration is known as George's ribbon, an insignia of the Russian Imperial military (orange and black, symbolizing fire and gunpowder, respectively). It had long been used at official Soviet celebrations of Victory Day, a Fourth of July–like national holiday commemorating Russia's vanquishing of the Nazis in World War II.

One of the women held a placard with a red star and a Russian man's name. We realized that the three had just taken part in a march in Manhattan. Early that day more than two thousand Russian Americans had marched along the Hudson River down to Battery Park while an aircraft sporting a giant orange and black ribbon flew over the Statue of Liberty. Most marchers carried placards featuring portraits of their ancestors who had fought in World War II. The marchers were partaking in a widespread initiative known as the Immortal Regiment, which began in Russia after Putin reassumed the presidency in 2012. The idea behind it was that the deceased veterans would be forever part of the victorious

Russian army if their descendants would remember them. In Moscow, the Immortal Regiment, promoted by the Kremlin, gathered millions of participants on Victory Day every year, and Putin routinely walked at the front of the march holding a portrait of his father. The Kremlin ensured a march was held in every major city in Russia.

Pro-Kremlin activists also introduced the initiative in the United States with the support of St. Nicholas Church, the headquarters of the Russian Orthodox Church in New York.[1] The Russian Youth of America, an obscure pro-Kremlin group led by a recent emigrant who was also a head of the youth department at St. Nicholas, took over organization of Immortal Regiment marches across the United States.

In May 2018, the marches took place in Washington, Boston, Denver, San Francisco, Seattle, Philadelphia, San Diego, Chicago, Detroit, Tallahassee (Florida), Orlando, Miami, Los Angeles, Houston, Portland (Oregon), Phoenix (Arizona), Raleigh (North Carolina), and Kansas City (Missouri). The largest event took place in New York, while a World War II costume party was held on the premises of an Orthodox church in New Jersey.

New Yorkers probably felt fine about this new march. The city was used to massive marches by Italians on Columbus Day and by the Irish on St. Patrick's Day, and then there was the Puerto Rican Day Parade, the West Indian Day Parade, and the Greek Independence Day Parade. This new Victory Day initiative was small and quiet by comparison. But for the Kremlin, it represented a significant projection of its power to America.

After the annexation of Crimea, the orange and black ribbon had become an ominous and aggressive political symbol. Putin's propagandists had adopted the ribbon as a symbol of an anti-Western, pro-Kremlin agenda. On the streets of Moscow, it became common to see cars with the ribbon attached to the antenna, sometimes in combination with a sticker that said, "1945—We Can Repeat," meaning that we, the Russian army, can get to the West again, if we feel like doing so.

Four years later, when Russian tanks rolled into Ukraine in February 2022, that ominous message became horrible reality.

But in May 2018, it was just a sign that the Kremlin had found a way to use pro-Kremlin civic movements run by Russian emigrants, including church organizations, to bring Putin's ribbon to the United States.

But was he ready to use those movements for bigger things?

The 2016 presidential election in the United States was, no doubt, a crucial moment for the Kremlin. Putin hated Hillary Clinton and believed he understood Donald Trump. Surely it was a good moment to use everything at his disposal to make life difficult for Clinton, so the Kremlin began sponsoring a massive cyberoperation that resulted in the largest active measure of election interference ever seen.

But the Kremlin still acted with restraint. The extensive network of organizations of pro-Kremlin compatriots on American soil was not activated. Instead, the Kremlin used hacking teams based in Russia and channeled the data they obtained to websites located beyond US borders. As we described in the 2017 revised paperback edition of *The Red Web*, many in Moscow believed that the political hacking campaign was a low-risk operation—and that the Kremlin's denial tactics would work forever.

They got caught red-handed almost immediately. CrowdStrike, the private information security company hired to handle the Democratic National Committee breach, published its report exposing Russian hackers in June 2016, before the first dump of stolen information came out. CrowdStrike's report was authored, ironically, by another Russian émigré, Dmitri Alperovitch.

Could the exposure, and the ensuing scandal over Russia's meddling, have had a deterrent effect on the use of pro-Kremlin compatriots in the United States? It seemed very probable.

But it didn't change the reality that Putin's regiment existed in the United States and could be activated at any time.

In the meantime, the émigrés kept raising the stakes with the Kremlin. A new opportunity to strike presented itself with the Russian oligarchs. They were an essential part of Putin's regime but were caught in the crossfire of Western sanctions imposed after the annexation of Crimea. The new Russian exiles turned up to campaign against the dirty Russian money in the West.

When the poisoning of a Russian former spy, Sergei Skripal, in Salisbury led the British Parliament to look into Russian oligarchs' money laundering in London, the new émigrés readily provided testimony. Garry Kasparov was among those who were more than happy to speak up.[2]

The new political émigrés saw this as their contribution to the fight against Putin's regime. If one couldn't get to Putin, one could reach his cronies—that was the logic.

Ilya Zaslavskiy, the former manager of the TNK-BP oil corporation, had been collateral damage in the fight between British and Russian shareholders and was one of those who readily joined the fight. He believed the Russian oligarchs abroad to be Kremlin enablers. If some oligarchs had treated him as a small fish, they greatly miscalculated. He started several campaigns exposing the oligarchs' sponsorship of the most respected Western universities. He campaigned against Soviet-born oligarchs who gave money to Oxford and Harvard in an effort to whitewash their reputations.

Being a diligent man, Zaslavskiy institutionalized his efforts. He joined the Free Russia Foundation as head of research, which meant leading the investigations into Russian oligarchs. The foundation's name resembled that of the institute Fischer and Kennan had launched in the 1950s to help the Russian political émigré cause. This time it was launched by the Russian emigrants, not the Americans. This time the Russians were campaigning on their own.[3]

The new émigrés also joined Vladimir Kara-Murza Jr. in his frantic activities in the corridors of the State Department and Congress in Washington, lobbying for more sanctions against Putin's people. And they kept flying people from Russia—opposition politicians, writers, activists, journalists—straight to Washington to talk to policy makers.

In Russia, the Kremlin kept up its fight against adverse opinions and information. Mostly, in the form of books.

In November 2018 Russian customs seized a copy of Masha Gessen's book *The Future Is History: How Totalitarianism Reclaimed Russia* that someone had ordered on Amazon. Customs claimed the book had "signs of propagandizing certain views and ideologies." The book was finally returned to the customer, but it was clear that Russian customs had started checking books coming into the country.[4]

The Kremlin's wise men knew that if a certain book reached a Russian audience, it could have a devastating effect on the country's political regime, whether it was Karl Marx's *Das Kapital* or Alexander Solzhenitsyn's *The Gulag Archipelago*.

Putin knew it too. He remembered how, back in his days in the KGB, thousands of Soviet citizens managed to read Solzhenitsyn's book despite all efforts by the omnipresent secret police to eliminate every copy.

At the same time, people kept leaving the country.

A year before we witnessed the Immortal Regiment march in New York, Olga Romanova had learned that the FSB was after her. Her contacts warned her that Russian authorities had started investigating her organization, Russia Behind Bars. The police raided the organization's offices, and her husband, Kozlov, got scared. He saw the threat of his own experience ten years prior, when a criminal case had been built against him that resulted in his arrest. Romanova was tough, but he didn't want that to happen to her.

Romanova and Kozlov left the country and moved to Berlin, Germany. There, Romanova went to work for a local Russian-speaking

TV channel. She joined the growing community of Russian journalists who had moved out of Russia and landed jobs elsewhere—in Kiev, Riga, Prague. Their voices were still heard at home; the borders remained porous.

Romanova and Kozlov also chose to do something more challenging: to run Russia Behind Bars from abroad. Romanova supervised things through Facebook and Skype. Kozlov took over management by making trips from Berlin to Moscow almost every month.

But their arrangement wouldn't last for long.

In September 2018 Kozlov and Romanova took a vacation in New York—Romanova wanted to visit the city where she had lived in the early 1990s. There, Kozlov broke the news: he was involved with another woman. Romanova and Kozlov split.

It was around that time when Kozlov told us that his mother had published Nahum Eitingon's letters from prison, with the introduction largely praising their famous ancestor.[5] On the last page of the book there was a photograph of Kozlov's son, now a teenager, in the uniform of a military cadet. One wonders what Nahum Eitingon, Stalin's top assassin, would think if he knew that his descendant was wearing the uniform of White émigré Alexei Jordan's Cadet Corps. We bet he would be surprised.

Romanova was hit hard by her split with Kozlov. But she still had one thing that was important to her: Russia Behind Bars. She started visiting Moscow, just for a few days at a time, testing the waters.

Vladimir Kara-Murza Jr., after his miraculous survival from the second poisoning, also started visiting Russia once again. He told us it was impossible for him, as a Russian politician, to stay away from the country.

That fragile coexistence of political émigrés shuttling between two worlds lasted a few more years. In the spring of 2020, Vladimir Putin had the Russian parliament approve amendments to the constitution that made it possible for him to stay in power forever, at least in theory. It was done in a rude and primitive manner, as if Putin decided to abandon all pretense of being a leader of a democratic country.

The pace of repressions increased, and they took a very personal turn. Andrei's father was put under criminal investigation, and the media license of our website Agentura.ru—which has been investigating the activities of the Russian security services since 2000—was canceled. We found the reason for cancellation quite disgusting: the official notice said the license was canceled "due to a death of the founder." But we were the founders of the website, and we took this as a threat aimed directly at us. The Kremlin also adopted a new policy of creating a list of "foreign agents" made up of individual journalists, with new names added every Friday. In the summer of 2020, many of our journalist friends began leaving the country. In September, it was our turn. We left Moscow just two weeks after Alexei Navalny, the most prominent opposition politician in the country, had gotten sick and lost consciousness on a plane to Omsk.

Navalny was taken to the local hospital in Omsk and put in a coma, and then he was transferred to Berlin, to the Charité hospital. He was still in a coma three weeks later when the German authorities made the statement that Navalny had been poisoned with Novichok, the same nerve agent that had been used to try to assassinate Sergei Skripal, a former Russian military intelligence officer, in Salisbury.

The blunt statement from the German authorities prompted an investigation that helped to answer the most difficult questions: who did the poisoning, what substance was used, and how exactly it was done. The investigation answered these questions not only in the Navalny case, but also in Kara-Murza Jr.'s two poisonings.

In December 2020, an investigative team from Bellingcat, in cooperation with CNN, *Der Spiegel*, the *Insider*, and Navalny's Anti-Corruption Foundation, published a joint report accusing the FSB of Navalny's poisoning. The very same day, Navalny posted,

"The case closed: I know who tried to kill me. We know the names, we know their ranks, and we have the photos." Before the report's publication, Navalny made a phone call to one of the FSB officers the joint team of investigative journalists had identified: Konstantin Kudryavtsev. He was a chemical expert with the FSB Research Institute N2, also known as the FSB Criminalistics Institute.

Navalny was well prepared for the call: he had a video camera on to record his conversation with the FSB officer and he installed special software to make his call look like it was coming from the FSB office directory number. He dialed Kudryavtsev's mobile number and introduced himself as an assistant to the head of the Security Council of Russia who was tasked with debriefing Kudryavtsev on the failure of the poisoning and the survival of Navalny. Kudryavtsev accepted Navalny's call and provided him with the details of the operation: Novichok had been applied to Navalny's underwear when he was staying in the hotel in Tomsk. The FSB officer blamed the medics for the failure of the operation.

The joint investigative team kept digging and soon a list of more victims was produced, with one detail in common: all of them were shadowed in their travels around the country by the same group of FSB operatives, including Kudryavtsev.

One of the targets of the FSB group was Vladimir Kara-Murza Jr., as was discovered in the report published on February 11, 2022. The report stated:

> Based on an analysis of travel records of known members of the poison squad from the FSB's Criminalistics Institute previously implicated in the poisoning of Alexey Navalny and three other Russian activists, we have now established that this unit also systematically tailed Vladimir Kara-Murza before both his first and second medical emergencies.[6]

According to the report, Kudryavtsev was part of the team of FSB operatives who shadowed Kara-Murza on two trips.

Finally, Kara-Murza's intrepid lawyer, Vadim Prokhorov, had found the answers to the questions he had asked himself for five years. Now he knew who had tried to kill his friend. The day the report was published Prokhorov posted on his Facebook page: "CHEKISTS ASSASSINS BELIEVE THEY CAN GET AWAY WITH IT. WRONG. THEY WILL BE CONDEMNED. WITH TIME."

Kara-Murza Jr. was in Moscow when the report emerged, and he stayed. He had made a decision to keep returning to Russia no matter what, and he didn't see why he should revisit that decision when he was given compelling evidence that it was the powerful FSB that had tried to kill him. Five days after the report was published, Kara-Murza discovered he was again under surveillance. A car with a plate assigned to the FSB was following him.

Kara-Murza kept visiting Russia and stayed for lengthy periods, adamant to remain in Russian domestic politics.

And then Russian troops attacked Ukraine.

Ten days later, the Russian parliament approved a law imposing a jail term of up to fifteen years for spreading "fake news" about the conflict in Ukraine. Even the word "war" was banned. Kara-Murza faced a difficult choice: either comply with the law and tread carefully to remain in the country or leave Russia, probably for good. He chose neither. He kept traveling, and whether he was in the United States or in Russia, he kept condemning Putin's war in his public appearances.

Two weeks later, Putin openly encouraged all those against the war to leave Russia for good. On March 16, Putin made a speech about national traitors and the fifth column and added, "The Russian people will always be able to distinguish true patriots from scum and traitors and simply spit them out like a fly that accidentally flew into their mouth."

If it was a hint to Kara-Murza Jr., he didn't take it. He stayed in Moscow. On April 12, police snatched him on the street outside his home and put him in jail. It happened just hours after he had been on CNN calling Putin's government "a regime of murderers."

Ten days later, he was charged with spreading fake news about the Russian military in Ukraine. The prosecutor cited the speech Kara-Murza had made in the Arizona House of Representatives in Phoenix about the brutality of Russian troops in Ukraine.[7] It looked like the Kremlin had decided to punish him not for what he did but for what he was—a Russian politician who had found a way to shuttle between two worlds, campaigning against Putin even during the war. Kara-Murza was placed in Vodnik prison in the north of Moscow, and Vadim Prokhorov, his lawyer, came to visit him in jail several times per week. Despite the threat to his safety, Prokhorov stayed in the country because of his friend.

In the meantime, we focused on investigating the role of the Russian security services in the war in Ukraine. We believed it important to expose the Kremlin's lies about the war. We also wanted to show that there were Russian voices against it. It didn't go unnoticed. In June, we learned that the Russian authorities had placed Andrei on both Russia's domestic and international wanted lists, meaning he would be immediately arrested if he returned to Russia.[8] The FSB initiated a criminal case, and the charges were similar to those Kara-Murza Jr. faced—"spreading false information about the Russian troops in Ukraine," with a jail term of up to ten years.

The rules for Russians abroad were changing, again. Less than three months into the war, evidence emerged of the FSB quietly approaching the families of those activists and journalists who had left the country. FSB agents summoned these relatives to meetings to get them to convince the new émigrés to return.[9] And though nobody was persuaded to come back to Russia, the émigrés took it as a sign that the FSB was treating their relatives in Russia as hostages—with understandable implications.

These kinds of tactics are exactly the same as what so many Russian exiles experienced after the revolution and throughout the Cold War. Russian history made a full circle.

When the war in Ukraine started, Gazprombank, in Zurich, sprang into action. It was a direct successor of the Wozchod bank, which was used successfully by the Kremlin in the 1970s and 1980s to sell Soviet gold and diamonds discreetly.

In March, the European Union kicked seven of the biggest Russian banks off the SWIFT global payments system. But Gazprombank, a subsidiary of the state-owned gas company Gazprom, was allowed to stay. The bank also avoided being placed under European sanctions, and though it was placed under British sanctions, the UK government granted it a license to operate. The bank could continue to receive payments to allow the flow of Russian gas to Europe.[10] The next month Putin signed a decree requiring companies from Western countries deemed "unfriendly" to pay for gas in rubles as a way to respond to the Western sanctions. Some countries rejected the demand, but others complied, opening accounts in rubles at Gazprombank in Zurich.[11]

The Swiss let it go, even though Swiss prosecutors had had an open criminal case for four years against the bank following the publication of the Panama Papers—a giant leak of millions of financial and legal documents from a Panama legal firm—which showed that the bank held the account of a company owned by Sergei Roldugin, a cellist and a personal friend of Putin.[12]

The Russian bank in Zurich found itself in the lucrative role of cutout between West and East, once again tasked by the Kremlin with a very sensitive mission, just as in the days of the Cold War.

After Russia invaded Ukraine, the regime immediately activated networks of pro-Kremlin compatriots abroad, most manifestly in Germany. Thousands marched the streets of German cities on May 9, 2022, on Russian Victory Day, with Russian flags and orange and black ribbons in support of Russia's war in Ukraine. It looked like Moscow, furious with growing international isolation, was eager to show that Russian people beyond Russia's borders were on Putin's side.

In the meantime, Russian émigrés kept fighting the Kremlin. When the war started, most members of Navalny's organization were already abroad, fleeing oppression. Now they began using every opportunity to campaign for sanctions and provided a list of targets that would hit Putin's regime the hardest. With these efforts, they joined the previous wave of political émigrés. It seems to have worked out quite well: the Western powers launched a massive campaign arresting the assets of Russian oligarchs and officials, including their palaces and yachts. Just three months into the war, the Italians seized a $700 million yacht linked to Putin.[13]

Since the beginning of the war, Romanova had put all her famously indomitable energy into organizing her Russian friends into a rapid relief force for refugees. During the first months of the war, she went to the main Berlin train station every day to help the Ukrainians fleeing to Germany. She spent her days buying body armor and first-aid kits to be sent back to Ukraine and connecting people in Germany, Ukraine, and all the countries in between to get people, and sometimes pets, out. She was very proud of the special operation to safely evacuate four cats from Odessa to Berlin.

Once again, Romanova found herself in the right place. She was needed, and she answered the call.

EPILOGUE

For decades, if not centuries, the Kremlin's main ideological line to justify Russia's autocracy was insisting that the country was unique.

It was its own Russian microcosm, totally incomprehensible from the outside, driven by rules and laws designed specifically for its vast territory. The universal norm was not applicable there. All kinds of evidence was presented, drawn from the wisdom of politicians and historians and great Russian writers. As a Russian poet famously put it:

> No, Russia can't be understood
> With mind or held to common standard: Her stature is unique for
>   good—
> Just faith in her is all we're granted.[1]

Thus—the logic goes, in lines that have been cited over and over again—Russia simply could not be turned into any semblance of a normal country, like, say, a Western democracy. Only autocrats could govern it efficiently, and only they could push it forward. The legacy was obvious: Peter the Great, Lenin and Stalin, Putin.

When Putin started the war in Ukraine, he immediately invoked the uniqueness of the country. For pro-Putin Russians, the sanctions supported by many countries and the near universal condemnation of the war were simply proof that the entire world was against Russia, again. The besieged fortress, standing alone, kept fortifying itself.

But for members of the intellectual and progressive part of Russian society, the war rendered their situation increasingly untenable. The reality of the Russian present became horrible, and the Russian future, at least the immediate one, appeared even bleaker. A joke that went viral on social media in the first month of the war claimed that English classes in Russian schools had stopped teaching the future simple tense. Russia no longer had a simple future.

Nor does the Russian past offer much hope anymore. After the Soviet Union collapsed, the new Russian leader Boris Yeltsin's narrative was straightforward: the Soviet period was a horrible deviation, and Russians simply needed to get back to what they had before 1917—the Russia of Leo Tolstoy, Anton Chekhov, and Pyotr Tchaikovsky. Thus, the emblem for Yeltsin's Congress of Compatriots in 1991 was made up of three lines—the white, blue, and red of the Russian tricolor—with a curve to symbolize the Soviet era's distortion of the otherwise smooth course of Russian history. But the invasion of Ukraine made the Russian Empire—with its bloody wars and self-imposed role as gendarme of Europe—look much less attractive.

A new national narrative is badly needed for Russia. Yet it cannot be produced in Putin's Russia, a place rampant with paranoia.

The long history of Russian emigration has at least one example of a successful effort beyond Russian borders: the Russian Free University, established in Prague in the 1920s and funded by the Czech government. It was dubbed the "Russian Oxford," and it managed to keep the Russian intellectual tradition alive and thriving until it was shut down by the Germans during the occupation.

Despite the false notion of it being "unique"—a narrative preached by Russian tyrants from the tsars to Putin—the country could produce something good, but only in cooperation with the West.

With so many Russian intellectuals abroad but still intimately connected to the country, there is a good chance, we believe, to make a new effort, and finally put the country on a path toward normalcy.

ACKNOWLEDGMENTS

Researching this book was a particular challenge for us. Our story embraces a hundred years, and as journalists, we are not used to working with such a long time frame. What became clear quite early is that in Russia, the history is less about archives, still jealously guarded, than it is about people.

When Irina went to the State Archive of Sociopolitical History, the former Communist Party Archive, the first person she met was an archivist, a charming lady in her seventies who turned out to be a niece of Stalin's successful spy Anatoly Gorsky, the chief of station in the United States who replaced Zarubin after Zarubin was recalled to Moscow. Such fortuitous encounters happened more than once and defined our approach. Everywhere we went, we tried to find and talk to people whose ancestors, relatives, friends, and colleagues were part of the story.

We are deeply grateful to Olga Romanova, Alexei Kozlov, Vladimir Kara-Murza Jr., and Vadim Prokhorov for their patience in the face of our never-ending questions. Thanks also to Evgeny Kiselev, one of the founders of NTV, now working in Ukraine— another Russian compatriot who was forced to leave the country.

We would like to thank the officers, veterans, and relatives of intelligence officers in Russia and in the United States whose help was crucial but whose names cannot be named. The book *Rezident,* by former FBI agent Robert K. Baker—a thorough and detailed research into the spy career of Vasily Zarubin—was of great help to us.

We are grateful to Natella Boltyanskaya for very generously sharing her research notes on the Jackson-Vanik amendment and to David Hoffman for reading chapters and offering suggestions.

Our friends Mindy Eng, Nick Fielding, and Marina Latysheva have always been supportive of us. We want to thank Katya and Egor, who tolerated us at their lively wooden dacha in the green hills sixty miles from Moscow in the summer of 2018—not an easy thing, given that we were fighting (sometimes very loudly) over every chapter.

We are also very grateful to Ivan Krastev for giving us the opportunity to spend December at IWM in Vienna—at exactly the moment when we needed a quiet place in which to turn our collection of outlines into a manuscript. And we are deeply thankful to Ivan, Dessy and Clemena in Vienna and Fiona, Laurie and Sam in London for their support when we started a new stage of our life—the life in emigration.

We also want to thank Evan Osnos, an incredible journalist at the *New Yorker*. In a way, it was Evan who gave us the idea for this book when, while treating us to lunch at the legendary Tabard Inn in Washington, he said, "Guys, you did a book about security, and then you did a book about technology. Now it's time to do a book about people."

We are deeply indebted to Evan's father, Peter Osnos, founder of PublicAffairs, who has been supportive of us since he agreed to read the proposal for our first book, *The New Nobility*, exactly ten years ago.

This book would have been impossible without Clive Priddle, publisher of PublicAffairs, who never flagged in his trust in us, even at a rather tricky moment in spring 2019.

We are immensely grateful to Athena Bryan at PublicAffairs and Lisa Kaufman, our editor, for helping us frame the manuscript on rather short notice!

And, as always, we thank Robert Guinsler at Sterling Lord Literistic, our agent and our friend.

NOTES

A NOTE ON SOURCES

We are grateful for the help of many people who spoke to us on condition that we protect their identities. For that reason, while we have documented our interviews with those people, we have elected not to provide detailed citations for readers, since information such as the date or location of the interview or the source's position or title increases the risk that they might be identified.

In addition, for dramatic purposes, we have taken the liberty in a very few instances of re-creating dialogue based on sourced information about the substance of a spoken conversation; in other cases, quoted dialogue represents our translation into English of conversation conducted in Russian. In all cases, we have attempted to represent the content of the conversation accurately, as the source conveyed it.

INTRODUCTION

1. Mike Eckel, "Chiefs of Three Russian Intelligence Agencies Travel to Washington," Radio Free Europe/Liberty, February 1, 2018, https://www.rferl.org/a/russia-spy-chiefs-washington/29010324.html.

2. Natalia Portyakova, "Dukhovno-Kulturny Center v Parizhe otkroyet diplomat" [The Spiritual-Cultural Center in Paris will be opened by a diplomat], *Izvestia*, August 7, 2017, https://iz.ru/627990/nataliia-portiakova/oplot-russkoi-kultury-i-dukhovnosti-v-parizhe-poluchit-glavu.

3. Vladimir Putin, "Opening Address at the World Congress of Russians Abroad" (English transcript), Kremlin, October 24, 2006, http://en.kremlin.ru/events/president/transcripts/23861.

4. Kremlin, interview with Vladimir Putin by *Russkaya Mysl* [in Russian], November 23, 2006, http://kremlin.ru/events/president/transcripts/23919.

5. UN Department of Economic and Social Affairs, *International Migration Report 2017: Highlights* (New York: United Nations, 2017), http://www.un

.org/en/development/desa/population/migration/publications/migrationreport/docs/MigrationReport2017_Highlights.pdf: "In 2017, India was the largest country of origin of international migrants (17 million), followed by Mexico (13 million). Other countries of origin with large migrant populations include the Russian Federation (11 million), China (10 million), Bangladesh (7 million), Syrian Arab Republic (7 million) and Pakistan and Ukraine (6 million each)."

CHAPTER 1: TALENT SPOTTING

1. Robert K. Baker, *Rezident: The Espionage Odyssey of Soviet General Vasily Zarubin* (Bloomington, IN: iUniverse, 2015).

2. Andrei Soldatov and Irina Borogan, "Vladimir Bukovsky: Rossia raspadetsa na sem chastey" [Vladimir Bukovsky: Russia will split up on seven parts], *Versyia* (November 2003).

3. F. E. Dzerzhinsky, "Zapiska V.R. Menzhinskomy o borbe s emigrantskimi terroristichikimi gruppami" [A note to Menzhinsky on fighting with the émigré terrorist groups], March 30, 1924 (no. 895):538, predsedatel VChK-OGPU, Rossia—XX vek (Moscow: Fond Demokratia, 2007).

4. Nicolas Ross, *Koutiepov: Le combat d'un général blanc: De la Russie à l'exil* (Geneva, Switzerland: Editions de Syrtes, 2016), 131.

5. The description of the romance is based on conversation with Alexei Kozlov, great-grandson of Zarubin, in March and April 2018, and the family chronicle written in 2012 by Petr Zarubin, son of Vasily Zarubin.

6. Ervin Stavinsky, *Zarubiny: Semyeynaya rezidentura* (Moscow: Olma, 2003).

7. Joseph Stalin, "October Revolution and the Tactics of the Russian Communists," first published as a preface to the book *On the Road to October* in December 1924. Available online, https://www.marxists.org/reference/archive/stalin/works/1924/12.htm.

8. Eduard Sharapov, *Naum Eitingon—karayushy mech Stalina* [Nahum Eitingon—a punishing sword of Stalin] (Moscow: Neva, 2003).

9. Sharapov, *Naum Eitingon.*

10. Stavinsky, *Zarubiny.*

CHAPTER 2: IDENTIFYING TARGETS

1. Sharapov, *Naum Eitingon*, 17; see also Mary-Kay Wilmers, *The Eitingons: A Twentieth-Century Story* (London: Verso, 2012), 147.

2. Evgeny Zhirnov, "V podvalnom pomeshenii Sovkonsulstva proiskhodilo sobranie" [In a cellar of the Soviet consulate, there was a meeting], *Kommersant*, June 8, 2009, https://www.kommersant.ru/doc/1176117.

3. "Politichesky carnaval, Moskva, Iun 1929" [Political carnival, Moscow, June 1929], https://cocomera.livejournal.com/267225.html.

4. "OGPU: Obzor politicheskogo sostoyania SSSR za iun 1929" [Overview of the political situation of the USSR, June 1929], http://istmat.info/node /25817.

5. V. K. H. Khaustov, V. P. Naumov, and N. C. Plotnikova. *Lubyanka. Stalin I VchK-OGPU-NKVD Yanvar 1921–Dekabr 1936* [Stalin and Lubyanka organs: VChK-OGPU-NKVD January 1921–December 1936] (Moscow: Fond Demokratia, 2003), 180–181; the full transcript of the conversation between Bukharin and Kamenev in Yuri Feltshinsky, *Razgovori s Bukharinim* [Conversations with Bukharin] (Moscow: IGL, 1993), 33, http:// lib.ru/HISTORY/FELSHTINSKY/buharin.txt.

6. Vyacheslav Menzhinsky was head of the Soviet secret police OGPU from 1924 to 1936.

7. Khaustov et al., *Lubyanka*.

CHAPTER 3: THE COST OF LOVE

1. Christopher Andrew, *The Secret World: A History of Intelligence* (New Haven, CT: Yale University Press, 2018), 285.

2. Khaustov et al., *Lubyanka*, Blyumkin's testimony, 193–212.

3. Oleg Goncharenko, *Izgnannaya Armia* [Exiled army] (Moscow: Veche, 2012), 188–193.

4. "K Istorii Chetvertogo Internatsionala" [To history of the fourth international], the online archive of the bulletins of the opposition, http://iskra-research .org/FI/BO/index.shtml.

5. Khaustov et al., *Lubyanka*, Blyumkin's testimony, 208–209.

6. Grigory Agabekov, *OGPU: The Russian Secret Terror* (New York: Brentano, 1931), 221.

7. Evgeny Matonin, "Partiynaya lubov Yakova Blyumkina" [A party love of Yakov Blyumkin], *Rodina*, March 1, 2016, https://rg.ru/2016/03/15/rodina -blumkin.html.

8. Khaustov et al., *Lubyanka*, 213.

9. The cars were described by several witnesses. One account in English can be found in James E. Hassel, "Russian Refugees in France and the United States between the World Wars," *American Philosophical Society* 81, pt. 7 (1991).

10. Ross, *Koutiepov*.

11. "La mystérieuse disparition du Général Koutiepoff," *Journal L'Illustration*, no. 4536 et 4537 (February 8 and 15, 1930), http://www.fangpo1.com/Koutiep off .htm.

12. The abduction account is based on the evidence of this sole witness, twenty-five-year-old August Steinmetz, that he provided to *L'Echo de Paris*, quoted in Ross, *Koutiepov*, 275–278.

13. Miller spent almost two years in Lubyanka prison until he was executed on May 11, 1939. For details, see also Nicolas Ross, *De Koutiepov a Miller: Le combat de russes blanc (1930–1940)* (Geneva, Switzerland: Editions de Syrtes, 2017), 213–241. See also V. L. Burtsev, *Bolshevitskie gangster v Parizhe: Pokhishenie generala Miller I generala Kutepova* [Bolshevik gangsters in Paris: Abduction of general Miller and general Kutepov] (Paris: printed by the author, 1939).

CHAPTER 4: "THE HORSE"

1. Victor Serge and Natalia Sedova Trotsky, *The Life and Death of Leon Trotsky* (London: Haymarket, 2016), 226–229.

2. Dmitry Volkogonov, *Trotsky: Demon Revolutsii* [Trotsky Devil of Revolution] (Moscow: Yauza, 2017), 518.

3. V. V. Poznyakov, *Sovetskaya razvedka v Amerike: 1919–1941* [Soviet Intelligence in America: 1919–1940] (Moscow: Mezhdunarodnie Otnoshenia, 2015), 450–452.

4. Baker, *Rezident.*

5. American aspects of assassination of Leon Trotsky. Hearings before the committee on Un-American Activities, House of Representatives, Eighty-First Congress, second session, July 26, August 30, October 18 and 19, and December 4, 1950.

6. His real name was Gregory Rabinowitz. He was an intelligence officer acting under disguise of the head of the office of the Soviet Red Cross in New York. See V. V. Poznyakov, *Sovetskaya Razvedka v Amerike 1919–1941* [Soviet Intelligence in America: 1919–1941] (Moscow: Mezhdunarodnie Otnoshenia, 2015), 425–426.

7. Poznyakov, *Sovetskaya Razvedka v Amerike.*

8. E. P. Sharapov, *Eitongon—Karaushiy Mech Stalina* [Eitingon—Punishing Sword of Stalin] (Moscow: Neva, 2003), 34.

9. Isaac Deutscher, *The Prophet: The Life of Leon Trotsky* (London: Verso, 2015), 1395, 1489.

10. P. Sudoplatov, *Spetsoperatsii 1930–1950 godi* [Special operations 1930–1950s] (Moscow: Olma, 1997).

11. Natalia Sedova, "Father and Son," Fourth International, August (1941): 196–200. https://www.marxists.org/archive/sedova-natalia/1940/misc/x001.htm.

12. Victor Serge and Natalia Sedova Trotsky, *The Life and Death of Leon Trotsky* (London: Haymarket, 2016).

13. *Guardian*, "Trotsky's assassination remembered by his grandson" (video), *YouTube*, August 21, 2012, https://www.youtube.com/watch?v=pI-arymQl94.

14. Serge and Sedova, *Life and Death*.

15. Deutscher, *The Prophet*, 1534.

16. E. P. Sharapov, *Eitongon*, 42.

17. Sudoplatov, *Spetsoperatsii*.

18. Deutscher, *The Prophet*, 1538.

CHAPTER 5: "THE MOTHER"

1. Wilmers, *The Eitingons*, 274; authors' conversations with Alexei Kozlov, December 2017–May 2019.

2. Sudoplatov, *Spetsoperatsii*.

3. He was issued a passport with the name "Frank Jacson"—apparently, Soviet intelligence misspelled the name. See also Harvard University, "American Aspects of Assassination of Leon Trotsky, Hearings before the Committee on Un-American Activities, House of Representatives, July 26, August 30, October 18 and 19, and December 4, 1950," https://archive.org/stream/americanaspectsoounit /americanaspectsoounit_djvu.txt.

4. E. P. Sharapov, *Eitongon*, 40.

5. Wilmers, *The Eitingons*.

6. Deutscher, *The Prophet*, 1539–1555.

7. Serge and Sedova, *Life and Death*, 265.

8. Serge and Sedova, 267. Mercader spent twenty years in a Mexican prison and then went to the Soviet Union. See Sudoplatov, *Spetsoperatsii*, 120.

9. The decision of Politburo of the Central Committee VKP (b) "About Awarding Mercader K.R., Eitingon N.I., Vasilevsky L.P. and others," June 6, 1941 (secret). The full list of agents awarded for Trotsky's assassination consists of Caridad Mercader, Nahum Eitingon (by Lenin's order); Lev Vasilevsky, Pavel Sudoplatov (by the Order of Red Banner); Iosif Grigulevich, Pastelnyak (by the Order of Red Star). Pastelnyak was an intelligence operative under disguise of a Soviet vice-consul in New York in 1940. Text of the decision is available at https://www.alexanderyakovlev.org/fond/issues-doc/58790.

CHAPTER 6: OPERATIONS AREA: UNITED STATES

1. "Syezd kompartii SCHA" [Congress of the Communist Party of the U.S.], *Pravda*, June 1, 1940, 6, http://istmat.info/files/uploads/43350/1940_g._1_polu-godie.pdf.

2. Pavel Sudoplatov and Anatoly Sudoplatov, *A Soviet Spymaster* (New York: Little, Brown, 1994).

3. Wilson Center, "Vassiliev White Notebook #1," 2009, http://digitalarchive
.wilsoncenter.org/document/112564.

4. Wilson Center, "Vassiliev White Notebook #1."

5. Baker, *Rezident.*

6. *International Wartime Parade in New York,* June 13, 1942, Grinberg, Para-
maunt, Pather Newsreels, https://www.gettyimages.com/detail/video/overhead-
views-of-parade-going-down-a-new-york-city-news-footage/502852465.

7. Family recollection of Zarubin's relatives. One of the sons of the prominent White émigré was lured to the Soviet Union and enlisted in the cavalry unit
of the Red army. He survived the war and became a close friend of Zarubin's
family.

8. To the FBI he was known as Benjamin W. Lassen or Lassov. See FBI files
on Koval available on the website of FBI online vault.

9. Yuri Lebedev was Koval's closest pupil in the Moscow Technical Chemical
Institute (Koval resumed his career at this facility after he got back to the Soviet
Union). For years, Lebedev was intrigued by Koval's spy past, and it became his
life passion to research Koval's life in archives and among those who knew him.
Much of the account about Koval is derived from Lebedev's research.

10. Allen Weinstein and Alexander Vassiliev, *The Haunted Wood: Soviet Espionage in America—The Stalin Era* (New York: Random House, 1998).

11. Abram Slutsky headed the Soviet foreign intelligence service from May
1935 to February 1938.

CHAPTER 7: THE TIDE TURNS

1. Hearings before the Committee on Un-American Activities, House of
Representatives, Eighty-First Session, March 31 and April 1, 1949, Government
Printing Office, Washington, DC, 1949.

2. Baker, *Rezident.*

3. FBIHQ file 10-340473: SF report to FBIHQ dated February 14, 1948,
quoted in Baker, *Rezident.* The transcript is also quoted in Gregg Herken, *Broth-
erhood of the Bomb* (New York: Henry Holt, 2002), as taken from two contem-
poraneous FBI reports on Nelson: Ladd to Hoover, April 16, 1943, 1–9, vol. 2;
and San Francisco field report, May 7, 1943, 10–22, vol. 1, Steve Nelson file, FBI.

4. CIA, "Part I: The American Response to Soviet Espionage," in *Venona:
Soviet Espionage and the American Response, 1939–1957,* March 19, 2007 (updated
June 19, 2013), https://www.cia.gov/library/center-for-the-study-of-intelligence
/csi-publications/books-and-monographs/venona-soviet-espionage-and-the
-american-response-1939-1957/part1.htm.

5. In the United States, Zarubin acted under an assumed name, Vassili Zubilin, Third Secretary of the Embassy of USSR, and he is referred to by this name in Hoover's letter.

6. J. V. Stalin. "The Dissolution of the Communist International: Answer to Reuter's Correspondent, May 28, 1943," https://www.marxists.org/reference /archive/stalin/works/1943/05/28.htm.

7. The letter named ten Soviet intelligence operatives and two American assets, but nine were specifically named as Zarubin's closest associates. CIA online library, Part I: American response to Soviet Espionage, Anonymous letter to Hoover, undated (received 7 August 1943), National Security Agency Venona Collection, 54-001, box D046 [Russian original with English translation], https:// www.cia.gov/library/center-for-the-study-of-intelligence/csi-publications/books -and-monographs/venona-soviet-espionage-and-the-american-response-1939 -1957/10.gif/image.gif.

8. Kathryn S. Olmsted, *Red Spy Queen: A Biography of Elizabeth Bentley* (Chapel Hill: University of North Carolina Press, 2002), 60.

9. Weinstein and Vassiliev, *Haunted Wood*, 276.

10. Weinstein and Vassiliev, *Haunted Wood*, 276.

11. N. V. Petrov, "Kto Rukovodil Organami Gosbezopasnosti 1941–1954" [Who headed the organs of state security in 1941–1954] (Moscow: Memorial, 2010), 951.

12. Authors' conversation with Alexei Kozlov, Zoya's grandson.

13. Stalin had his own "death doctor"—Grigory Mairanovsky, professor, and colonel of state security, the head of Laboratory N1 (poisoning) within the Soviet secret police. He used political prisoners for experiments with poisons.

14. Authors' conversation with Koval's biographer Yuri Lebedev, December 2016. See also Andrei Soldatov, "The Soviet Atomic Spy Who Asked for a U.S. Pension," *Daily Beast*, May 28, 2016, https://www.thedailybeast.com/the-soviet -atomic-spy-who-asked-for-a-us-pension.

15. Based on research done by Yuri Lebedev and provided to the authors.

16. Kremlin, "President Vladimir Putin Handed Over to the GRU (Military Intelligence) Museum the Gold Star Medal and Hero of Russia Certificate and Document Bestowed on Soviet Intelligence Officer George Koval," Kremlin.ru, November 2, 2007, http://en.kremlin.ru/events/president/news/43173.

CHAPTER 8: WARRING NARRATIVES

1. CIA, "Russian Emigrant Organizations," Confidential report, March 29, 1950, available on the website of the CIA's Freedom of Information Act

Electronic Reading Room, https://www.cia.gov/library/readingroom/docs/CIA -RDP82-00457R004400040003-3.pdf.

2. Letter to George Kennan from William H. Jackson, July 2, 1951, released on January 18, 2002, CIA website, https://www.cia.gov/library/readingroom /document/cia-rdp80r01731r000500560001-9.

3. CIA, "Russian Emigre Politics," CIA-RDP57-00384R00100050068-3, July 20, 2000, https://www.cia.gov/library/readingroom/document/cia-rdp57 -00384r00100050068-3.

4. Kevin C. Ruffner, "Review: Soldiers, Spies, and the Rat Line: America's Undeclared War against the Soviets," *Studies in Intelligence* (1995):117, https:// numbers-stations.com/cia/Studies%20In%20Intelligence%20Nazi%20-%20 Related%20Articles/STUDIES%20IN%20INTELLIGENCE%20NAZI%20 -%20RELATED%20ARTICLES_0010.pdf.

5. Deutscher, *The Prophet*, 1366.

6. Markus Wolfe, "Troe is 30-kh" [Three from the 1930s] (Moscow: Progress, 1990), 66.

7. And he was right to be cautious—already in 1936 the Soviet authorities got suspicious of Fischer's *The Nation*, calling the magazine "the main Trotskyist horn in the US" and wondering whether Fischer was ready to attack his journal and defend the Soviet position. See the letter of K. A. Umansky, Soviet diplomat in the United States to the Soviet Foreign Ministry with proposals of increasing the Soviet Union information influence in the United States, October 20, 1936, Alexander Yakovlev Foundation, https://www.alexanderyakovlev.org/fond/issues -doc/71001.

8. Hede Massing, *This Deception* (New York: Duell, Sloan, & Pierce, 1951), 258; Baker, *Rezident*.

9. In December 1950, Sir Bill Slim, the chief of the Imperial General Staff of the United Kingdom, returned from a visit to Washington and warned his fellow service chiefs that "the United States were convinced that war was inevitable, and that it was almost certain to take place within the next eighteen months; whereas we did not hold [this view], and were still hopeful that war could be avoided. This attitude of the United States was dangerous because there was the possibility that they might think that because war was inevitable, the sooner we got it over with the better, and we might as a result be dragged unnecessarily into World War III." Richard J. Aldrich, *The Hidden Hand: Britain, America, and Cold War Secret Intelligence* (Woodstock, NY: Overlook, 2001), 11.

10. US State Department, "NSC 20/1, US Objectives With Respect to Russia," August 18, 1948, https://archive.org/details/NSC201-USObjectivesWith RespectToRussia/. Drafted by the Policy Staff in the State Department, PSC 38, the NSC report states that "in the event of a disintegration of Soviet power . . . our best course would be to permit all the exiled elements to return to Russia as

rapidly as possible and to see to it, in so far as this depends on us, that they are all given roughly equal opportunity to establish their bids for power." No clear protégé so far: "among the existing and potential opposition groups there is none which we will wish to sponsor entirely and for whose actions, if it were to obtain power in Russia, we wish to take responsibility."

11. Wilson Center, "George Kennan on Organizing Political Warfare [Redacted Version]," April 30, 1948, https://digitalarchive.wilsoncenter.org /document/114320.

12. CIA, "Russian Emigrant Organizations," Confidential report, March 29, 1950, available on the website of the CIA's Freedom of Information Act Electronic Reading Room, https://www.cia.gov/library/readingroom/docs/CIA -RDP82-00457R004400040003-3.pdf.

13. Princeton University Library, "Fischer Louis, 1896–1970," https:// findingaids.princeton.edu/names/73845816.

14. Hugh Wilford, *The Mighty Wurlitzer: How the CIA Played America* (Cambridge, MA: Harvard University Press, 2008), 42.

15. Authors' conversation with British historian Richard Aldrich.

16. Eric Thomas Chester, *Covert Network: Progressives, the International Rescue Committee, and the CIA* (Abingdon: Routledge, 1995).

17. Pavel Tribunskiy, "The Ford Foundation, the Cultural Cold War, and the Russian Diaspora in the USA: A Case Study of the Free Russia Fund/East European Fund (1951–1961)," Issuelab, January 1, 2016, https://www.issuelab .org/resource/ford-foundation-the-cultural-cold-war-and-the-russian-diaspora -in-the-usa-a-case-study-of-the-free-russia-fund-east-european-fund-1951-1961 .html.

18. George Fischer, ed., *Russian Émigré Politics* (New York: Free Russia Fund, Inc., 1951), 5.

19. In 1952, George Fischer published a second book, titled *Soviet Opposition to Stalin*. This book repeated the same argument but tailored it to a broader audience. It was greeted by glowing reviews in academic journals.

20. CIA, "Russian Emigrant Organizations," Confidential report, March 29, 1950, available on the website of the CIA's Freedom of Information Act Electronic Reading Room, https://www.cia.gov/library/readingroom/docs/CIA -RDP82-00457R004400040003-3.pdf.

21. CIA employment of Russian émigrés was not limited by the NTS. George Kiselvater was born in St. Petersburg in 1910, brought to the United States in 1915, and remained in America when the Bolsheviks seized power. Kiselvater joined the US Army during World War II and, as a fluent Russian speaker, was involved in the lend-lease program. When the CIA was formed, he joined and became a legend at Langley as a branch chief in the Soviet Division. As a handler, he ran several Soviet spies, including Oleg Penkovsky. CIA, "A Look

Back . . . George Kisevalter: Legendary Case Officer," January 14, 2011 (updated April 30, 2013), https://www.cia.gov/news-information/featured-story-archive/2011-featured-story-archive/george-kisevalter.html.

CHAPTER 9: STALIN'S DAUGHTER

1. A colonel Lev Vasilevsky—by the secret Stalin's order, he was given the Red Banner award for his role in the assassination of Trotsky.

2. M. A. Tumshis and V. A. Zolotarev, *Evrei v NKVD SSSR 1936–1938* [Jews in NKVD USSR, 1936–1938] (Moscow: Russkij fond sodejstvija obrazovaniju i nauke, 2017), 710.

3. CIA, "Soviet Use of Assassination and Kidnapping: A 1964 Review of KGB Methods," September 22, 1993 (updated August 4, 2007), https://www.cia.gov /library/center-for-the-study-of-intelligence/kent-csi/vol19no3/html/v19i3a01p _0001.htm.

4. Simo Mikkonen, "Mass Communications as a Vehicle to Lure Russian Émigrés Homeward," *Journal of International and Global Studies* 2, no. 2 (2011): 44–61, http://www.lindenwood.edu/files/resources/44-61.pdf.

5. *New York Times*, "Émigrés' Fears Cited: Countess Tolstoy Calls Exiles in US Target of Soviets," May 24, 1956.

6. The Free Russia Fund was renamed the East European Fund at the end of 1951. See Pavel Tribunskiy, "The Ford Foundation, the Cultural Cold War, and the Russian Diaspora in the USA: A Case Study of the Free Russia Fund/East European Fund (1951–1961)."

7. Association for Diplomatic Studies and Training, "Ambassador Mark Palmer," Foreign Affairs Oral History Project, October 30, 1997, https://www .adst.org/OH%20TOCs/Palmer,%20Mark.toc.pdf.

8. US Department of State, "A 'Controlled' Freeze, January 1966–May 1967: Telegram from Secretary of State Rusk to the Ambassador to the Soviet Union (Thompson), March 6, 1967," US Department of State Archive, https://2001 -2009.state.gov/r/pa/ho/frus/johnsonlb/xiv/1396.htm.

9. WNYC, "Svetlana Alliluyeva," April 26, 1967 (audio recording), NYPR Archive Collections, https://www.wnyc.org/story/svetlana-alliluyeva/.

10. WNYC, "Svetlana Alliluyeva."

11. Grace Kennan Warnecke, "My Secret Summer with Stalin's Daughter," *Politico*, May 2, 2018.

12. Warnecke, "My Secret Summer."

13. Lesley Rimmel, "How Do You Solve a Problem Like Svetlana?" Wellesley Centers for Women, https://www.wcwonline.org/Women-s-Review-of-Books -Nov/Dec-2016/how-do-you-solve-a-problem-like-svetlana.

14. "Faculty Unit Urges Transfer of Power," *Columbia Spectator*, May 6, 1968, https://archive.org/stream/ldpd_8603880_000#page/n9/mode/2up/search /sociolo.

15. WNYC, "Svetlana Alliluyeva," April 26, 1967 (audio recording), NYPR Archive Collections, https://www.wnyc.org/story/svetlana-alliluyeva/.

16. Boris Pasternak, "Ona pytalas osvoboditsa ot mertvoy khvatki otsa" [She tried to break from the deadly grip of her father], *Moskovskie Novosti*, December 2, 2011, http://www.mn.ru/friday/76166.

17. Authors' conversations with Alexander Cherkasov, a chairman of Memorial Human Rights organization.

CHAPTER 10: NOW IT'S OFFICIAL

1. Ford Library and Museum, "Memorandum of Conversation," March 1, 1973, https://www.fordlibrarymuseum.gov/library/document/0314/1552563.pdf.

2. Adam Nagourney, "In Tapes, Nixon Rails about Jews and Blacks," *New York Times*, December 10, 2010, https://www.nytimes.com/2010/12/11/us/politics /11nixon.html.

3. "What it is, is it's the insecurity," Nixon once said. "It's the latent insecurity. Most Jewish people are insecure. And that's why they have to prove things"; Nagourney, "In Tapes."

4. Nagourney, "In Tapes."

5. The source of the transcript of Politburo's meeting held on March 20, 1973: "Spisok Brezhneva" [Brezhnev's list], *Novaya Gazeta*, March 13, 2006, https:// www.novayagazeta.ru/articles/2006/03/13/29888-spisok-brezhneva.

6. Andrei Sakharov, "Open Letter to the United States Congress," December 13, 1974, http://insidethecoldwar.org/sites/default/files/documents/Jackson -Vanik%20Amendment%20to%20the%20trade%20reform%20act%20of%20 1972,%20january%204,%201975.pdf.

7. Fred A. Lazin, *The Struggle for Soviet Jewry in American Politics* (Lanham, MD: Rowman & Littlefield, 2005), 47.

8. Christopher Andrew and Vasili Mitrokhin, *The Mitrokhin Archive: The KGB in Europe and the West* (London: Penguin, 1999), 413.

9. *New York Times*, "Ford Signs the Trade Act; Soviet Issued Is Unresolved," January 4, 1975.

10. *New York Times*, "What Price a Soviet Jew?" February 22, 1981, https:// www.nytimes.com/1981/02/22/opinion/what-price-a-soviet-jew.html. The *New York Times* argued: "Just look at the pattern since 13,000 Soviet Jews were unexpectedly allowed to leave in 1971: With the signing of SALT I, the first big wheat deal and the promise of more trade, the number rose in 1972 and 1973 to

32,000 and 35,000. Then came the Jackson-Vanik amendment, impeding trade unless Jews were allowed to leave freely, and the departures declined sharply, to 21,000 in 1974, 13,000 in 1975, 14,000 in 1976 and 17,000 in 1977. The amendment remains in force, but with progress toward SALT II and a further wheat deal, emigration rose again to 29,000 in 1978 and to a record total of 51,000 in 1979. Then came Afghanistan, the wheat embargo and other trade restrictions, and the 1980 figure fell to 21,000."

11. Authors' conversation with Nikita Petrov, memorial historian of the KGB and Stalin's secret services.

12. *New York Times*, "Remember the Refuseniks?" December 14, 1990, https://www.nytimes.com/1990/12/14/opinion/remember-the-refuseniks.html.

CHAPTER 11: BEAR IN THE WEST

1. Nina Alovert, *Mikhail Baryshnikov: Ya vybral svoyu sudbu* [Mikhail Baryshnikov: I chose my destiny] (Moscow: AST, 2006).

2. Kevin Plummer, "Historicist: Centre Stage in the Cold War" *Torontoist*, July 2, 2001, https://torontoist.com/2011/07/historicist_centre_stage_in_the _cold_war/.

3. John Fraser, *Private View: Inside Baryshnikov's American Ballet Theatre* (New York: Bantam, 1988).

4. The account of Baryshnikov's escape is derived largely from Fraser, *Private View*; Alovert, *Mikhail Baryshnikov*; and Plummer, "Historicist."

5. Plummer, "Historicist."

6. Plummer, "Historicist."

7. Authors' conversation with a former agent of the KGB station in Ottawa, Canada.

8. Eva Merkacheva, "Solist Bolshogo Teatra rasskazal o rabote na vneshnuyu razvedku" [A dancer of the Bolshoy Theater tells of his work on foreign intelligence], *Moskovsky Komsomolets*, March 22, 2019, https://www.mk.ru/social/2019/03/21/solist-bolshogo-teatra-rasskazal-o-rabote-na-vneshnyuyu-razvedku.html.

CHAPTER 12: THE KGB THINKS BIG

1. "A case of Solzhenitsyn" [in Russian], Solzhenitsyn.ru, http://www.solzhenitsyn.ru/upload/text/Delo_o_pisatele_A.I._Solzhenitsyne_(Istochnik._1993._3._S._87101).pdf.

2. Andrew and Mitrokhin, *Mitrokhin Archive*, 415.

3. In fact, US president Ford refused to invite Solzhenitsyn to the White House, apparently honoring the agreement with the Soviet Union. See *New York Times*, "Solzhenitsyn-White House Issue Revived," August 13, 1975, https://www.nytimes.com/1975/08/13/archives/solzhenitsynwhite-house-issue-revived.html.

4. See, e.g., Mikhail Gorbachev, "On the Abolition of the Decrees of the Presidium of the Supreme Soviet of the USSR on the Stripping of the Citizenship of the USSR of Certain Persons Living Outside the USSR" [in Russian], August 15, 1988, http://www.alexanderyakovlev.org/fond/issues-doc/68189.

5. Authors' conversation with Nikita Petrov, September 2018.

6. On July 21, 1973, the FBI arrested Victor Chernyshev, the first secretary of the Soviet embassy in Washington, on espionage charges after he was caught meeting with Air Force Office of Special Investigations Special Agent Sergeant James David Wood. Wood had sent a letter volunteering his services to the KGB. Edward Mickolus, *The Counterintelligence Chronology: Spying by and against the United States* (Jefferson, NC: McFarland, 2015), 77.

7. Federal Bureau of Investigation, "FOIPA Request No.: 1348465-000, Subject: Kryuchkov, Vladimir" (Letter), April 22, 2016, https://ia800409.us.archive.org/2/items/VladimirKryuchkov/Kryuchkov%2C%20Vladimir.pdf.

8. *Pervoye Glavnoye Upravlenie* is sometimes translated as First Chief Directorate and sometimes as First Main Directorate. We use the translation used by Andrew and Mitrokhin in their seminal 1999 book, *The Mitrokhin Archive: The KGB in Europe and the West*.

9. Authors' conversation with Oleg Kalugin, a head of the Department K (external counterintelligence) of the PGU KGB, February 2018; "KGB in the Baltic States: Documents and Researches," documents of Lithuanian KGB online archives, www.kgbdocuments.eu.

10. Richard H. Cummings, *Cold War Radio: The Dangerous History of American Broadcasting in Europe, 1950–1989* (Jefferson, NC: McFarland, 2009), 177.

11. The sailor's name was Yuri Marin (Pyatakov). He redefected to the Soviet Union in 1973, and in 1973 a book was published bearing his name about his life as a KGB agent at Radio Liberty. Almost identical was a fate of another agent—Oleg Tumanov. Tumanov jumped a Soviet ship outside Libya in 1965. He moved to Germany and joined Radio Liberty in 1966. In a year, officers of the Department K located him in Munich and successfully recruited him. He fled to the Soviet Union in 1986 and held a press conference exposing the CIA presence at Radio Liberty. For details, see Cummings, *Cold War Radio*.

12. Authors' conversation with Nikita Petrov.

13. Andrew and Mitrokhin, *Mitrokhin Archive*, 417.

14. Milton Bearden and James Risen, *The Main Enemy: The Inside Story of the CIA's Final Showdown with the KGB* (New York: Ballantine, 2003).

15. Oleg Kalugin, *Spymaster: My Thirty-Two Years in Intelligence and Espionage against the West* (Philadelphia: Perseus, 2009), 108.

16. Kalugin, *Spymaster*, 104, 203.

CHAPTER 13: MOVING PEOPLE

1. Authors' conversation with Maria Phillimore-Slonim, June 2018.

2. Jo Thomas, "Afghan War: Russians Tell of the Horror," *New York Times*, June 28, 1984, https://www.nytimes.com/1984/06/28/world/afghan-war-russians-tell-of-the-horror.html.

3. A note to Allen Dalles, Paris, January 11, 1951, in Albert Jolis, *A Clutch of Reds and Diamonds: A Twentieth Century Odyssey* (New York: East European Monographs, Columbia University Press, 1996), 385.

4. Bukovsky came into trouble with the Soviet authorities already in school—he was thrown out for publishing a handwritten journal, and later he was excluded from the university for his antigovernment activities.

5. Jolis, *Clutch of Reds*.

6. Authors' conversation with Vladimir Bukovsky, June 2018.

7. Authors' conversation with Vladimir Bukovsky, June 2018.

8. Authors' conversation with Maria Phillimore-Slonim, June 2018.

9. Associated Press, "Deserters Return to Soviet from London," *New York Times*, November 12, 1984.

10. Authors' conversation with Valeri Shirayev, July 2018.

11. Authors' conversation with Galina Ackerman, a member of Resistance International in the 1980s.

12. Aleksandr Solzhenitsyn, *Invisible Allies* (Berkeley, CA: Counterpoint, 1995).

13. Statement of LTG William E. Odom, USA Director, NSA/CSS on Soviet émigrés, before the Permanent Subcommittee on Investigations of the Senate Committee on Governmental Affairs, United States Senate, October 8, 1987. Available on the site of the CIA library, online reading room.

14. Gorbachev, "On the Abolition."

15. The documents scanned by Vladimir Bukovsky are available at "Soviet Archives" at Info-RUSS, http://psi.ece.jhu.edu/~kaplan/IRUSS/BUK/GBARC/buk-rus.html.

CHAPTER 14: THE OTHER RUSSIA

1. "The Other Russia" was the term for this diaspora coined by Michael Glenny and Norman Stone in their excellent 1990 book of that title, an anthology of oral interviews with three generations of Russian émigrés; Glenny and Stone, *The Other Russia: The Experience of Exile* (New York: Viking, 1991).

2. The text is available on the website of the Yeltsin center, "Predsedatel Verkhovnogo Soveta RSFSR Yeltsin B.N. Obrashenie Predsedatelya Verkhovnogo Soveta RSFSR B.N. Yeltsina k sootechestvennikam za rubezhom, 25.12.1990" [Address of the chairman of the Supreme Council of RSFSR Boris Yeltsin to compatriots abroad, December 25, 1990], https://m.yeltsin.ru/archive/paperwork/9590/.

3. Douglas Smith, *Former People* (London: Pan, 2013), 334–335.

4. *The Emigrants* was published in late 1930, Kutepov was snatched from the streets of Paris in January of the same year, and his disappearance caused enormous scandal, harming the Soviet reputation in the country.

5. Mikhail Tolstoy, "Pervy Kongress Sootechestvennikov" [The first Congress of Compatriots], *St. Petersburg Historical Journal*, no. 3 (2014), 72.

6. Authors' email exchange with Mikhail Tolstoy, May–December 2018.

7. Authors' conversation with Mikhail Tolstoy; see Mikhail Tolstoy, "Pervy Kongress Sootechestvennikov" [The first Congress of Compatriots], *St. Petersburg Historical Journal*, no. 3 (2014).

8. Authors' conversation with Mikhail Tolstoy.

9. Broadcasting Board of Governors, "Resolution Honoring 65th Anniversary of Radio Free Europe/Radio Liberty's Russian Service," March 14, 2018, https://www.bbg.gov/wp-content/media/2018/03/Resolution-65th-Anniversary-of-RFERL-Russian-Service.pdf.

10. Mikhail Tolstoy, "Pervy Kongress Sootechestvennikov" [The first Congress of Compatriots], *St. Petersburg Historical Journal*, no. 3 (2014), 86.

CHAPTER 15: MOVING THE MONEY

1. US District Court, Central District of California, United States of America v. Stanley Mark Rifkin, No CR 78-1050 (A)—WMB, quoted by Jay Becker, "Rifkin, a Documentary History, 2 Computer L.J.471 (1980)," *John Marshall Journal of Information Technology and Privacy Law* 2, no. 1 (1980), http://repository.jmls.edu/jitpl/vol2/iss1/23; BookRags, "Stanley Rifkin," https://www.social-engineer.org/wiki/archives/Hackers/hackers-Mark-Rifkin-Social-Engineer-furtherInfo.htm.

2. Rifkin's testimony in court, February 22, 1979, quoted by Jay Becker, "Rifkin, a Documentary History, 2 Computer L.J.471 (1980)," *John Marshall Journal of Information Technology and Privacy Law* 2, no. 1 (1980), http://repository.jmls.edu/jitpl/vol2/iss1/23.

3. Kevin D. Mitnick and William L. Simon, *The Art of Deception: Controlling the Human Element of Security* (Indianapolis, IN: Wiley, 2002), 5.

4. Mitnick and Simon, *Art of Deception*, 5.

5. Andrew Tully, *Inside the FBI* (1980; Lake Oswego, OR; eNet, 2015), 12.

6. This was how Eurodollars were born. *Istoria Sovetskikh I Rossikskikh bankov za granitsey: Vospominania Ochevidtsev, Documenti* [The history of Soviet and Russian banks abroad: Witness testimonies, documents] (Moscow, 2007) 1, no. 29. See also M. M. Boguslavskii, *Private International Law: The Soviet Approach* (Dordrecht, Netherlands: Martinus Nijhoff Publishers, 1988).

7. Authors' email exchange with Stan Rifkin, April 28–29, 2019.

8. "Technologicheskoye Ograblenie" [Technological heist], *Rovesnik* Magazine 11, 1980.

9. Authors' conversation with the press office of ALROSA; the ALROSA corporate website, http://eng.alrosa.ru/alrosa-and-ddc-sign-a-memorandum-of-understanding/.

CHAPTER 16: THE SCHEME DEVISED

1. Sarah Bartlett, "The Clumsy Quest for Irving Bank," *New York Times*, September 18, 1988, https://www.nytimes.com/1988/09/18/business/the-clumsy-quest-for-irving-bank.html.

2. Robert A. Bennett, "Irving Suitor a Tough Banker," *New York Times*, September 29, 1987, https://www.nytimes.com/1987/09/29/business/irving-suitor-a-tough-banker.html.

3. Father Vasili Khvostenko was a mountain engineer, and upon his return, he was promptly executed by Stalin's secret police. His son Lev founded school 213 in Leningrad, and his grandson became the great Russian poet Alexei Khvostenko ("Khvost").

4. Authors' conversation with Natasha Gurfinkel, December 2018.

5. According to the *New York Times*.

6. Simon Sebag Montefiore, *The Romanovs: 1613–1918* (New York: Vintage, 2016), 22.

7. Joseph Berger, "Soviet Turmoil," *New York Times*, September 17, 1991.

8. Authors' conversation with Natasha Gurfinkel, December 2918.

9. Authors' conversation with Mikhail Khodorkovsky, June 2018. In 1994, Natasha Gurfinkel married Russia's representative to the IMF, Konstanin Kagalovsky, who later joined Khodorkovsky's bank as his deputy. Natasha became known as Mrs. Gurfinkel-Kagalovsky.

CHAPTER 17: MUDDYING THE WATERS

1. Timothy O'Brien and Lowell Bergman, "The Money Movers: A Special Report; Tracking How Pair Went from Russia to Riches," *New York Times*, October 19, 1999, https://www.nytimes.com/1999/10/19/world/the -money-movers-a-special-report-tracking-how-pair-went-from-russia-to -riches.html.

2. O'Brien and Bergman, "Money Movers."

3. O'Brien and Bergman, "Money Movers."

4. Raymond Bonner and Timothy L. O'Brien, "Activity at Bank Raises Suspicions of Russia Mob Tie," *New York Times*, August 19, 1999, https://www .nytimes.com/1999/08/19/world/activity-at-bank-raises-suspicions-of-russia -mob-tie.html.

5. Authors' conversation with Natasha Gurfinkel.

6. Bonner and O'Brien, "Activity at Bank."

7. Bonner and O'Brien, "Activity at Bank."

8. Testimony of Thomas A. Renyi, CEO of BoNY, US House of Representatives, "Russian Money Laundering, Hearing before the Committee on Banking and Financial Services, September 21, 1999," https://archive.org/details /russianmoneylaunoounit.

9. Robert O'Harrow Jr. and Sharon LaFraniere, "Yeltsin's Son-in-Law Kept Offshore Accounts, Hill Told," *Washington Post*, September 23, 1999.

10. Authors' conversation with Mikhail Khodorkovsky, June 2018.

11. Testimony of Thomas A. Renyi, US House of Representatives, "Russian Money Laundering."

12. See, e.g., "Delo Bank of New York—kak ochernyali Rossiyu" [The case of the Bank of New York: How Russia was slandered], *Kommersant*, March 7, 2003, https://www.kommersant.ru/doc/369918.

13. Authors' conversation with Natasha Gurfinkel, December 2018.

14. Timothy L. O'Brien with Raymond Bonner, "Banker and Husband Tell of Role in Laundering Case," *New York Times*, February 17, 2000, https:// www.nytimes.com/2000/02/17/world/banker-and-husband-tell-of-role-in -laundering-case.html.

15. Jonathan Sibun, "Ex-BoNY Executive Sentenced for Money-Laundering," *Financial News*, June 27, 2006, https://www.fnlondon.com/articles/ex-bony-executive-sentenced-for-money-laundering-1-20060727.

16. Timothy O'Brien, "Bank Settles US Enquiry into Money Laundering," *New York Times*, November 9, 2005, https://www.nytimes.com/2005/11/09/business/bank-settles-us-inquiry-into-money-laundering.html.

17. Denis Uvarov, "'Russkuyu mafiu' ne posadili" ["Russian mafia" was not sent to jail], *Vremya Novostey*, July 28, 2006, http://www.vremya.ru/2006/133/8/157547.html.

18. US House of Representatives, "Russian Money Laundering."

CHAPTER 18: SOME HABITS DIE HARD

1. First Chief Directorate, *Pervoye Glavnoye Upravlenie* (PGU) of the KGB.

2. Pete Earley, *Comrade J: The Untold Secrets of Russia's Master Spy in America after the End of the Cold War* (New York: Penguin, 2007), 62–63.

3. Leonid Shebarshin, *Posledniy Boy KGB* [The last fight of the KGB] (Moscow: Algoritm, 2013); authors' conversations with Shebarshin, 2001–2003.

4. Authors' conversations with Rolf Mowatt-Larssen, a chief of the CIA's Moscow station in the early 1990s, November 2018.

5. Earley, *Comrade J*, 62–63.

6. The idea was initially suggested by Leonid Nikitenko, chief of the Department K. See Shebarshin, *Posledniy Boy KGB*, 29.

7. Shebarshin, *Posledniy Boy KGB*.

8. KGB major-general Leonid Makarov. He shared the room with Shebarshin in a KGB foreign intelligence school no. 101 in the 1960s.

9. Shebarshin, *Posledniy Boy KGB*, 37.

10. Argumenti I Fakti, no. 34, 1990.

11. "Bez Plasha I Kinzhala" [Without cloak and dagger], *Pravda*, April 22, 1990.

12. The text of the 1993 report "Novy vyzov posle Kholodnoy Voini" [A new challenge after the Cold War], on the website of the SVR, http://svr.gov.ru/material/2-1.htm. The second report, "Perspektivi rasshirenia NATO i interesi Rossii" [Prospects of the NATO expansion and the interests of Russia], presented in November 1993, concerning the expansion of NATO to the east, was highly critical of NATO, but it's not available online.

CHAPTER 19: COOPERATION AND REBRANDING

1. Authors' conversations with Rolf Mowatt-Larssen; see Rolf Mowatt-Larssen, "US and Russian Intelligence Cooperation during the Yeltsin Years," Belfer Center for Science and International Affairs, February 11, 2011, https://www.belfercenter .org/publication/us-and-russian-intelligence-cooperation-during-yeltsin-years.

2. Viktor Abakumov, the head of the dreaded military counterintelligence agency SMERSH (SMErt SHpionam—Death to Spies) during World War II and then a minister of state security of the Soviet Union from 1946 to 1951. He was arrested and shot after Stalin's death.

3. "Shef Rossiyskoy Razvedki posetil SCHA" [Chief of Russian Foreign Intelligence visited the United States], *Kommersant*, June 22, 1993, https://www .kommersant.ru/doc/51323?query=CBP%20и%20ЦРУ.

4. Authors' conversation with Rolf Mowatt-Larssen.

5. Authors' conversation with Alexander Vassiliev.

6. The SVR hastened to announce that it reached an understanding with Random House in July 1992, but the talks continued until 1993. See the following: V SCHA izdayut patiknizhic o geroiakh-razvedchikakh [Five-volume set about hero-spies to be published in the United States], *Kommersant*, July 6, 1992, https://www.kommersant.ru/doc/5536.

7. John Castello and Oleg Tsarev, *Deadly Illusions: The KGB Orlov Dossier Reveals Stalin's Master Spy* (New York: Crown, 1993).

8. Only three books were published according to the initial plan: Nigel West and Oleg Tsarev, *The Crown Jewels: The British Secrets at the Heart of the KGB Archives* (New Haven, CT: Yale University Press, 1999); David E. Murphy, Sergei A. Kondrashev, and George Bailey, *Battleground Berlin: CIA vs. KGB in the Cold War* (New Haven, CT: Yale University Press, 1997); Aleksandr Fursenko and Timothy J. Naftali, *"One Hell of a Gamble": Khrushchev, Castro, and Kennedy, 1958–1964* (New York: Norton, 1998).

9. Authors' email exchange with James O'Shea Wade.

10. Phillip Knightly, "Disinformation," *London Review of Books*, July 8, 1993, https://www.lrb.co.uk/v15/n13/phillip-knightley/disinformation.

11. Authors' conversation with Alexander Vassiliev, July 2018.

12. Authors' conversation with Alexander Vassiliev, July 2018.

13. Weinstein and Vassiliev, *Haunted Wood*; Harvey Klehr, John Earl Haynes, and Alexander Vassiliev, *Spies: The Rise and Fall of the KGB in America* (New Haven, CT: Yale University Press, 2009).

14. Wilson Center, Vassiliev Notebooks, http://digitalarchive.wilsoncenter .org/collection/86/vassiliev-notebooks.

15. We described this operation in our book *The New Nobility* (New York: PublicAffairs, 2010), 116 (Assistance directorate of the FSB).

16. Andrei Soldatov, "The True Role of the FSB in the Ukrainian Crisis," *Moscow Times*, April 15, 2014, https://www.themoscowtimes.com/2014/04/15/the -true-role-of-the-fsb-in-the-ukrainian-crisis-a33985.

17. Earley, *Comrade J*, 22–23; authors' conversations with Sergei Tretyakov and with former SVR operatives previously based in New York.

18. Earley, *Comrade J*, 195.

19. Authors' conversations with Tretyakov.

20. Brian Ross, Pete Madden, and Michelle McPhee, "Russian Spy Evgeny Buryakov Deported from the United States, April 5, 2017," *ABC News*, https:// abcnews.go.com/International/russian-spy-evgeny-buryakov-deported-united -states/story?id=46601947.

CHAPTER 20: A FRESH START

1. Kremlin, transcript of Putin's address to the First World Congress of Compatriots, http://kremlin.ru/events/president/transcripts/21359.

2. The full name is the Federal Agency for the Commonwealth of Independent States, Compatriots Living Abroad and International Humanitarian Cooperation.

3. The KGB 1968's manual, "The Use of the Soviet Culture Committee for Cultural Ties with Compatriots Abroad in Intelligence Activity" (39), published by Michael Weiss at the *Interpreter*. This tradition was never broken; in autumn 2013, Yuri Zaytsev, the head of the Russian Center for Science and Culture in Washington, was investigated by the FBI as a possible spy. The FBI then suspected that a cultural exchange program funded by Rossotrudnichestvo and run by Zaytsev was clandestinely recruiting Americans. See Molly Redden, "FBI Probing Whether Russia Used Cultural Junkets to Recruit American Intelligence Assets," *Mother Jones*, October 2013, https://www.motherjones.com/politics/2013 /10/fbi-investigating-yury-zaytsev-russian-diplomat-spy/; and Sari Horwitz, "Head of D.C.-Based Russian Cultural Center Being Investigated as Possible Spy," *Washington Post*, October 23, 2013, https://www.washingtonpost.com/world /national-security/head-of-dc-based-russian-cultural-center-being-investigated -as-possible-spy/2013/10/23/63a0bb54-3c02-11e3-a94f-b58017bfee6c_story.html ?utm_term=.2a4bde2a419e.

4. Congress Sootechestvinnikov, 11–12 Oktabrya 2001, Itogovie Materiali [Congress of Compatriots, October 11–12, 2001, the final materials] (Moscow: Drofa, 2001).

5. "Znakomie vse Vice" [Familiar all vice], *Kommersant*, October 23, 2001, https://www.kommersant.ru/doc/288415.

6. Obituary for Alexei Jordan: "Pamyati moego druga" [In memoriam of my friend], http://www.fskk.ru.

7. Alexei Jordan, "Alexei Jordan: Ya veryu v velikoye budushee Rossii" [Alexei Jordan: I believe in the great future of Russia], PMJ, http://www.pmg-online.ru /article_jordan2.htm.

CHAPTER 21: THE SIEGE

1. Authors' conversations with Victor Shenderovich, Evgeny Kiselev, and Vladimir Kara-Murza Sr.

2. Authors' conversation with Evgeny Kiselev, August 2018.

3. His name was Leonid Rozhetskin. Rozhetskin was part of the third wave of emigration—he had been brought to the United States by his mother in 1980, when he was fourteen years old. A brilliant student, he won a scholarship to Columbia University, from which he graduated with distinction, and in 1990 he graduated cum laude from Harvard Law School. He disappeared in March 2008 in Jurmala, Latvia, when he was forty-one years old. His body was found in Latvian woods in 2012.

4. Richard W. Stevenson, "An American in Moscow," *New York Times*, September 20, 1995, https://www.nytimes.com/1995/09/20/business/an-american-in -moscow.html.

5. Yuri Sagaidak was a former colleague of Vassiliev—in the late 1980s, he had served in London under disguise of a journalist of *Komsomolskaya Pravda* until 1989. For details, see Valentine Low, "My Friend Yuri . . . the Communist Spy," *The Times* (London), February 24, 2018, https://www.thetimes.co.uk/article /valentine-low-my-friend-yuri-the-communist-spy-g9z5q7qt9.

6. Authors' conversations with Evgeny Kiselev.

7. Authors' conversations with Kara-Murza Sr., December 2017–April 2019.

8. "Takeover of NTV," Radio Svoboda, April 15, 2001, https://www.svoboda .org/a/24197943.html.

9. NTV report on a takeover of NTV, April 14, 2001, "Vipuski novostei o zakhvate NTV 14.04.2001" [News reports about the seizure of NTV April 14, 2001], https://www.youtube.com/watch?v=ueF9mDOCCGE.

10. Mila Kuzina, "Putin I Dobrodeev ponyali drug druga" [Putin and Dobrodeev understood each other], Gazeta.Ru, April 16, 2001, https://www .gazeta.ru/2001/04/16/putinidobrod.shtml; see also Radio Svoboda reporting, April 15, 2001, https://www.svoboda.org/a/24197943.html.

11. News reports on a takeover of NTV, April 14, 2001, "Vipuski novostei o zakhvate NTV 14.04.2001" [News reports about the seizure of NTV April 14, 2001], https://www.youtube.com/watch?v=ueF9mDOCCGE.

12. NTV, "Itogi with Evgeny Kiselev," April 3, 2001, https://www.youtube.com/watch?v=fD9hU8fkwBo&t=2407s.

CHAPTER 22: GETTING OUT THE MESSAGE

1. "NTV popytalos prervat translatsiyu program Inter-TV za rubezh" [NTV tried to interrupt the translation of Inter-TV abroad], Newsru.com, September 28, 2001, https://www.newsru.com/russia/28sep2001/inter.html.

2. "Bush nazval Putina reformatorom" [Bush called Putin a reformer], *Kommersant*, November 15, 2001, https://www.kommersant.ru/doc/926509.

3. Peter Baker, "'I'm Thrilled He's Here,' Bush Says as Putin Visits His Texan Ranch," *Washington Post*, November 15, 2001, https://www.washingtonpost.com/archive/politics/2001/11/15/im-thrilled-hes-here-bush-says-as-putin-visits-his-texas-ranch/d9928257-b7e4-428c-9d44-865a1ce6e5f5/?noredirect=on&utm_term=.f9766e0f64c5.

4. Boris Jordan, "Control of Russian TV," *New York Times*, December 7, 2001, https://www.nytimes.com/2001/12/07/opinion/l-control-of-russian-tv-547751.html.

5. TSN, "Shuster v 60-letniy yubiley priznalsa v antisovetskoy deyatelnosti" [Shuster at his 60th jubilee admitted his anti-Soviet activity], November 23, 2012, https://ru.tsn.ua/politika/shuster-v-60-letniy-yubiley-priznalsya-v-antisovetskoy-deyatelnosti-i-zvanii-agenta-cru.html.

6. Edward Glazarev, "Russian Immigrants' CNN RTVI Broadcasts Lots of News—and Soaps," *New York Daily News*, December 15, 2002, http://www.nydailynews.com/archives/boroughs/russian-immigrants-cnn-rtvi-broadcasts-lots-news-soaps-article-1.500196.

CHAPTER 23: THE CRISIS

1. For details, see our 2010 book, *The New Nobility*.

2. Susan B. Glasser, "NTV Feeling Kremlin's Wrath," *Washington Post*, November 22, 2002, https://www.washingtonpost.com/archive/politics/2002/11/22/ntv-feeling-kremlins-wrath/b2edc32a-1666-43b5-95c7-eb8b8506e70d/?utm_term=.8098c4625963.

3. C-SPAN, "Media Coverage of Terrorism," November 18, 2002, https://www.c-span.org/video/?173903-1/media-coverage-terrorism.

4. Glasser, "NTV Feeling Kremlin's Wrath."

5. Kremlin, "President Vladimir Putin Met with Representatives of the Media and State Duma Deputies," November 25, 2002, http://en.kremlin.ru/events/president/news/27753.

6. Kremlin, full transcript of Putin's angry remarks, November 25, 2002, http://kremlin.ru/events/president/transcripts/21788.

7. PBS, "Commanding Heights: Boris Jordan," https://www-tc.pbs.org/wgbh/commandingheights/shared/pdf/int_borisjordan.pdf.

8. Authors' conversations with Kara-Murza Jr.

CHAPTER 24: COURTING THE WHITE CHURCH

1. Berel Lazar is the chairman of the Confederation of Jewish Communities of Russia.

2. Andrei Kolesnikov, "K nim priekhal, k nim priekhal Vladimir Vladimirich dorogoy" [To them came Dear Vladimir Vladimirovich], *Kommersant*, November 15, 2001, https://www.kommersant.ru/doc/292187.

3. CNN, "Transcript: Bush, Putin News Conference," June 18, 2001, http://www.cnn.com/2001/WORLD/europe/06/18/bush.putin.transcript/index.html.

4. Gregory L. Freeze, "Russian Orthodoxy and Politics in the Putin Era," Carnegie Endowment for International Peace, February 9, 2017, https://carnegieendowment.org/2017/02/09/russian-orthodoxy-and-politics-in-putin-era-pub-67959.

5. Kremlin, "Gosudarstvenny visit v Soedinennie Shati Ameriki" [State visit to the United States of America], November 7–16, 2001, http://kremlin.ru/events/president/trips/45476.

6. Authors' conversation with Boris Jordan, December 2018.

7. In the conversation with the authors, Jordan claimed that it was he who raised the topic of reunification, not Putin.

8. Sophia Kishkovsky, "2 Russian Churches, Split by War, Reuniting," *New York Times*, May 17, 2007, https://www.nytimes.com/2007/05/17/world/europe/17russia.html.

CHAPTER 25: REUNION

1. Authors' conversation with Sophia Kishkovsky, who was raised in Sea Cliff. See Lois Morton, "A Village Tinged with Old Russia," *New York Times*, April 10, 1997, https://www.nytimes.com/1977/04/10/archives/long-island-weekly-a-village-tinged-with-old-russia-in-sea-cliff.html.

2. Authors' conversation with Boris Jordan.

3. Hanna Kozlowska, "As the American UN Delegation Moves Out of the Waldorf-Astoria Hotel, Putin Books a Suite," https://qz.com/497342/as-the-american-un-delegation-moves-out-of-the-waldorf-astoria-hotel-putin-books-a-suite/.

4. "Vladimir Putin dorozhit vtorim mestom" [Vladimir Putin praises the second place], *Kommersant*, September 29, 2003, https://www.kommersant.ru/doc/414468.

5. Authors' conversation with Holodny, November 2018. Holodny claimed he picked up a blue cassock purely by chance.

6. "Putin rasporyadilsa postavit v Moskve Pamyatnik Andropovu" [Putin ordered to erect a monument to Andropov in Moscow], *Lenta*, October 6, 2003, https://lenta.ru/news/2003/10/06/monument/.

7. Kishkovsky, "2 Russian Churches."

8. We documented this process in our book, Andrei Soldatov and Irina Borogan, *The New Nobility: The Restoration of Russia's Security State and the Enduring Legacy of the KGB* (New York: PublicAffairs, 2010).

9. "Vstrecha delegatsii ot Russkoy Zarubezhnoy Tserkvi s Patriarkhom Moskovskim i vseya Rusi Aleksiem i chlenami Sinoda RPTs MP" [The meeting of the delegation of the Russian Church Abroad with the Moscow and all Russia's Patriarch Alexei, and with the members of Synod of the Russian Orthodox Church], Vestnik Germanskoy Eparkhii Russkoy Pravoslavnoy Tservki za Granitsey, December 3, 2003, http://ruskline.ru/monitoring_smi/2003/12/03/vstrecha_delegacii_ot_russkoj_zarubezhnoj_cerkvi_s_patriarhom_moskovskim_i_vseya_rusi_aleksiem_i_chlenami_sinoda_rpc_mp/.

10. Authors' conversation with Kiselev.

11. The mastermind of Klebnikov's assassination was never identified.

12. Peter Baker and Susan B. Glasser, "American Optimist Mourned in Moscow," *Washington Post*, July 15, 2004, https://www.washingtonpost.com/archive/politics/2004/07/15/american-optimist-mourned-in-moscow/c2076f2a-a86d-4701-b355-406a9959c297/.

13. Authors' email exchange with Musa Klebnikov, widow of Paul.

14. Authors' email exchange with Musa Klebnikov, widow of Paul.

15. Officially titled "IV All-Diaspora Council of the Russian Orthodox Church Outside of Russia of the Clergy and Laity."

16. The remains of Anton Denikin, the commander in chief of the White army, along with the remains of Ivan Ilyin, a chief ideologue of the White army in exile, were transferred to Moscow in October 2005 and given a full-honor military funeral in the Moscow Donskoy monastery.

17. Authors' conversation with Boris Jordan.

18. We documented this process in our 2010 book, *The New Nobility*.

19. "Putin otkryl v Krimy pamyatnik, Chto s nim ne tak" [Putin opened a monument in Crimea: What's wrong with it], Korrespondent.net, November 20, 2017, https://korrespondent.net/ukraine/events/3908485-putyn-v-krymu-otkryl-pamiatnyk-chto-s-nym-ne-tak.

CHAPTER 26: POLITICAL EMIGRATION: RESTART

1. Authors' conversation with Evgeny Kiselev, who confirmed the conversation between Alexander Voloshin and Gusinsky.

2. Sergey Lukyanov, "Russia, Inc.," *Moscow Times*, November 12, 1996, http://old.themoscowtimes.com/sitemap/free/1996/11/article/russia-inc/316250.html.

3. "Kolokol Berezovskogo nauchit grazhdan otstaivat svoi prava pered gosu-darstvom" [Berezovsky's Kolokol will teach citizens to protect their rights before the state], *Lenta*, October 5, 2001, https://lenta.ru/news/2001/10/05/kolokol/.

4. Soldatov and Borogan, *The New Nobility*, 102–103.

5. Authors' conversation with Alexander Litvinenko, 2004, London.

6. We provided our version of the 1999 apartment bombings in our 2010 book, Soldatov and Borogan, *New Nobility*.

7. The Russian edition was published in 2002 (New York: Liberty Publishing House), available online, http://www.terror99.ru/book.htm; the English edition: Alexander Litvinenko and Yuri Felshtinsky, *Blowing Up Russia: The Secret Plot to Bring Back KGB Terror* (New York: Encounter Books, 2007).

8. For instance, Georges Agabekov, an officer of OGPU, defected in Istanbul in 1929, published his book, *OGPU: The Russian Secret Terror* in 1931, and got killed in 1937 in the Pyrenees; or Walter Krivitsky, a Soviet intelligence officer who defected in 1937, published his memoirs *In Stalin's Secret Service* in 1939, and was assassinated in Washington in 1941.

9. Ian Cobain, Matthew Taylor, and Luke Harding, "'I Am Plotting a New Russian Revolution,'" *Guardian*, April 13, 2007, https://www.theguardian.com/world/2007/apr/13/topstories3.russia.

10. Luke Harding, "Berezovsky Charged with Coup Plot over Guardian Interview," *Guardian*, July 3, 2007, https://www.theguardian.com/news/2007/jul/03/russia.pressandpublishing.

CHAPTER 27: ILLUSIONS CRUSHED

1. Echo Moskvy, Semya Zaslavskikh [Family of the Zaslavskiys], May 6, 2007, https://echo.msk.ru/guests/14021/.

2. Authors' conversations with Ilya Zaslavskiy.

3. Sergei Mashkin, "Taina porkitaya srokom" [Secret covered by the prison term], *Kommersant*, May 8, 2008, https://www.kommersant.ru/doc/1165775.

4. Authors' conversations with Alexei Kozlov.

5. To name just a few: Alexander Lebedev, an officer with the London KGB station in the 1980s, helped Soviet capitalists to open bank accounts in London banks in the late 1980s and became one of the top Russian bankers, working with Russian debts. A former intelligence officer was head of Vnesheconomobank, a state bank in charge of raising export and financial credits for the Soviet Union and then Russia; in the early 1990s, the chairman of the Central Bank—a Russian analogue of the Federal Reserve system—was a KGB foreign intelligence officer.

6. Authors' conversations with Olga Romanova.

7. Kozlov denied this.

8. Authors' conversations with Romanova and Kozlov; see also Olga Romanova, *Butyrka, Turemnaya Tetrad* [Butyrka, Prison's Notebook] (Moscow: Angedonia, 2016).

CHAPTER 28: "WE NEED SOME TARGETED HITS"

1. BBC, "At the Pro-Kremlin Rally, the Opposition Was Planted on the Stake" [in Russian], July 27, 2010, https://www.bbc.com/russian/russia/2010/07/100727_russia_seliger_mockery.

2. Authors' conversations with Kara-Murza Jr.

3. Michael McFaul, *From Cold War to Hot Peace: An American Ambassador in Putin's Russia* (Boston: Houghton Mifflin Harcourt, 2018), 365.

4. "Nemtsov protiv Putina" [Nemtsov against Putin], Voice of America, January 18, 2011, https://www.golos-ameriki.ru/a/nemtsov-vestus-putin-2011-01-18-114149549/192376.html.

5. Executive Office of the President, "Proclamation 8697, Suspension of Entry as Immigrants and Nonimmigrants of Persons Who Participate in Serious Human Rights and Humanitarian Law Violations and Other Abuses," August 9, 2011, https://www.federalregister.gov/documents/2011/08/09/2011-20395/suspension-of-entry-as-immigrants-and-nonimmigrants-of-persons-who-participate-in-serious-human.

6. "Boris Nemtsov and Chirikova poluchayut instruktsii v Vashingtone," YouTube, September 21, 2011, https://www.youtube.com/watch?v=ZemHhZcpKsQ.

CHAPTER 29: DESPERATE TIMES

1. One such figure was Alexei Navalny, who had come to prominence in the late 2000s as an anticorruption campaigner and popular blogger.

2. Steven Lee Myers, *The New Tsar: The Rise and Reign of Vladimir Putin* (New York: Knopf, 2016).

3. Natalia Rostova, "Kara-Murza mladshy govorit, chto uvolen iz-za spiska Magnitskogo" [Kara-Murza said he was fired because of the Magnitsky list], *Republic*, July 14, 2012, https://republic.ru/posts/l/811013.

4. This was the next logical development in Gusinsky's long journey into exile. A few years earlier, Gusinsky had publicly asked Putin to let him back into Russia. In an interview with the Israeli newspaper *Haaretz*, he praised Putin. But the Kremlin rejected Gusinsky's plea.

5. Authors' conversation with Gary Kasparov, March 2018.

6. Ian Cobain, "No Evidence Boris Berezovsky Was Murdered, Oligarch's Inquest Hears," *Guardian*, March 27, 2014, https://www.theguardian.com/world/2014/mar/27/no-evidence-boris-berezovsky-murdered-russian-oligarch-inquest.

7. Khodorkovsky and Putin's conversation in the Kremlin, February 2003, https://www.youtube.com/watch?v=u6NKb79VN8U.

8. Mikhail Khodorkovsky, "Ten Years as a Prisoner," *New York Times*, October 24, 2013, https://www.nytimes.com/2013/10/25/opinion/international/ten-years-a-prisoner.html.

9. Authors' conversation with Mikhail Khodorkovsky.

10. Authors' conversation with Gary Kasparov.

11. Carl Schreck, "Russian Asylum Applications in US Hit 24-Year Record," Radio Free Europe/Radio Liberty, May 2, 2018, https://www.rferl.org/a/russian-asylum-applications-in-u-s-hit-24-year-record/29204843.html.

12. Authors' conversation with Mikhail Khodorkovsky.

CHAPTER 30: WHEN THE PARTY'S OVER

1. Rebecca Mead, "Black Hole," *New Yorker*, November 15, 2010, https://www.newyorker.com/magazine/2010/11/15/black-hole-rebecca-mead.

2. Rachel Morarjee, "Snob Appeal," *Fortune*, October 27, 2010, http://archive.fortune.com/2010/10/26/news/international/Snob_magazine_Prokhorov.fortune/index.htm.

3. "O Proekte" [About the project], *Snob*, https://snob.ru/basement.

4. Mead, "Black Hole"; Sam Dolnick, "Oligarchs and Absinthe Shots," *New York Times*, October 29, 2010, https://cityroom.blogs.nytimes.com/2010/10/29/oligarchs-and-absinthe-shots/.

5. See details in our book, Andrei Soldatov and Irina Borogan, *The Red Web: The Kremlin's Wars on the Internet* (New York: PublicAffairs, 2017).

6. Megan Davies, "Prokhorov Reassures Investors as He Focuses on Politics," Reuters, October 28, 2012, https://www.reuters.com/article/russia-prokhorov/prokhorov-reassures-investors-as-he-focuses-on-politics-idUSL1E8LS06Q20121028.

7. Richard L. Cassin, "OFAC Adds Five Russians to Magnitsky Sanctions List," FCPA Blog, January 10, 2017, http://www.fcpablog.com/blog/2017/1/10 /ofac-adds-five-russians-to-magnitsky-sanctions-list.html.

8. Ingrid Nordgaard, "Lost Opportunities and Newfound Possibilities: Awaiting a New Cold War or a New Generation," NYU Jordan Center for Advanced Study of Russia, April 9, 2013, http://jordanrussiacenter.org/event -recaps/lost-opportunities-and-newfound-possibilities-awaiting-a-new-cold-war -or-a-new-generation/#.XDO8ZM_YrOQ.

9. Masha Gessen, "Flying Putin, Fired Editor," *New York Times*, September 10, 2012, https://latitude.blogs.nytimes.com/2012/09/10/flying-putin-fired -editor/.

10. Amie Ferris-Rotman, "Masha Gessen, 2017 *Foreign Policy's* Global Thinkers profile," https://2017globalthinkers.foreignpolicy.com/2017/profile/masha -gessen?c0244ec121=; Masha Gessen's page on the website of *New Yorker*, https:// www.newyorker.com/contributors/masha-gessen/page/2.

11. Authors' conversation with Luke Harding, July 2018.

12. Interview of Masha Gessen [in Russian], TV Rain, October 19, 2016, https://tvrain.ru/teleshow/harddaysnight/gessen-419223/.

13. Authors' conversation with Masha Gessen, September 2018.

14. "Putin Has Been Good for Russia," IQsquared, YouTube, June 3, 2013, https://www.youtube.com/watch?v=CjDTtgAkCSo.

15. Interview of Boris Jordan [in Russian], *Delovoy Peterburg*, June 14, 2014, https://www.dp.ru/a/2014/04/11/Putin_otvetil_i_na_jetot_v.

16. An author of the idea, Vladimir Yakovlev, emigrated to Israel. In 2017 he said that there are no Global Russians anymore, only refugees. Vladimir Yakovlev, "Upotreblyat termi Global Russians segodnya v principe nepristoino" [Vladimir Yakovlev: To use the term Global Russians today is unfair], *Zima*, July 3, 2017, https://zimamagazine.com/2017/07/vladimir-yakovlev-upotreblyat -termin-global-russians-segodnya-v-printsipe-nepristojno/.

CHAPTER 31: ELIMINATING THE PROBLEM

1. This chapter is largely based on recollections of Vadim Prokhorov, Vladimir Kara-Murza Jr., and his wife, Zhenya, as well as the documents provided by Prokhorov.

2. Authors' conversation with Vadim Prokhorov.

3. Authors' conversation with Vadim Prokhorov.

4. Authors' conversations with Kara-Murza Jr.

5. Yevgenia Albats, *The State within a State: The KGB and Its Hold on Russia—Past, Present, and Future* (New York: Farrar Straus & Giroux), 1994.

6. "Vladimir Kara-Murza—zagadka otravlenia" [Kara-Murza, a mystery of poisoning], *Current Time*, January 18, 2016, https://www.currenttime.tv /a/27493037.html.

7. "Vladimir Kara-Murza," *Current Time*.

8. Maria-Luisa Tirmaste, "Otravlenie Vladimira Kara-Murzi Mladshego vnov zainteresovalo Sledstevenny Komitet" [Investigative Committee took a renewed interest in the poisoning of Vladimir Kara-Murza Jr.], *Kommersant*, April 16, 2018, https://www.kommersant.ru/doc/3605068.

9. Authors' conversation with Zhenya Kara-Murza, January 2019.

CHAPTER 32: CHASING A POISON

1. Authors' conversations with Vadim Prokhorov.

2. X-Pertise Consulting, "Oberhuasbergen, Ref: case of Vladimir Kara-Murza, 17A035-bis" [Report about the examination of hair, blood, and urine], author's copy provided by Prokhorov, March 17, 2017.

3. Alexander Dobrovolsky, "Moskovsky Komsomolets, Smertelny ukus Lenina" [Lethal bite of Lenin], https://www.mk.ru/editions/daily/article/2006 /12/26/173541-smertelnyiy-ukus-lenina.html. Research done by Nikina Petrov also supports this statement.

4. Andrew E. Kramer, "More of Kremlin's Opponents Are Ending Up Dead," *New York Times*, August 21, 2016, https://www.nytimes.com/2016/08/21/world /europe/moscow-kremlin-silence-critics-poison.html.

5. Authors' conversation with Vadim Prokhorov.

6. Mike Eckel, "FBI Silent on Lab Results in Kremlin Foe's Suspected Poisoning," Radio Free Europe/Radio Liberty, October 26, 2018, https://www.rferl .org/a/fbi-silent-on-lab-results-in-kremlin-foe-s-suspected-poisoning/29564152 .html.

CHAPTER 33: EVERYTHING OLD IS NEW AGAIN

1. The details in this section are derived from the authors' conversation with Sergei Tretyakov and from Earley, *Comrade J*.

2. Interview with Sergei Tretyakov by Andrei Soldatov, *Novaya Gazeta*, January 2, 2008, https://www.novayagazeta.ru/articles/2008/02/01/39469-beglyy -i-pushistyy.

3. On March 21, 2001, the US State Department announced the expulsion of fifty Russian diplomats: four accused of direct involvement with a former FBI agent, agent-turned-spy Robert Hanssen, to be expelled immediately and an

additional forty-six to leave by July. The scandal was considered to be the most serious spy row between the United States and Russia since the end of the Cold War: the last time the United States expelled dozens of Russian diplomats was in 1986. On March 25, the *Sunday Times* claimed that British prime minister Tony Blair, during the two-day EU summit in Stockholm, warned Vladimir Putin of the growth of Russian intelligence activity in Britain. On March 29, the German Federal Agency for the Protection of the Constitution (German counterintelligence service) released the annual report stating that Russia increased the number of spies operating out of its diplomatic missions in Germany. It seemed to merely echo British claims: "The number of intelligence operatives has increased as the amount of embassy personnel has grown."

4. Authors' conversations with Sergei Tretyakov.

5. Federal Bureau of Investigation, "Operation Ghost Stories: Inside the Russian Spy Case," October 11, 2011, https://www.fbi.gov/news/stories/operation -ghost-stories-inside-the-russian-spy-case.

6. In 2003 Putin okayed the plan of the Russian domestic agency FSB to form an intelligence department. It was called the Department of Operative Information. The department was meant to become a cross point between counterintelligence and intelligence; it was formed out of the sections in charge of collecting "intelligence from the territory," a euphemism for recruiting foreign nationals in Russia, with an eye to subsequently running them as agents in their home countries. As its official symbol, the department adopted a globe, the same symbol of world-spanning reach used in the insignia of the Russian foreign intelligence agency (for details, see Soldatov and Borogan, *New Nobility*). It was this department that was put, apparently, in charge of dealing with compatriots; since 2010, the deputy head of the department was made a permanent member of the government commission on the issues of compatriots abroad.

7. "Sluzhba, kotoroy ne vidno" [Service which is not visible], a report from the SVR HQ, *Vesti, TV Saturday show*, October 8, 2016, https://www.vesti.ru /doc.html?id=2807761.

CHAPTER 34: THE FEARS OF THE SUPER-RICH

1. Conversation with Eugene Kaspersky at the German Economic Forum in 2017; Convent Kongress GmbH, "Deutsches Wirtschaftsforum 2017: Eugene Kaspersky," YouTube, November 27, 2017, https://www.youtube.com/watch?v= XjXymYcGoGQ.

2. Hearing before the Select Committee on Intelligence of the US Senate, March 30, 2017, https://www.intelligence.senate.gov/hearings/open-hearing -intelligence-matters-1.

3. Gordon Lubold and Shane Harris, "Russian Hackers Stole NSA Data on US Cyber Defense," *Wall Street Journal*, October 5, 2017, https://www.wsj.com /articles/russian-hackers-stole-nsa-data-on-u-s-cyber-defense-1507222108.

4. For more details, see Soldatov and Borogan, *The Red Web*.

5. Soldatov and Borogan, *The Red Web*.

6. In February 2019, Kaspersky's employee Ruslan Stoyanov was sentenced to twenty-two years in prison.

7. Authors' conversation with Alexander Lebedev, July 2018.

8. In 2006–2008, we worked in *Novaya Gazeta*, and we didn't notice any interference in our reporting.

9. Alexander Lebedev, *Ochota na bankira* [Hunting a banker] (Moscow: Izdatelstvo E., 2017).

10. Anne Applebaum, "In from the Cold," *New York Times Style Magazine*, March 8, 2013, https://www.nytimes.com/2013/03/08/t-magazine/evgeny -lebedev-in-from-the-cold.html.

11. Shaun Walker, "Putin Tells Journalists to Keep 'Snotty Noses' Out of His Business," *Independent*, April 19, 2008, https://www.independent.co.uk/news /world/europe/putin-tells-journalists-to-keep-snotty-noses-out-of-his-business -811794.html.

12. "Billionaire Lebedev Sells Red Wings for 1 Ruble," *Moscow Times*, April 5, 2013, https://themoscowtimes.com/articles/billionaire-lebedev-sells-red-wings -for-1-ruble-22992.

13. Lebedev YouTube channel [in Russian], "Prosto grazhdanskoye obshestvo. Reportazh s mitinga" [Just a civic society, a reportage from the manifestation], December 25, 2011, https://www.youtube.com/watch?v=0TYX8zAzbW8.

14. Authors' conversation with Vladimir Kara-Murza Sr.

CHAPTER 35: ON THE PATH TO WAR

1. Coordination Council of the Russian Compatriots Abroad, "The Immortal Regiment in the United States," https://ksors.org/?p=17627.

2. He was not alone; two recent Russian exiles also spoke up at the hearings: Vladimir Ashurkov, of the Anti-Corruption Foundation, and Roman Borisovich, of ClampK. For details, see UK Parliament, "Moscow's Gold: Russian Corruption in the UK," May 21, 2018, https://publications.parliament.uk/pa /cm201719/cmselect/cmfaff/932/93202.htm.

3. Free Russia Foundation website, https://www.4freerussia.org/about/.

4. *Meduza*, "St. Petersburg Court Upholds Customs Seizure of Masha Gessen's New Book about Modern-Day Russian 'Totalitarianism,'" January 16, 2019, https:// meduza.io/en/news/2019/01/16/a-search-of-masha-gessen-s-book-in-russian

-customs-was-based-on-the-author-s-reputation-not-the-book-s-contents-a-st
-petersburg-court-has-nonetheless-ruled-the-seizure-was-legal.

5. Leonid Eitingon, *Pisma in Vladimirskoy turmi* [Letters from Vladimir
prison] (Moscow: Algoritm, 2018).

6. Bellingcat, "Vladimir Kara-Murza Tailed by Members of FSB Squad Prior
to Suspected Poisonings," February 11, 2021, https://www.bellingcat.com/news
/uk-and-europe/2021/02/11/vladimir-kara-murza-tailed-by-members-of-fsb
-squad-prior-to-suspected-poisonings/.

7. Editorial Board, "In the Case Against Vladimir Kara-Murza, Russia
Turns Truth into a Crime," *Washington Post*, April 22, 2022, https://www
.washingtonpost.com/opinions/2022/04/22/case-against-vladimir-kara-murza
-russia-turns-truth-into-crime/.

8. *Washington Post*, "How a Russian Investigative Reporter Found Out
He Was a Kremlin Target," June 23, 2022, https://www.washingtonpost.com
/world/2022/06/23/andrei-soldatov-russia-ukraine-fsb.

9. *Mediazona*, "Pervy otdel: FSB pitaetsa ugovorit rossian vernutsa v
stranu, vyzyvaia na besedi ikh rodstvennikov," May 3, 2022, https://zona.media
/news/2022/05/03/vernis.

10. *Financial Times*, "EU Plans to Evict Largest Russian Lender from Swift
but Spare Energy Bank," May 4, 2022, https://www.ft.com/content/deb36bec
-41df-44eb-83fd-cbfbce7aac2b.

11. Bloomberg, "Four European Gas Buyers Made Ruble Payments to Russia," April 27, 2022, https://www.bloomberg.com/news/articles/2022-04-27/four
-european-gas-buyers-made-ruble-payments-to-russia.

12. Dirk Schütz, "Gazprombank: Zürcher Staatsanwaltschaft ermittelt gegen
CEO" [Gazprombank: Zurich public prosecutor investigates CEO], *Bilanz*,
February 1, 2022, https://www.handelszeitung.ch/bilanz/gazprombank-zurcher
-staatsanwaltschaft-ermittelt-gegen-ceo.

13. BBC, "Italy Orders Seizure of Yacht Linked to Putin," May 6, 2022,
https://www.bbc.com/news/61357256.

EPILOGUE

1. Fyodor Tyutchev, "No, Russia Can't Be Understood," trans. St. Sol, Lyr-
ics Translate, https://lyricstranslate.com/en/умом-россию-не-понять-no-russia
-cant-be-understood.html.

INDEX

Credit: Irina Borogan, Konstantin Zavrazhin

Andrei Soldatov and **Irina Borogan** are cofounders of Agentura.ru and authors of *The Red Web* and *The New Nobility*. Their work has been featured in the *New York Times, Moscow Times, Washington Post, Online Journalism Review, Le Monde, Christian Science Monitor*, CNN, and BBC. The *New York Times* has called Agentura.ru "a web site that came in from the cold to unveil Russian secrets."

Soldatov and Borogan left Russia in 2020. They cannot get back: when the war started, Soldatov was placed on Russia's wanted list because of their antiwar position and reporting.

PublicAffairs is a publishing house founded in 1997. It is a tribute to the standards, values, and flair of three persons who have served as mentors to countless reporters, writers, editors, and book people of all kinds, including me.

I. F. STONE, proprietor of *I. F. Stone's Weekly*, combined a commitment to the First Amendment with entrepreneurial zeal and reporting skill and became one of the great independent journalists in American history. At the age of eighty, Izzy published *The Trial of Socrates*, which was a national bestseller. He wrote the book after he taught himself ancient Greek.

BENJAMIN C. BRADLEE was for nearly thirty years the charismatic editorial leader of *The Washington Post*. It was Ben who gave the *Post* the range and courage to pursue such historic issues as Watergate. He supported his reporters with a tenacity that made them fearless and it is no accident that so many became authors of influential, best-selling books.

ROBERT L. BERNSTEIN, the chief executive of Random House for more than a quarter century, guided one of the nation's premier publishing houses. Bob was personally responsible for many books of political dissent and argument that challenged tyranny around the globe. He is also the founder and longtime chair of Human Rights Watch, one of the most respected human rights organizations in the world.

·   ·   ·

For fifty years, the banner of Public Affairs Press was carried by its owner Morris B. Schnapper, who published Gandhi, Nasser, Toynbee, Truman, and about 1,500 other authors. In 1983, Schnapper was described by *The Washington Post* as "a redoubtable gadfly." His legacy will endure in the books to come.

Peter Osnos, *Founder*